AMIGURUMI TOY BOX

16 SUPER CUTE
AMIGURUMI TOYS TO CROCHET

LANA CHOI

LANAdolls
Creation Lab

tuva

Tuva Publishing
www.tuvapublishing.com

Address Merkez Mah. Cavusbasi Cad. No71
Cekmekoy - Istanbul 34782 / Turkey
Tel +9 0216 642 62 62

Amigurumi Toy Box

First Print 2020 / October

Content Crochet

Editor in Chief Ayhan DEMİRPEHLİVAN
Project Editor Kader DEMİRPEHLİVAN
Author Lana CHOI
Technical Editors Leyla ARAS, Büşra ESER
Graphic Designers Ömer ALP, Abdullah BAYRAKÇI, Tarık TOKGÖZ
Crochet Tech Editor Wendi CUSINS

ISBN 978-605-7834-17-1

TuvaYayincilik TuvaPublishing
TuvaYayincilik TuvaPublishing

16 Super Cute Amigurumi Toys to Crochet

INTRODUCTION

"How much are these?"

"I'm sorry, these toys are not for sale. They're all my children, so I cannot sell them. But I can show you how to make them. It's very easy to learn, and then you can make some yourself."

I've been working as an optician for the last ten years, and now every corner of the front office is full of the crochet dolls I started making six years ago. Thanks to them, I meet new customers who come in to look at the dolls and want to buy them. My answer is always the same, "Sorry, these dolls are not for sale."

Some people think I'm overreacting because they're just toys. But I've poured my time and emotions into each stitch while making my precious children. I can't sell them.

Instead, I started sharing how to make these dolls on my blog. Many people were interested and enjoyed crocheting them. Thanks to this, I created an internet community called "LANAdolls Creation Lab" as well as a website and YouTube channel.

People have shared their stories with me... The success someone felt after making a doll for the first time; the family who used a crocheted doll to communicate with their child; a few people who overcame their depression by crocheting toys. Hearing all these happy stories and experiences, made me realize I enjoy crocheting together with many different people. Through this book, I hope to share the joy of making crocheted dolls with more people.

Thank you to my parents and family, who gave me passion; and also to my supportive friends, Jaehee, Jeongsook, and Hee Seon. I appreciate you all.

LANA

CONTENTS

PART 01

GET READY?

BEFORE MAKING YOUR DOLL FRIENDS

PART 02

LET'S PLAY!

HAVING FUN MAKING YOUR DOLL FRIENDS

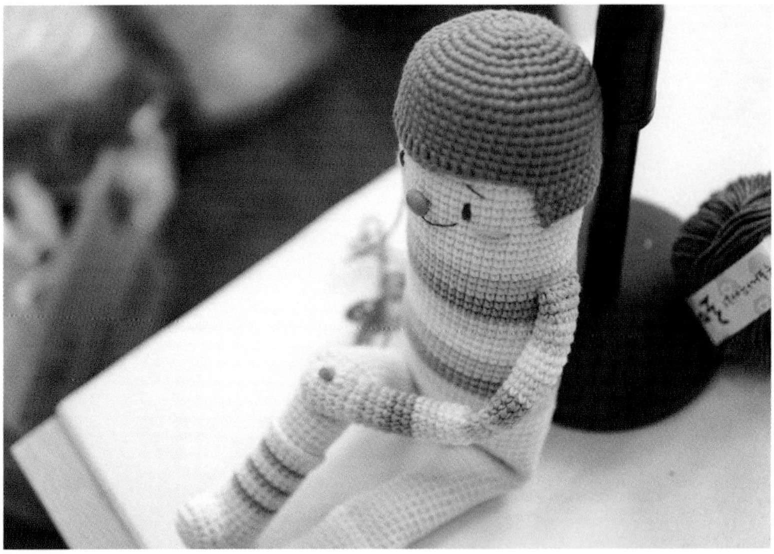

The GREAT GATSBY
F SCOTT FITZGERALD

MAHAL
ALOHA STATE

LA PR

LIKE

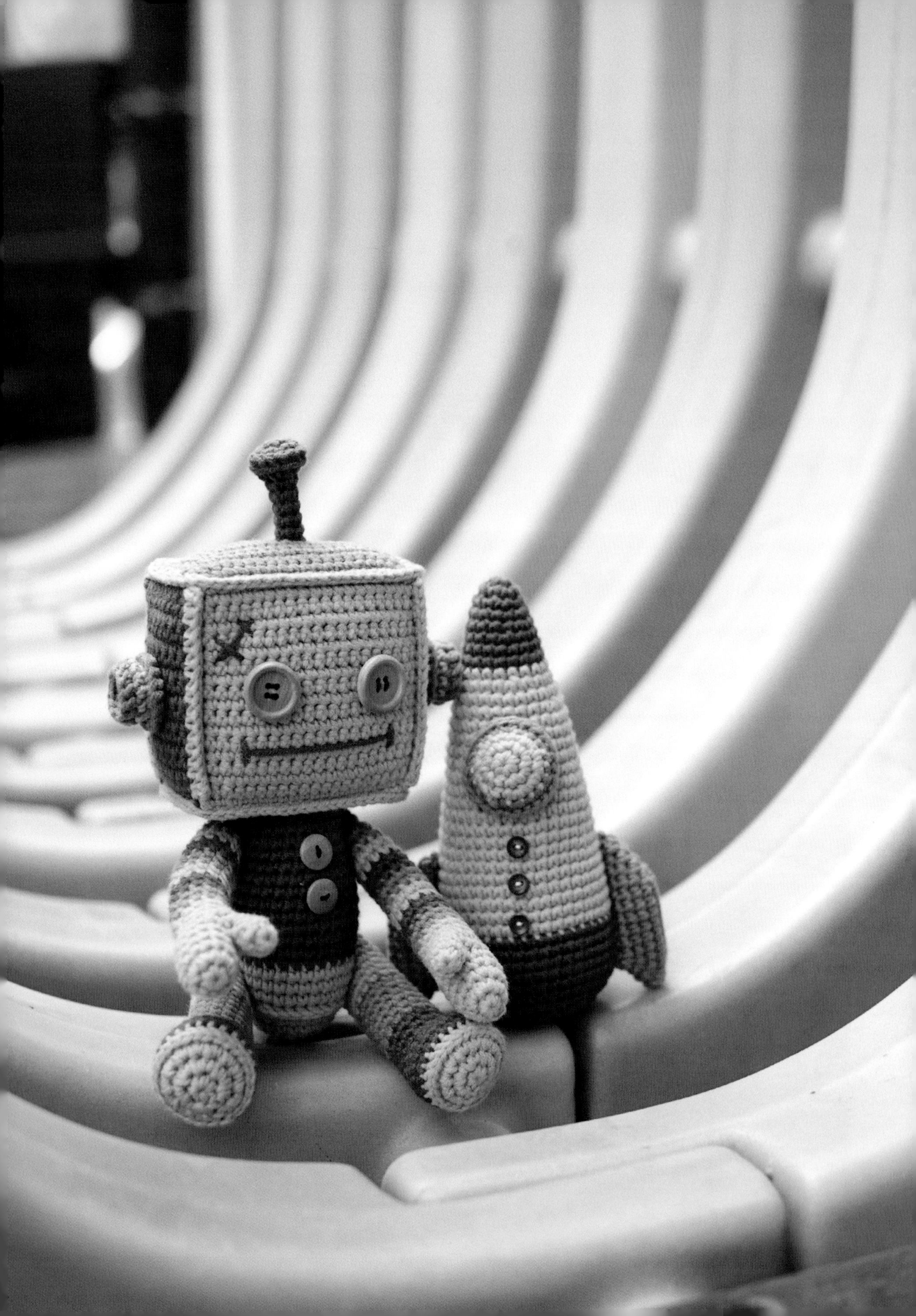

Materials & Tools

Yarn

Cotton Yarn is the preferred choice to use when making dolls.

NOTE: Medium Weight (Worsted)yarn or Light Weight (DK) yarn is suitable for the projects.

Crochet Hooks

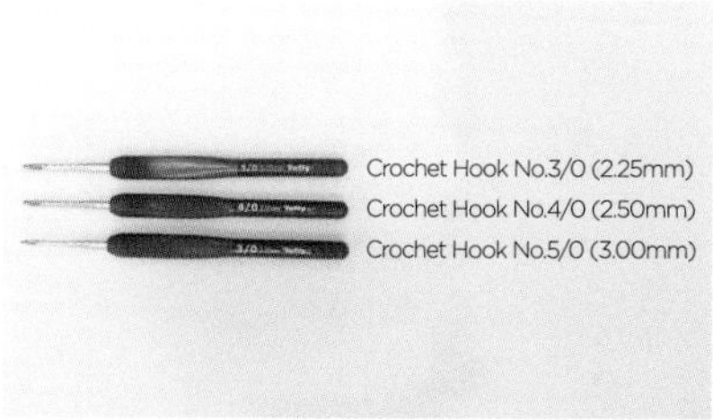

For the dolls, it is important to crochet tightly so that the stuffing doesn't come out. Use a hook which is size or two smaller than the hook size recommended on the yarn label.

Yarn Needles

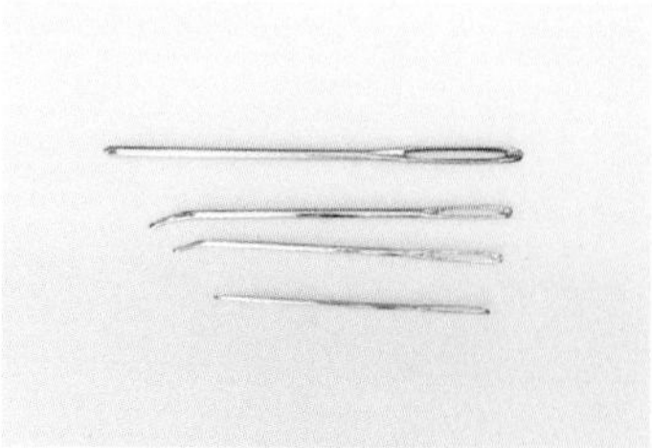

A selection of different sized tapestry needles is needed for both finishing off and assembling the various parts of the dolls.

Yarn Weight	Yarn Types
1 SUPER FINE	Sock, Fingering, Baby
2 FINE	Sport, Baby
3 LIGHT	DK, Light Worsted
4 MEDIUM	Worsted, Afghan, Aran
5 BULKY	Chunky, Craft, Rug

Metric	US	UK	Japan
2.25 mm	B-1	13	3/0
2.50 mm	-	12	4/0
2.75 mm	C-2	-	
3.00 mm	-	11	5/0
3.25 mm	D-3	10	
3.50 mm	E-4	9	6/0
3.75 mm	F-5	-	
4.00 mm	G-6	8	7/0
4.50 mm	#7	7	7.5/0
5.00 mm	H-8	6	8/0

Straight Pins

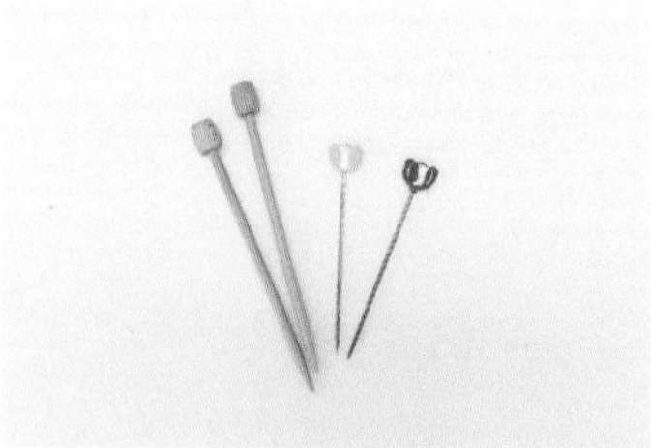

These are used to either mark the exact location before sewing, or to secure pieces together.

Locking Stitch Markers

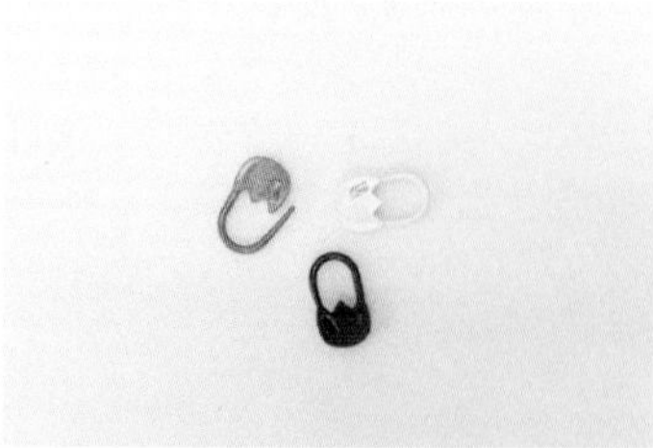

These handy markers are used to mark the beginning stitch of each round, or to mark off a number of stitches.

Water-Soluble Marking Pen

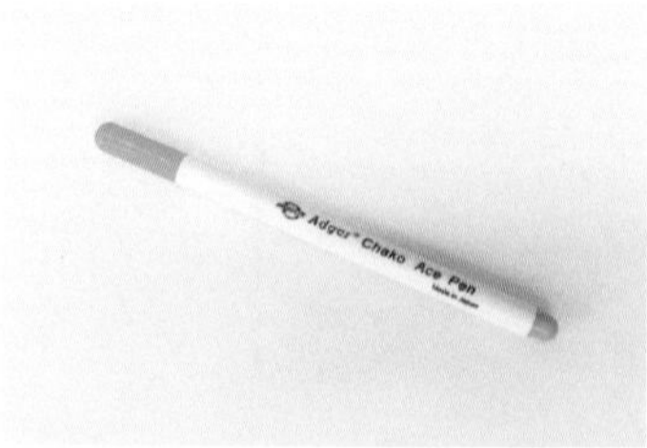

The marks made with this pen are easily removed with water, making it useful to mark the position on each piece before assembling.

Forceps

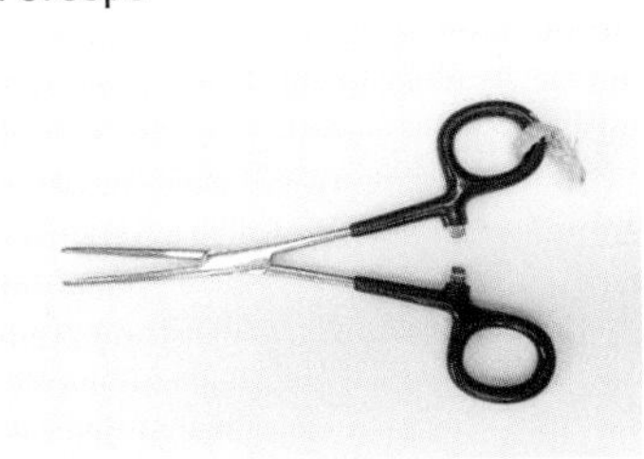

These are used to insert the stuffing into deep narrow spaces where it is difficult to use your fingers, especially all the way into the tips of the feet and arms.

Sharp Pointed Tweezers

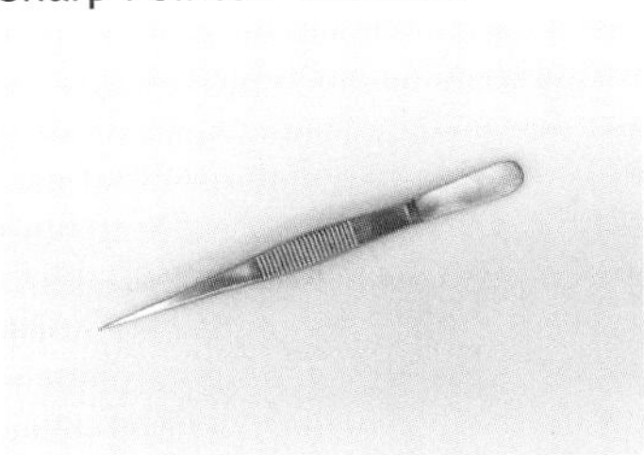

This can be used instead of the forceps when stuffing the doll. They are also used to hide the yarn tails inside the doll.

Buttons

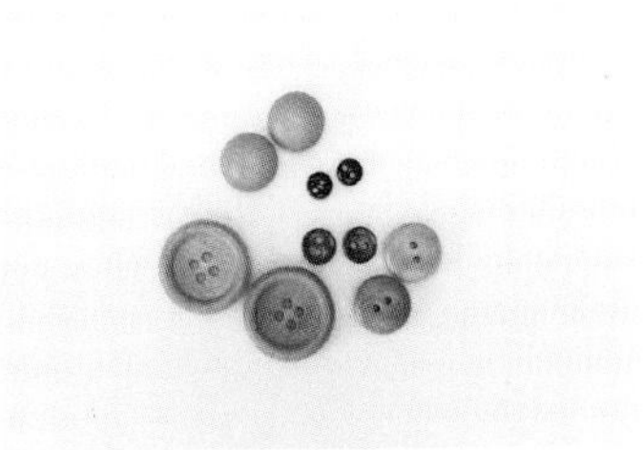

These are used as the eyes or nose on the faces of the dolls. Depending on the size and shape of the buttons, you can change the whole expression and mood of the doll. They are also used to decorate the dolls.

Bean Button

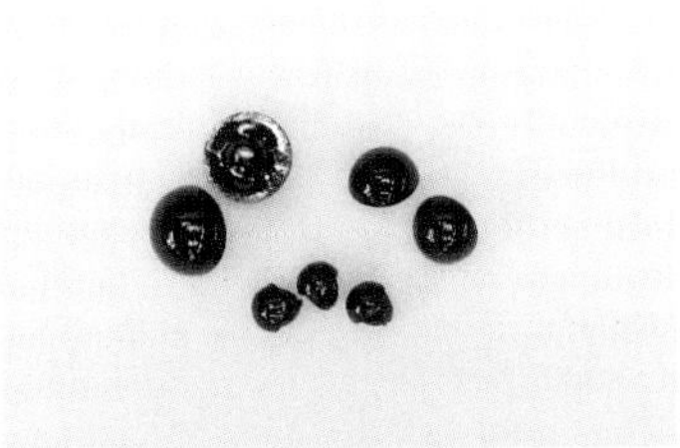

These are also used as the eyes or nose of a doll to create different expressions. They're called bean buttons, because they look like beans.

Toy Stuffing

When making the dolls, it is a good idea to use stuffing that does not clump together. It should hold its shape well and be suitable (and safe) for children.

Scissors

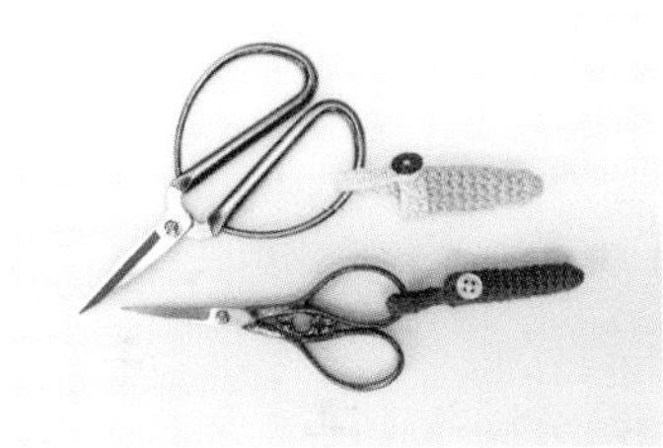

These are needed to cut and trim the yarn and threads, as well as to cut out felt or fabric shapes. Make sure they are sharp enough to cut through the yarn cleanly.

Sewing Thread

Used for embroidering facial features on the dolls, and to sew on buttons. I use a thread which is thicker and stronger than normal thread, which is more suitable when sewing on crochet fabric.

Sewing Needles

These are used with the sewing threads. The different sizes and lengths are for the various purposes needed for the dolls.

Craft Wire

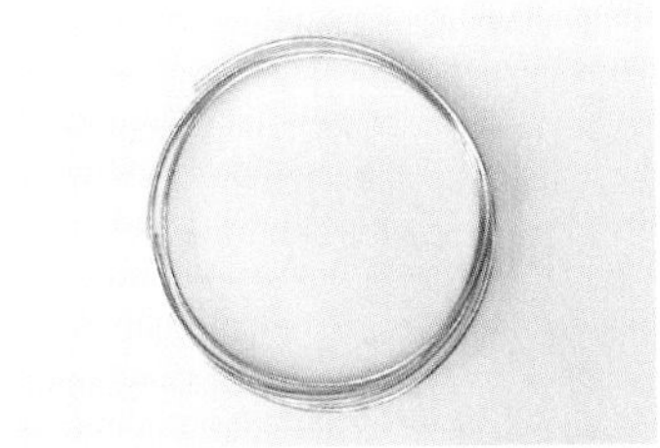

When this is used inside the dolls, the arms and legs are bendable. However, if the doll is for a young child, please do not use wire.

How to Hold a Crochet Hook

Pencil Hold

With the hook pointing down, hold the hook with your middle finger and thumb, as if it were a pencil.

Knife Hold

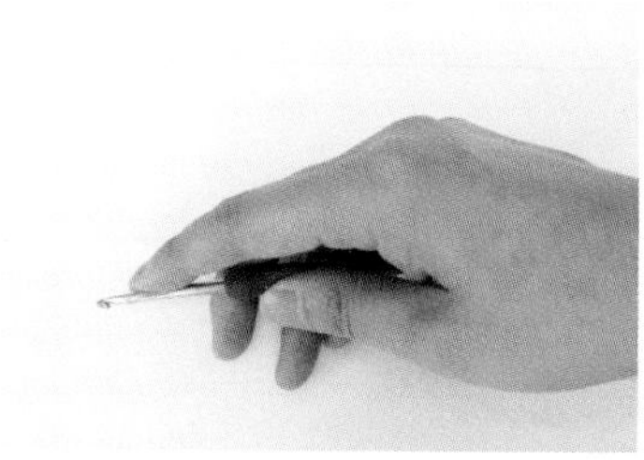

With the hook pointing down, hold the hook with your index finger extended, as if you were holding a knife.

How to Hold the Yarn

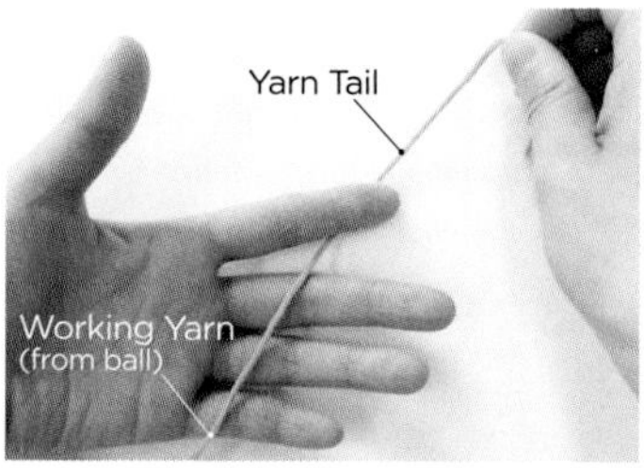

1. Place the yarn across your left hand with the yarn tail under your index finger.

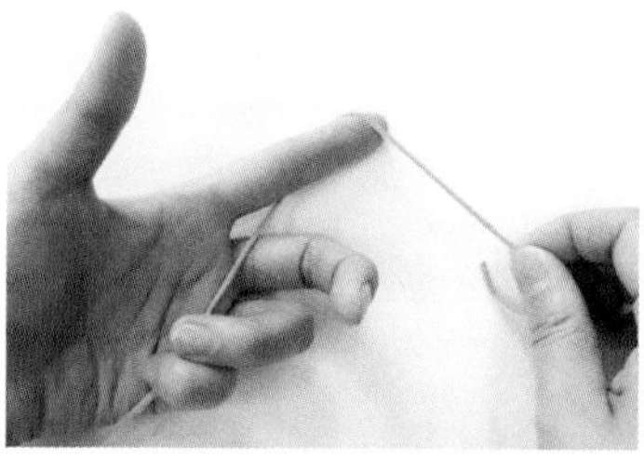

2. Wrap the yarn tail over your index finger and hold the working yarn with your left hand ring finger.

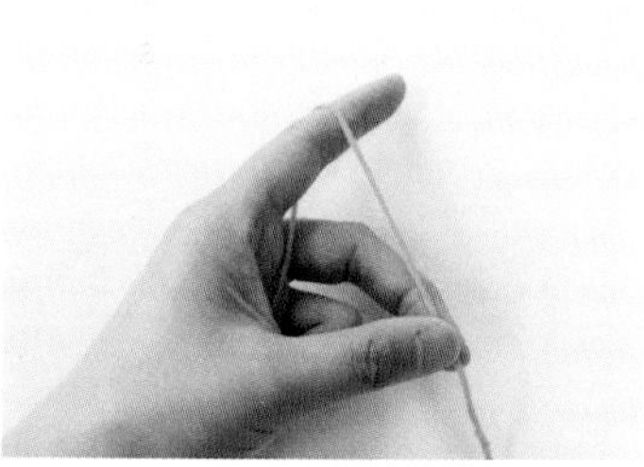

3. Hold the tail between your thumb and middle finger. Adjust the tension of the yarn by bending and flexing the index finger.

How to Wrap the Yarn Over the Hook

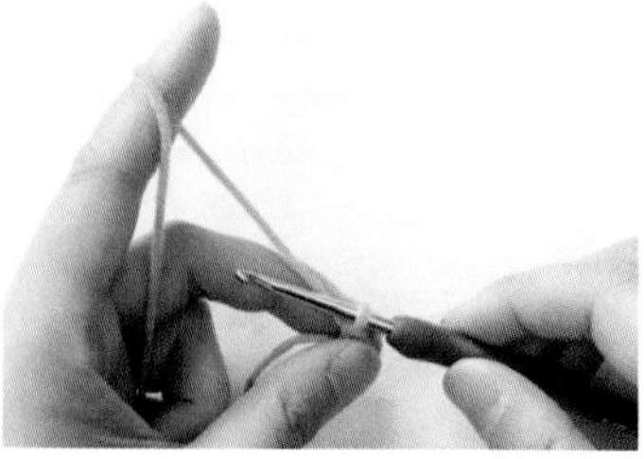

1. Place the hook in front of the yarn.

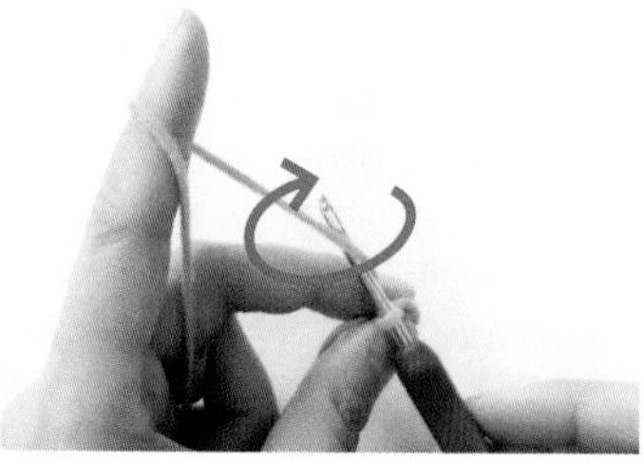

2. Move the hook under the yarn and upwards in a circular motion, so that the yarn wraps around the hook.

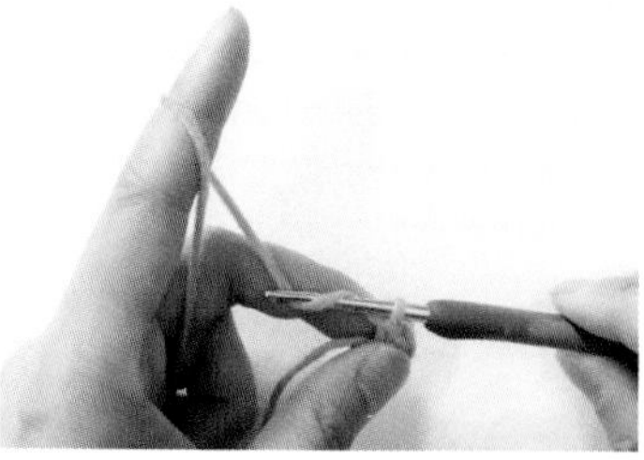

3. Pull the yarn through the loop on the hook. Use this method to wrap the yarn for every crochet stitch.

Finding the Correct Hook for the Yarn

Finding the correct hook size to match the thickness of the yarn is important when crocheting toys. Generally, one would choose a hook one or two sizes smaller than that recommended on the yarn label, so that a tighter fabric is created. However, because each person works at a different tension, and each yarn company uses different standards to determine the hook sizes, it is a good idea to work up yarn swatches before making the dolls. Work the swatches using different sized hooks - larger and smaller - than what you would normally use, and compare the results, before making a doll.

» Using a 4.00 mm hook

Using a larger hook with the yarn, the crochet piece stretches easily. Holes are formed between the stitches, where the stuffing can easily come out.

» Using a 3.00 mm hook

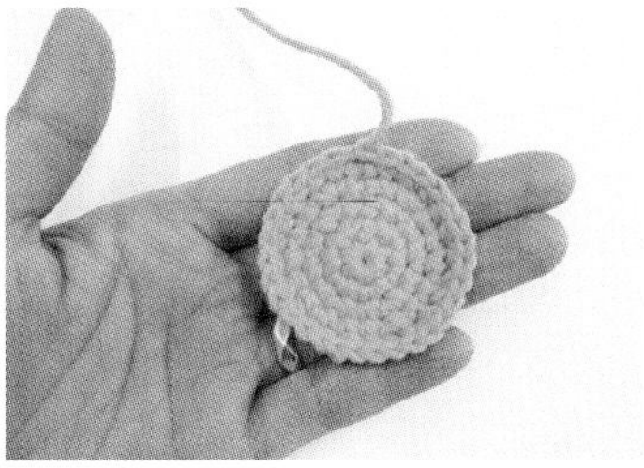

Here the crochet piece does not stretch well. Stitches are formed tightly with no visible holes between them.

» Using a 2.25 mm hook

Using a smaller hook, the fabric is denser and feels stiff.

GET READY!

PART 01

BEFORE MAKING YOUR DOLL FRIENDS

○ BASIC CROCHET STITCHES ○

Chain Stitch (ch)

This stitch is the basis of many crochet projects. It is used as a foundation when working in rows or when making ovals. It is good to practice this stitch.

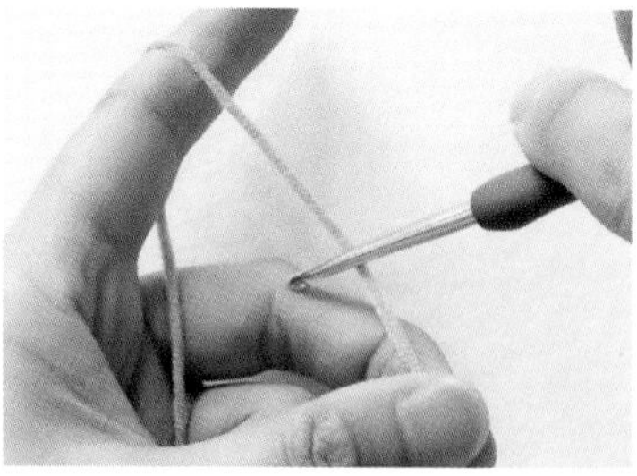

1. Place the hook on the yarn.

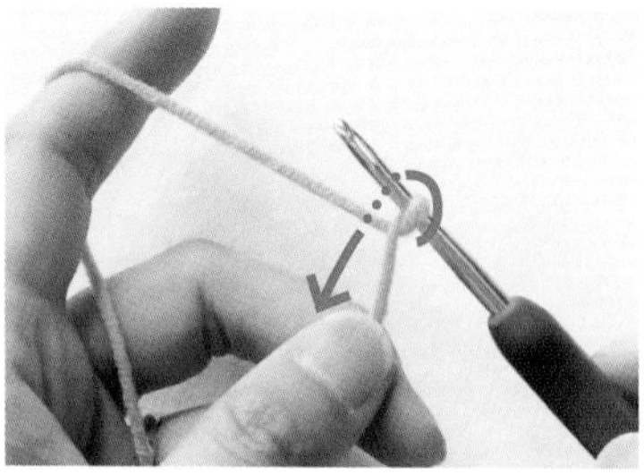

2. Turn the hook downwards under the yarn, and then lift the hook up to form a loop on the hook.

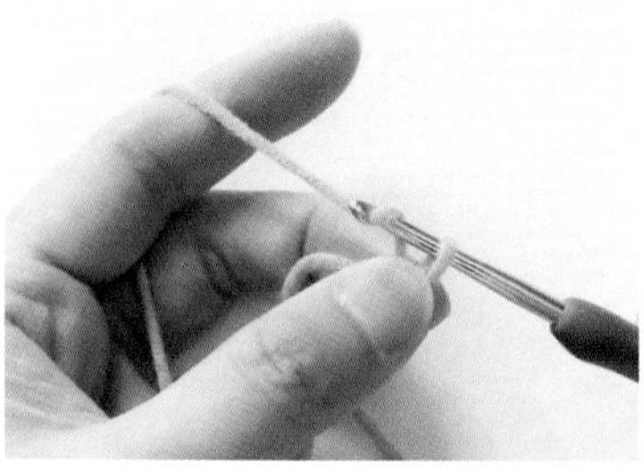

3. Hold the twist in the yarn tightly with your thumb and middle finger, and wrap the yarn over the hook.

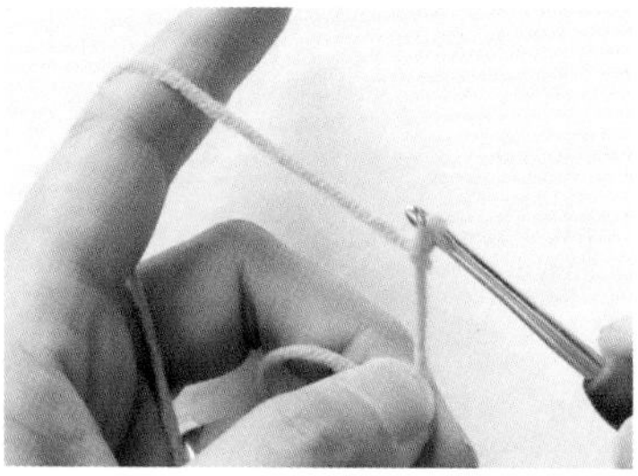

4. Pull the wrapped yarn through the loop on the hook to make a knot. This is not the first chain stitch.

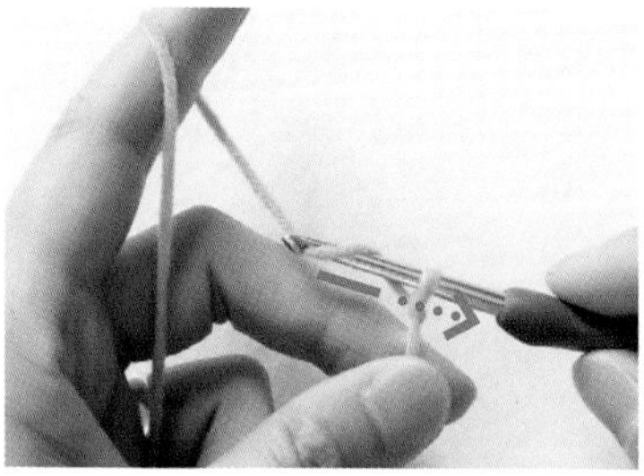

5. Wrap the yarn over the hook and pull the wrapped yarn through the loop on the hook to make the first chain stitch.

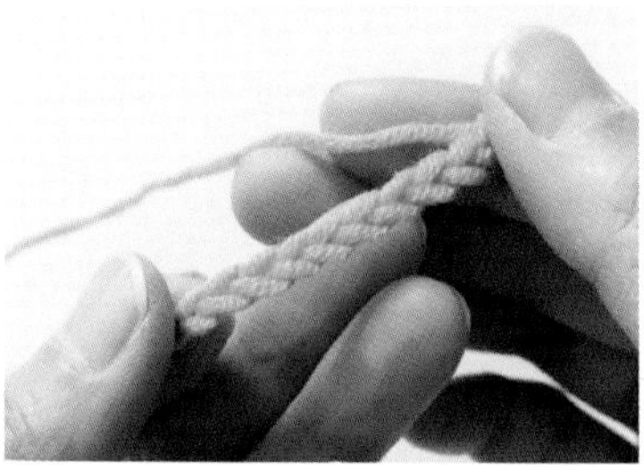

6. Repeat this process to make as many chain stitches as you need. In the photo, there are 10 chain stitches made.

tip

Chain Front: The shape of a "V" is at the front of a chain stitch.

Back Ridge: An arch shape is on the back of a chain stitch.

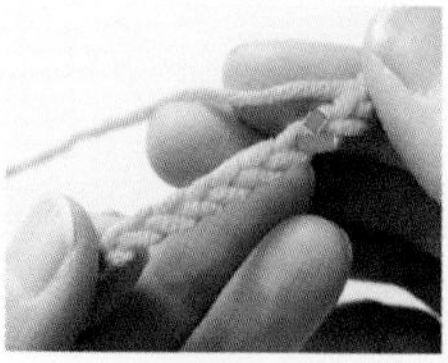

Chain Front

Back Ridge

Single Crochet (sc)

X

This is the stitch most used when crocheting dolls. It is also the most suitable stitch to use because of its tight structure. It is used to form the overall shape of every doll's body and head, so be sure to learn and practice it.

1 Insert the hook under both loops of the next stitch on the previous round.

2 Wrap the yarn over the hook.

3 Pull the wrapped yarn through the stitch to make a loop. There are now two loops on the hook.

4 Wrap the yarn over the hook again. Pull the yarn through the two loops on the hook to complete the single crochet stitch.

5 Repeat the process in steps 1-4 for every single crochet stitch, as many times as necessary. The photo shows 5 single crochet stitches.

Back Loop Only (blo)

Working in the back loop only is a technique often used in stitch patterns, where the hook in inserted only in the back loop of a stitch instead of under both loops of the stitch. The process of making the stitch is the same, only where the hook gets inserted is different. If you are confused, please refer to the Single Crochet explanation.

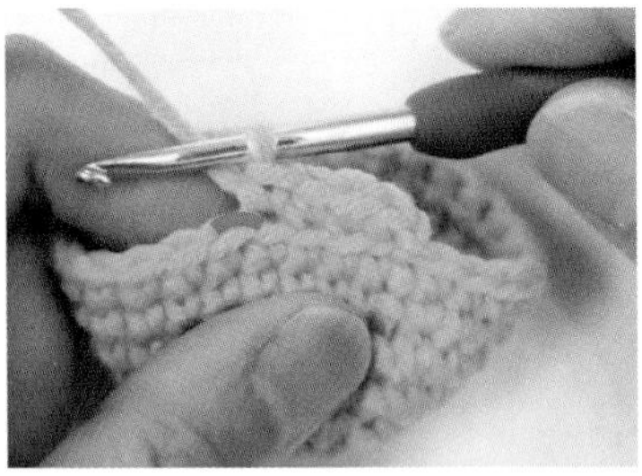

1 The colored part is where to insert the hook.

2 Insert the hook into the back loop only of the next stitch on the previous round.

3 Wrap the yarn over the hook and pull it through the back loop.

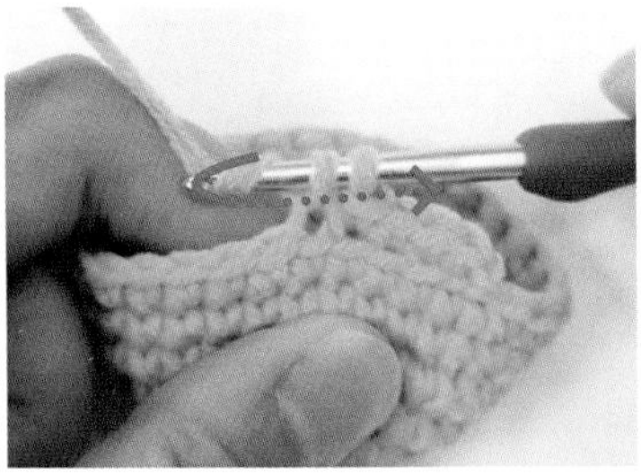

4 Wrap the yarn over the hook again and pull it through the two loops on the hook to complete a back loop only single crochet stitch.

5 Repeat the process in steps 2-4 as many times as necessary. The photo shows a round of back loop only stitches completed. You can see a horizontal line (formed by the unused front loops) under the current round.

tip

Different stitches can be worked in the back loop only or front loop only, including decreases, increases and other basic crochet stitches.

Back loop only

Front loop only

Front Loop Only (flo)

This technique is used when you need your work to fold outwards, or have a shaped part, like a visor on a hat. Working in the front loop only is where the hook is inserted under the front loop of a stitch. Please note that this technique can be used with various crochet stitches.

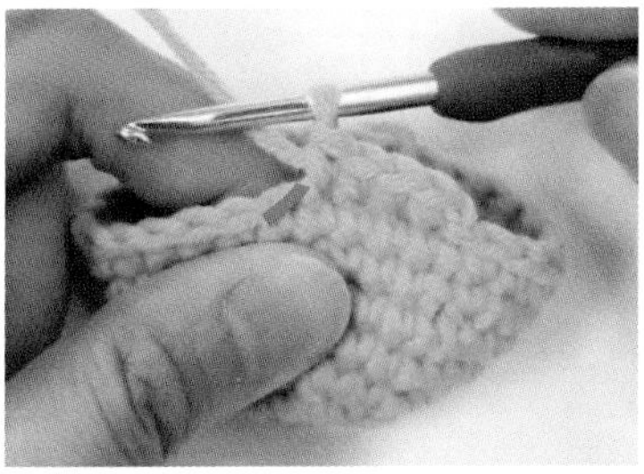

1. The colored part is where to insert the hook.

2. Insert the hook into the front loop only of the next stitch on the previous round.

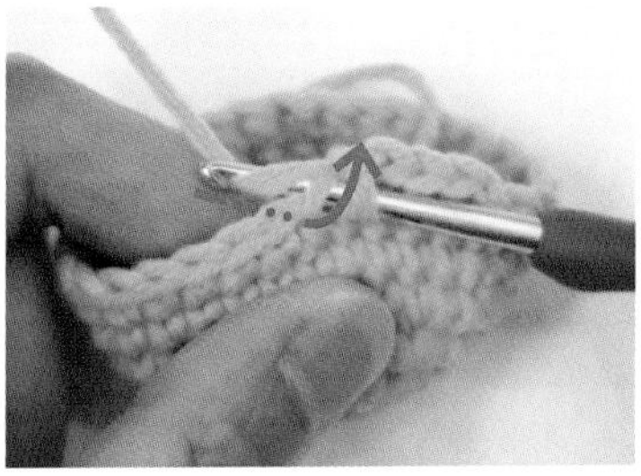

3. Pull the yarn through the front loop.

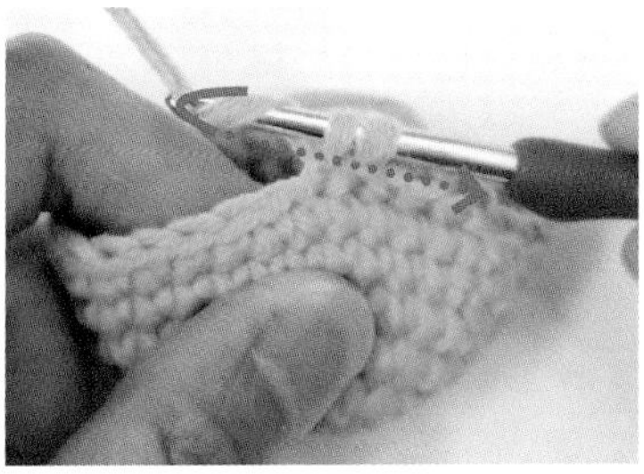

4. Wrap the yarn over the hook again and pull it through the two loops on the hook to complete the stitch.

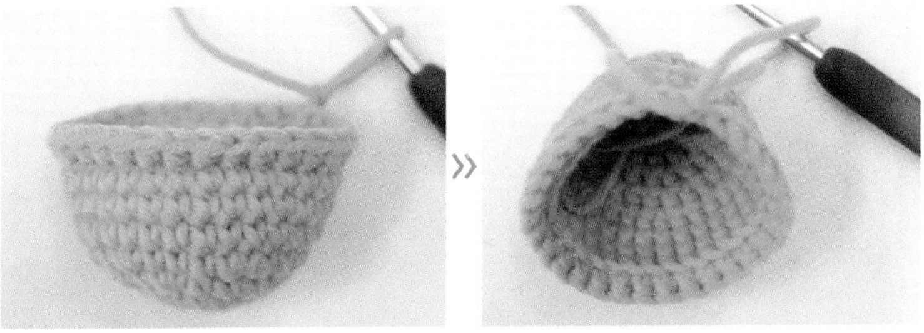

5. Repeat the process in steps 2-4 as many times as needed. The photos show a round of front loop only stitches completed. On the inside, you can see the horizontal line (formed by unused back loops) under the last round.

Single Crochet Increase (sc-inc or 2sc)

This is a crochet technique that increases the number of stitches so that the total area of the doll becomes larger as you progress. Working another single crochet stitch into the same stitch, increases one stitch to two stitches.

1 Complete 1 single crochet.

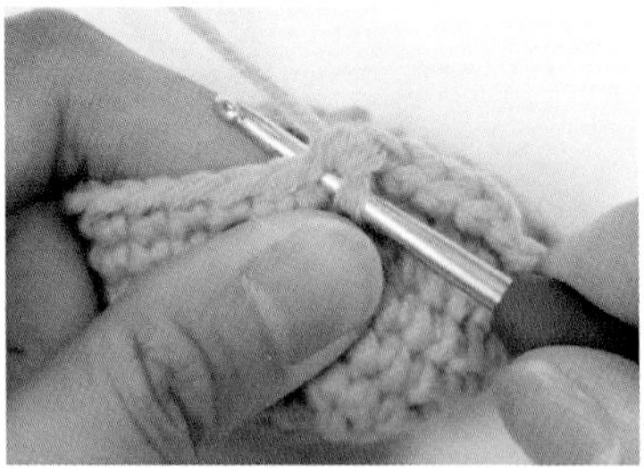

2 Insert the hook into the same stitch and work one more single crochet.

3 When that is done, it shows the 2 single crochets worked into the 1 stitch. You can see the 1 stitch extended at the end.

Single Crochet Decrease (sc-dec or sc2tog)

This is how to reduce two stitches to one stitch. We'll show you both the normal decrease and the invisible decrease, which is more suitable for doll making, so practice both ways.

» A normal decrease

1 Insert the hook into the next stitch on the previous round.

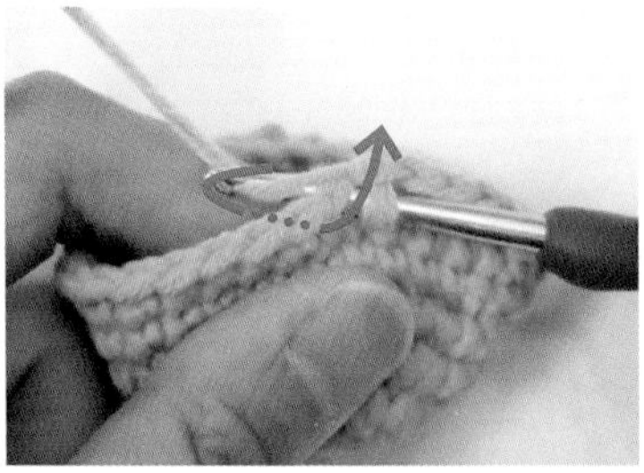

2 Wrap the yarn over the hook and pull the wrapped yarn through the stitch to make a loop. There are now two loops on the hook.

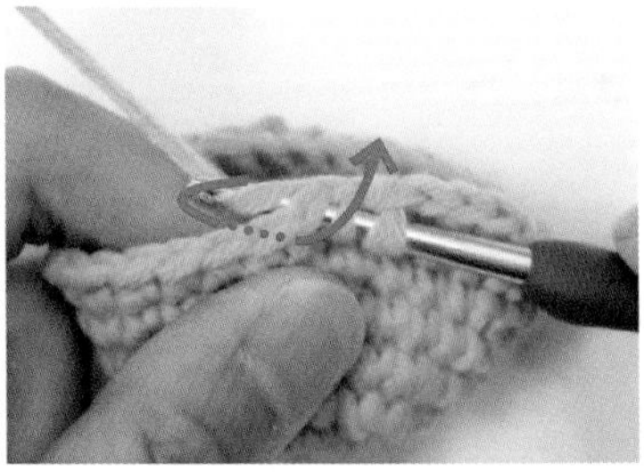

3 Then insert the hook in the following stitch, wrap the yarn over the hook and pull the wrapped yarn through the stitch. There are now three loops on your hook.

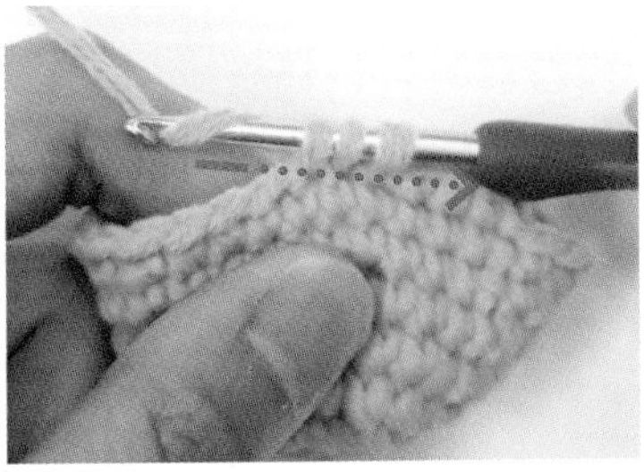

❹ Wrap the yarn over the hook and pull through all three loops on hook.

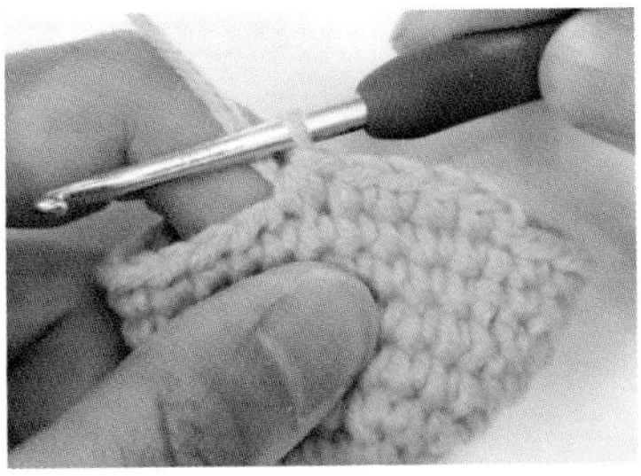

❺ After making 4 single crochets, the following 2 stitches were reduced to 1 single crochet.

» Invisible decrease (suitable for making dolls)

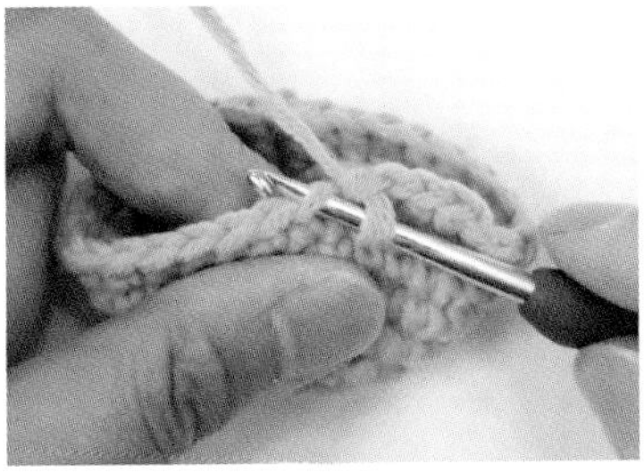

❶ Insert the hook into the front loop only of the next stitch on the previous round.

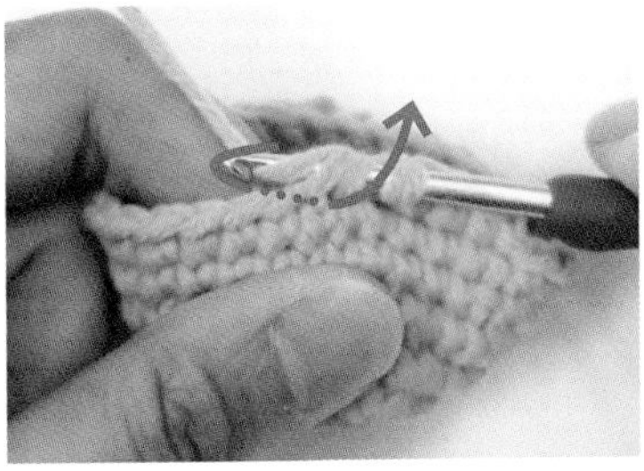

❷ Then insert the hook under the front loop only of the following stitch and pull the yarn through both these front loops. There are now two loops on the hook.

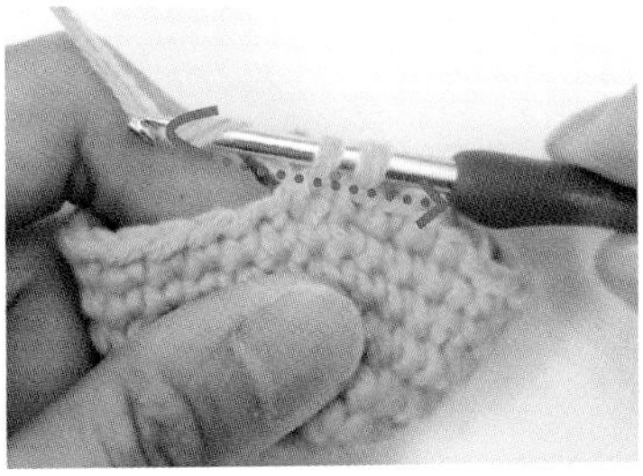

❸ Wrap the yarn over the hook and pull through both loops on hook.

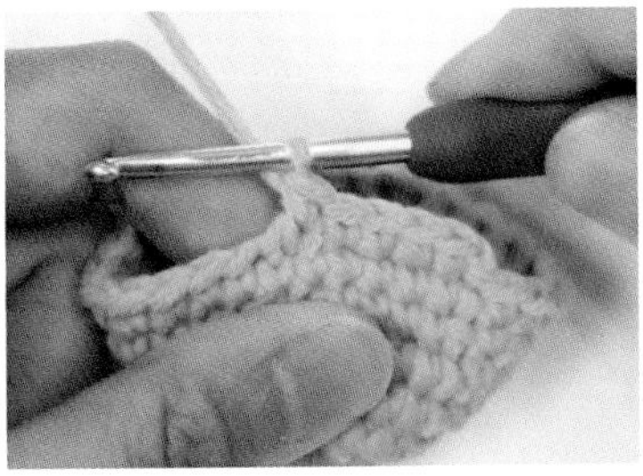

❹ After 4 single crochets, the following 2 stitches were reduced to 1 single crochet with an invisible decrease.

Back Post Single Crochet (BPsc)

This technique bends the tops of the stitches on the previous round towards you and is achieved by working between the stitches around the post of the stitch.

1. Insert the hook from the back and around the post of the stitch.

2. Wrap the yarn over the hook and pull the wrapped yarn through the stitch post to make a loop. There are now two loops on the hook.

3. Wrap the yarn over the hook again, and pull through both loops on the hook to complete the single crochet.

4. Repeat the process in steps 1-3 for each back post single crochet. The photo shows one round worked in back post single crochet stitches.

tip

Stitch Height: The height of the stitch in terms of chain stiches.
The photo shows the height of single crochet (one chain), half-double crochet (two chains), and double crochet (three chains) stitches respectively.

Single Crochet

Half-Double Crochet

Double Crochet

Slip Stitch (sl st)

When working in rounds, a slip stitch is used to join the last stitch of the round to the first stitch. It can also be used to move across to another stitch position, or to secure the ends when finished crocheting.

» Joining with a slip stitch

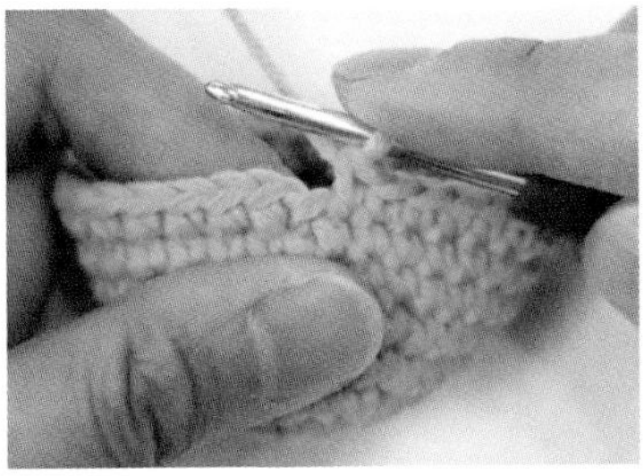

1 When the last stitch is made, it's time to join to the first stitch to finish the round.

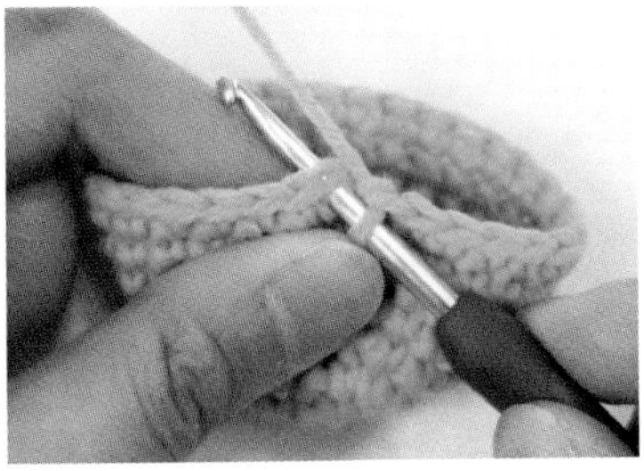

2 Insert the hook in the first stitch.

3 Wrap the yarn over the hook, and pull the yarn through the stitch and through the loop on the hook.

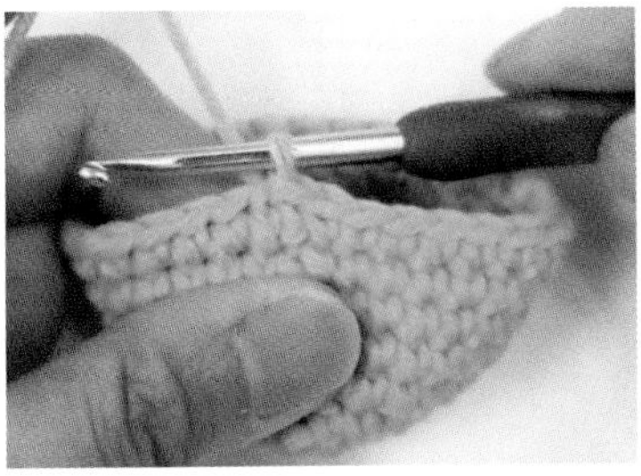

4 The photo shows the finished slip stitch join.

» Slip stitches to move position

1 Insert the hook in the next stitch.

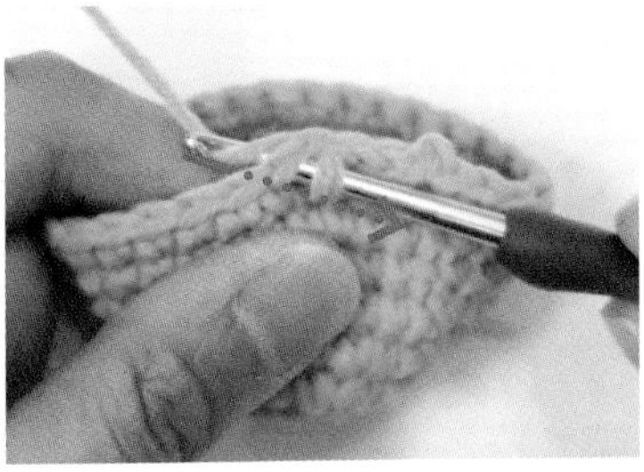

2 Wrap the yarn over the hook and pull it through the stitch and loop on the hook.

3 The position has been moved by 5 slip stitches.

Half-Double Crochet (hdc)

The height of this stitch is twice as long as the single crochet, and can work up more quickly. However, due to the longer length, there's a chance of the stuffing escaping, so this stitch is used mainly for clothes and accessories.

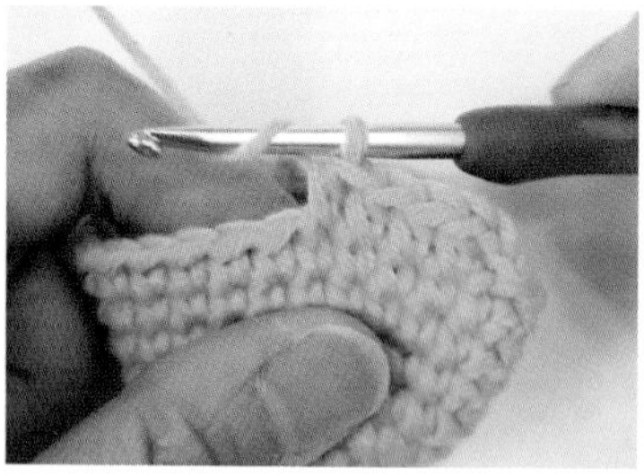

1 Wrap the yarn over the hook.

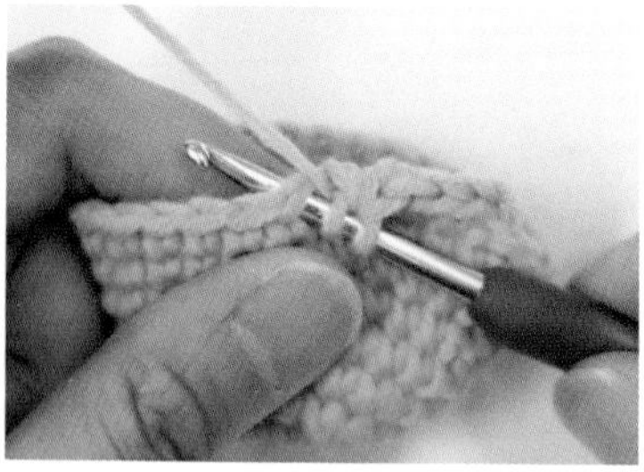

2 Insert the hook into the next stitch on the previous round.

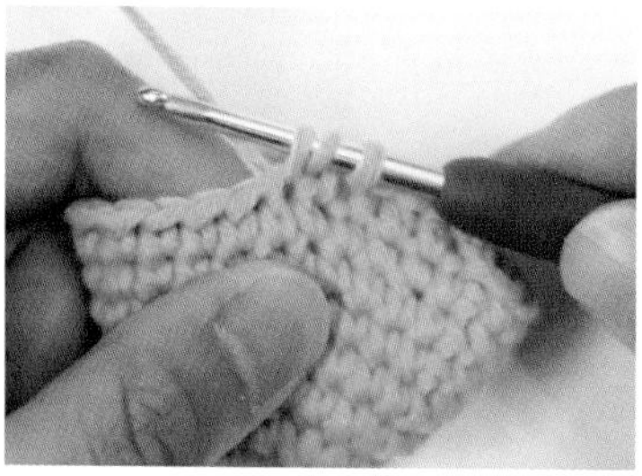

3 Wrap the yarn over the hook and pull it through the stitch. There are now three loops on the hook.

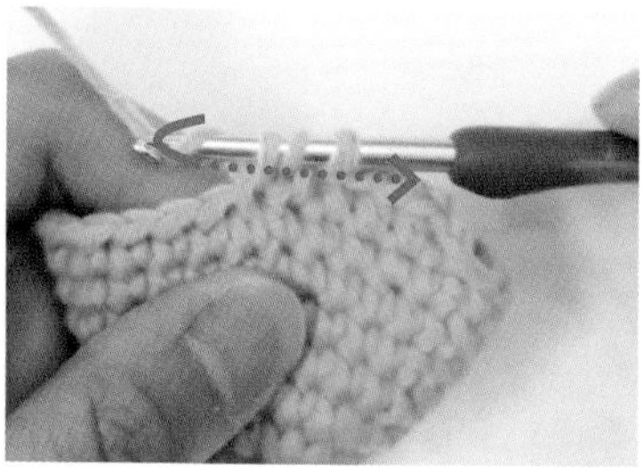

4 Wrap the yarn over the hook again and pull through all three loops on the hook, to complete a half-double crochet stitch..

5 Repeat steps 1-4 for each half-double crochet as needed. The first photo shows 5 half-double crochet stitches, and the next photo shows a finished round of half-double crochets.

Double Crochet (dc)

The height of the double crochet is three times as long as the single crochet. These longer stitches are better suited to use when making clothes and accessories.

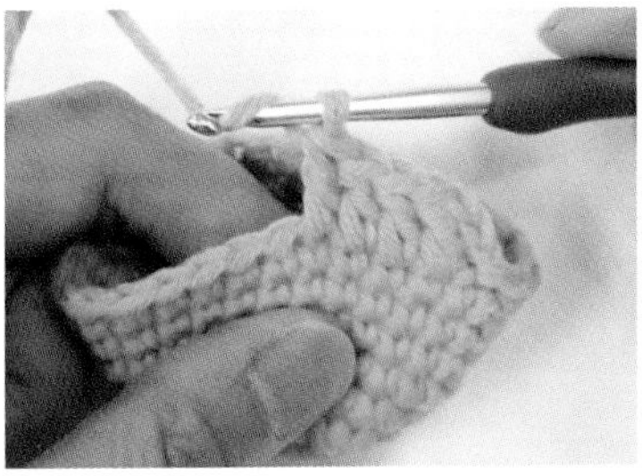

1. Wrap the yarn over the hook.

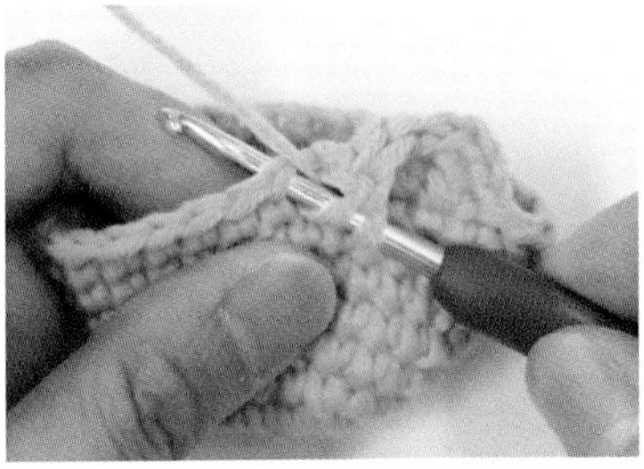

2. Insert the hook into the next stitch.

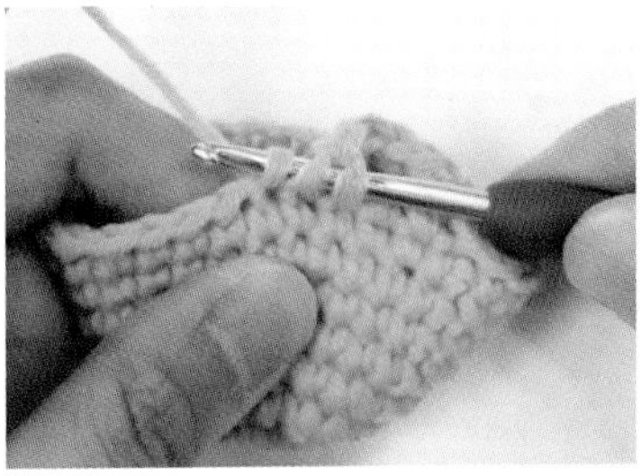

3. Wrap the yarn over the hook and pull it through the stitch. There are now three loops on the hook.

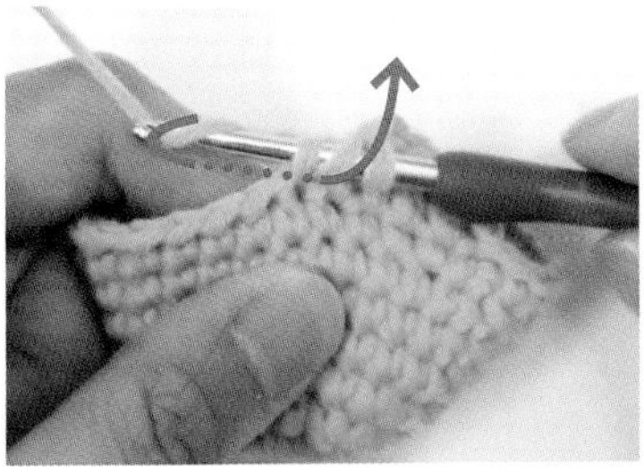

4. Wrap the yarn over the hook and pull it through the first two loops on the hook. There are now two loops left on the hook.

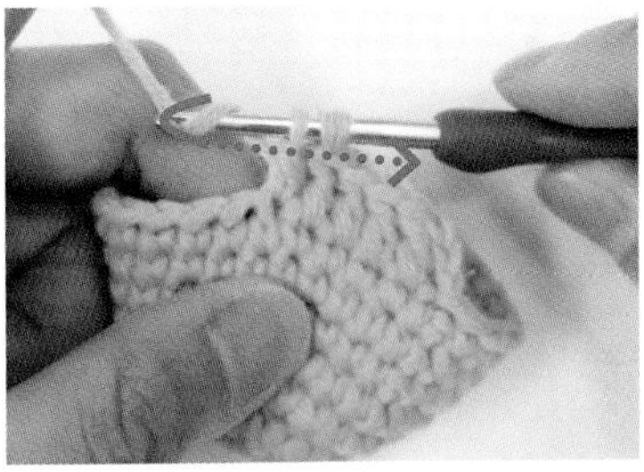

5. Wrap the yarn over the hook once more and pull it through the remaining two loops to complete the double crochet stitch.

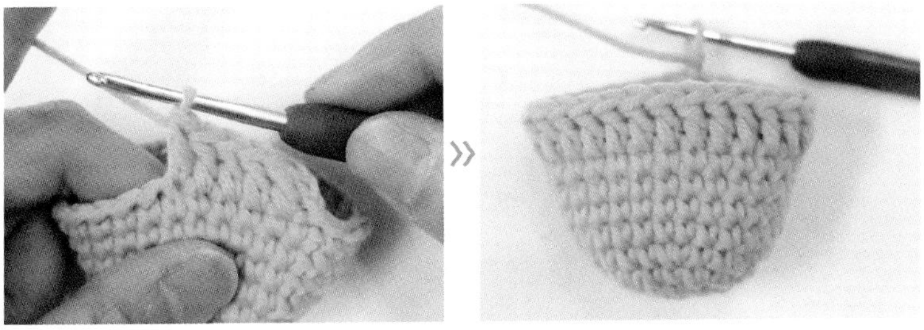

6. Repeat steps 1-5 for each double crochet needed. The first photo shows 5 double crochet stitches, and the next photo shows a finished round of double crochets.

Double Crochet Increase (dc-inc or 2dc)

This crochet technique makes the pieces bigger by increasing the number of stitches. As with the single crochet increase, you can increase the number of double crochet stitches, by working two stitches into one stitch.

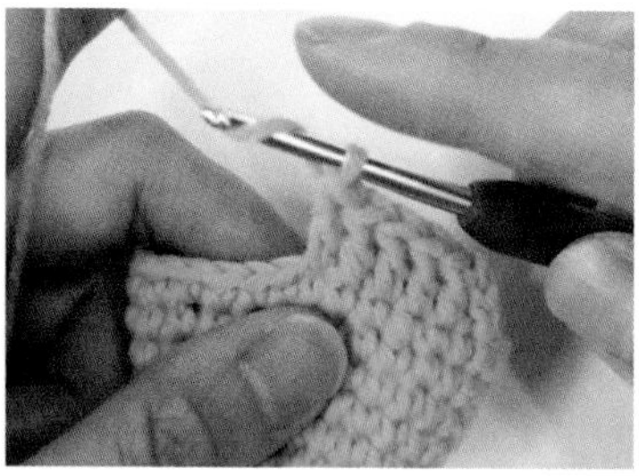

1. Complete a double crochet stitch. Wrap the yarn over the hook.

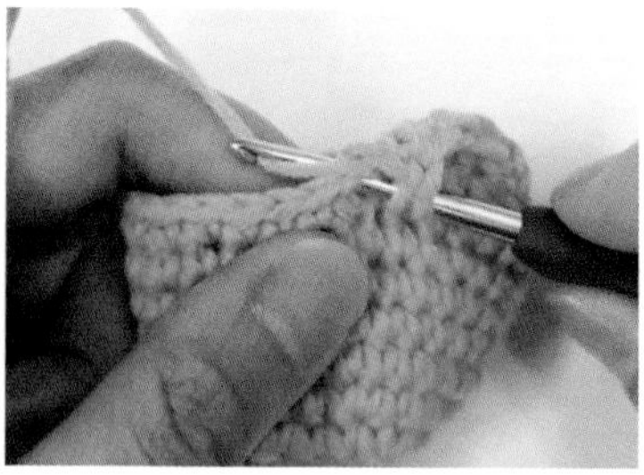

2. Insert the hook into the same stitch and work one more double crochet.

3. In the photo, after the first 4 double crochets, there is a double crochet increase. You can see the 1 stitch extended at the end.

Double Crochet Decrease (dc-dec or dc2tog)

This crochet technique reduces two stitches from the previous row into one stitch, using double crochet stitches.

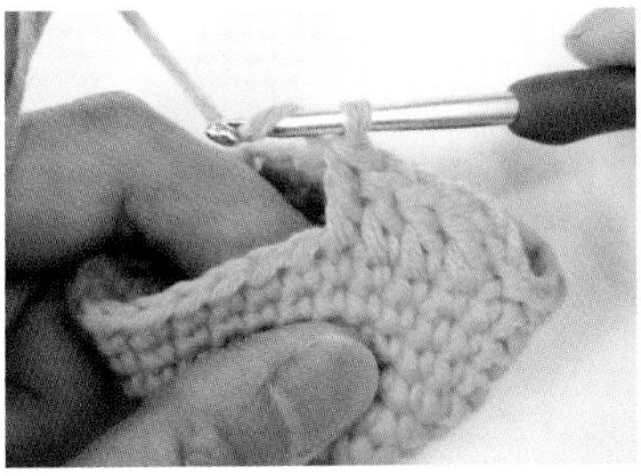

1 Wrap the yarn over the hook.

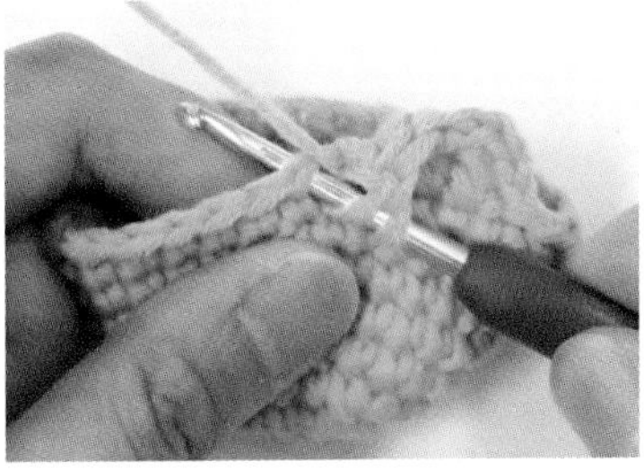

2 Insert the hook into the next stitch.

3 Wrap the yarn over the hook and pull it through the stitch. There are three loops on the hook.

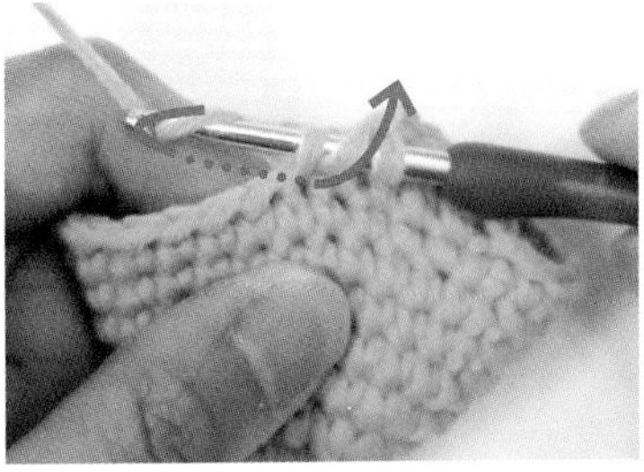

4 Wrap the yarn over the hook and pull it through the first two loops on the hook. Two loops remain on the hook.

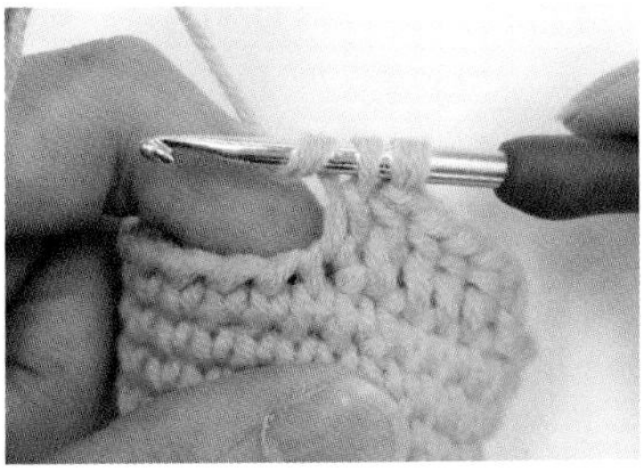

5 Wrap the yarn over the hook again.

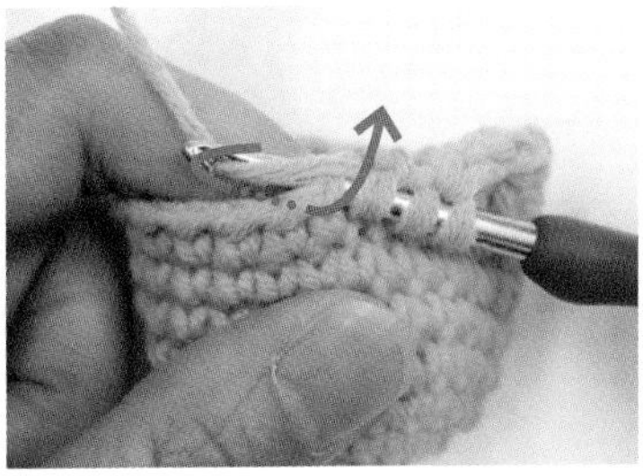

6 Then insert the hook in the following stitch, wrap the yarn over the hook and pull it through the stitch. There are now four loops on your hook.

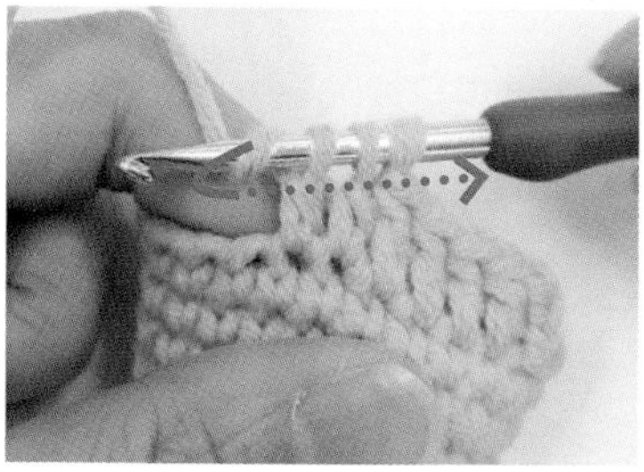

7 Wrap the yarn over the hook and pull it through the first two loops on the hook.

8 Wrap the yarn over the hook once more and pull it through the remaining three loops on the hook.

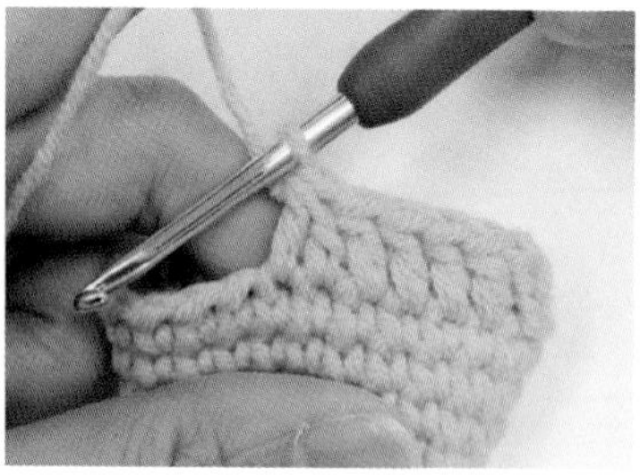

9 In the photo, after the first 4 double crochets, there is a double crochet decrease. You can see that 2 stitches on the previous round are now reduced to 1 stitch.

Double Crochet Shell (shell or 5dc-shell)

This crochet technique makes a fan-like shape using double crochet stitches. It looks like a sea shell, so it's called a shell stitch. In this book, it is often used as a decorative border at the bottom of skirts or as hair bangs.

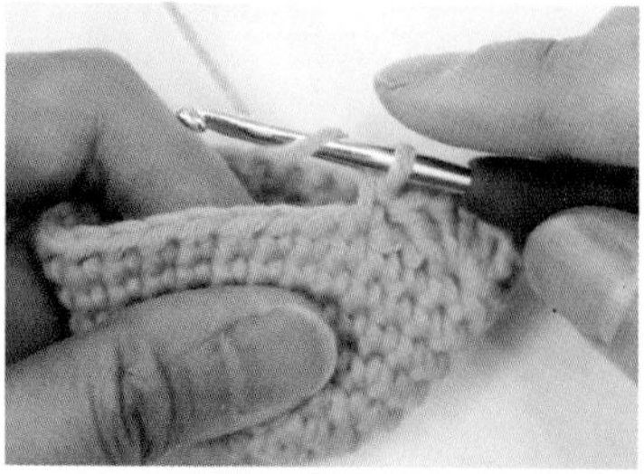

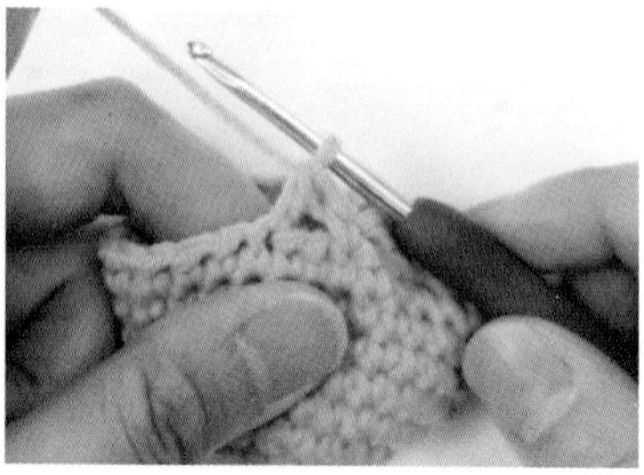

1 After a single crochet stitch is made, wrap the yarn over the hook.

2 Skip the next 2 stitches, insert the hook in the third stitch and make a double crochet stitch. The photo shows one completed double crochet.

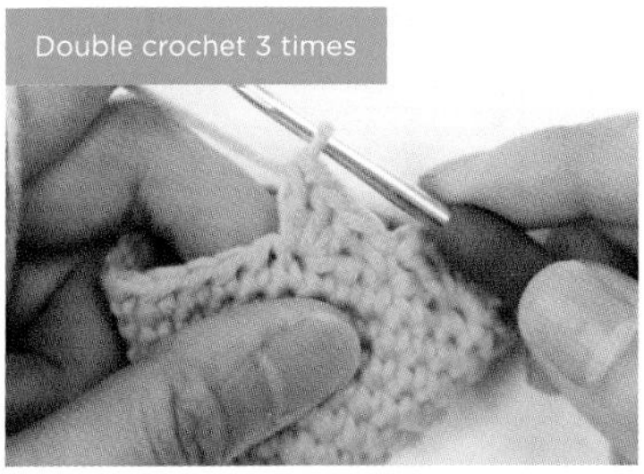

3 Make 4 more double crochets in the same stitch. The photos show the series of double crochets made - 2 times, 3 times, 4 times, & 5 times - all in the one stitch.

4 Then skip the next 2 stitches, insert hook in the following stitch and make a single crochet. The single crochet stitches are made before and after each shell.

5 Repeat steps 1-4 for as many shells as needed. The photo shows a finished round of double crochet shell stitches.

◦ CROCHET SHAPES ◦

Working in Rows

This is the basic style of crocheting. At the end of each row, change direction and work back across the stitches of the previous row. This style can be used to make flat faces, and in this book is used to make suspender straps, bow ties, ribbons, collar, and Ricky's head.

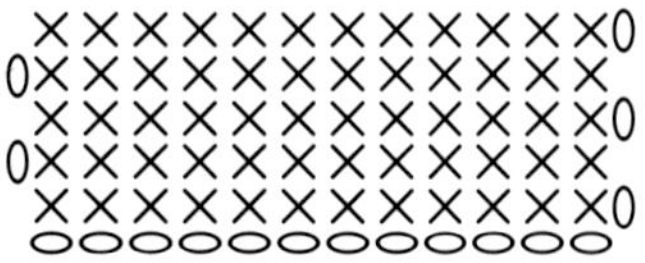

1 Make a string of chain stitches (**O**). This is the foundation chain.

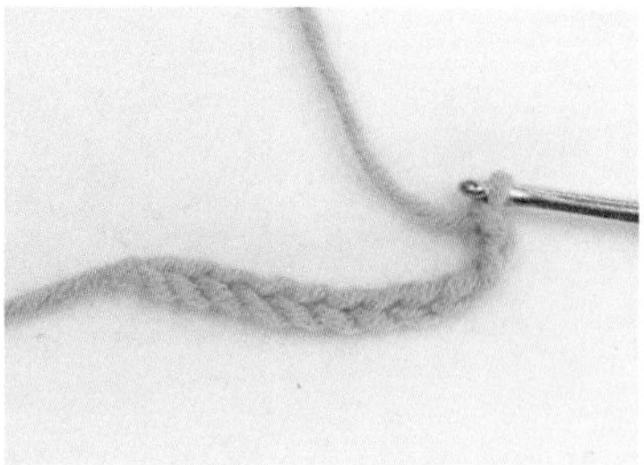

2 Add one more chain stitch. This stitch is known as the "turning chain" (**0**) and brings the row up to the height of the stitches. It is not included in the stitch count of the row.

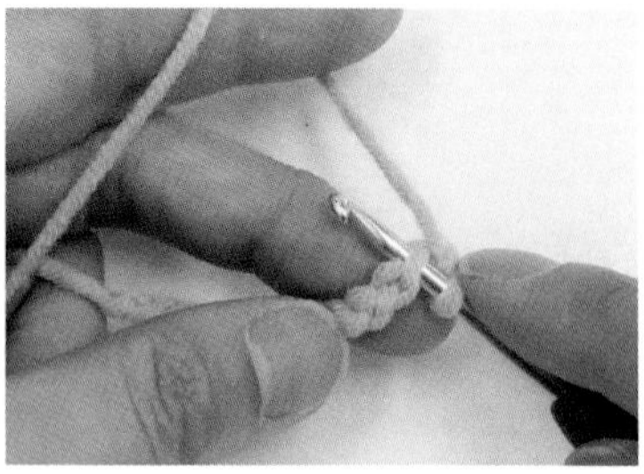

3 Skip the turning chain and insert the hook in the next chain and make a single crochet (**X**).

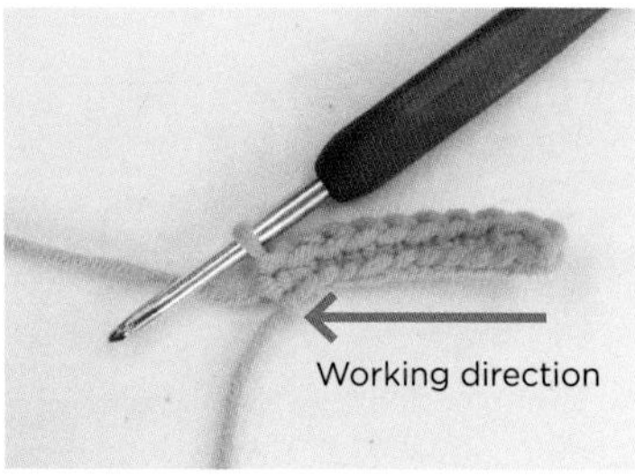

4 Work a single crochet in each of the remaining chain stitches to finish the row.

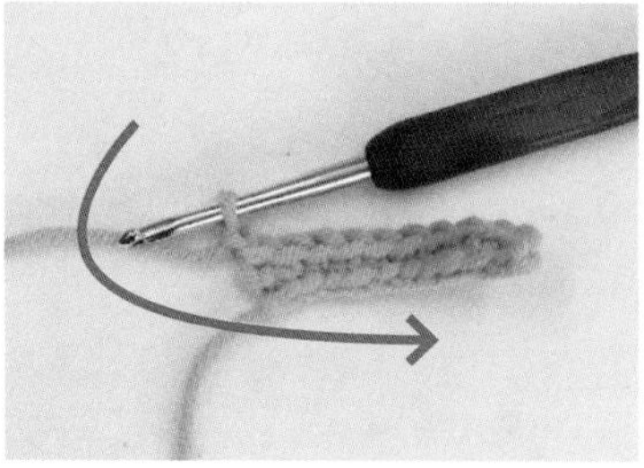

5 At the end of the row work one chain stitch (turning chain), and then turn your work around.

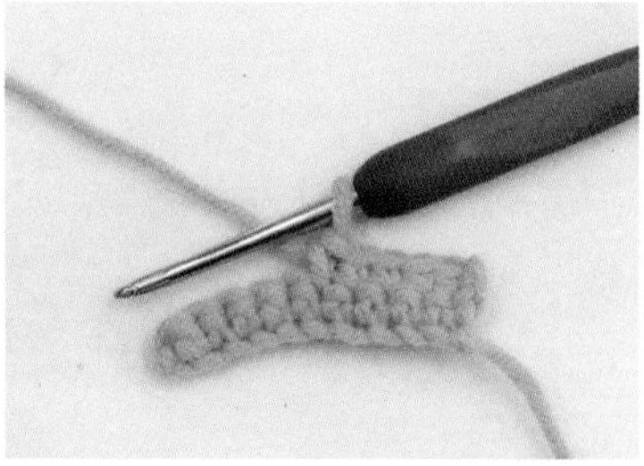

6 Insert your hook in the stitch at the base of the turning chain and work a single crochet. Continue working single crochet stitches across the row. Repeat steps 5 & 6 as needed.

7 The photo shows the unique pattern created by alternating right side rows and wrong side rows of single crochet stitches.

Working in Rounds

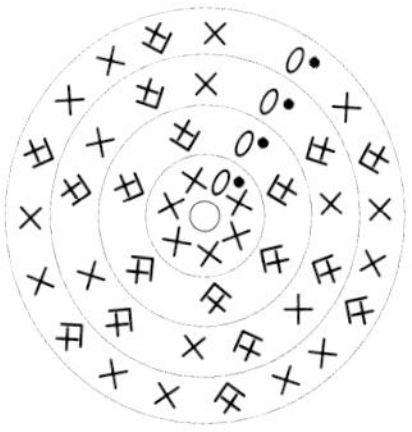

This style is most frequently used when making dolls, as it creates a pouch which can be stuffed. There is a formula which needs to be learnt, so practice it well.

» Starting Ring (Magic / Adjustable Ring)

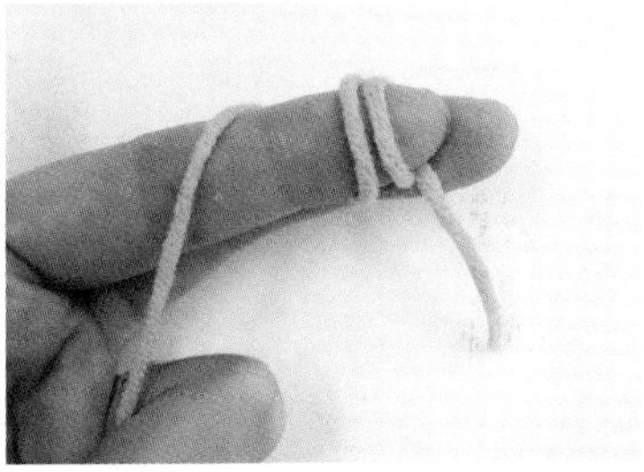

1 Wind the yarn tail twice around the index finger on your left hand.

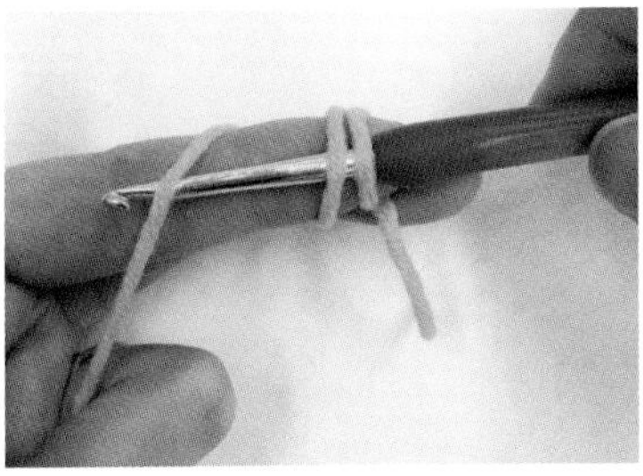

2 Insert the hook under the wound yarn and under the working yarn.

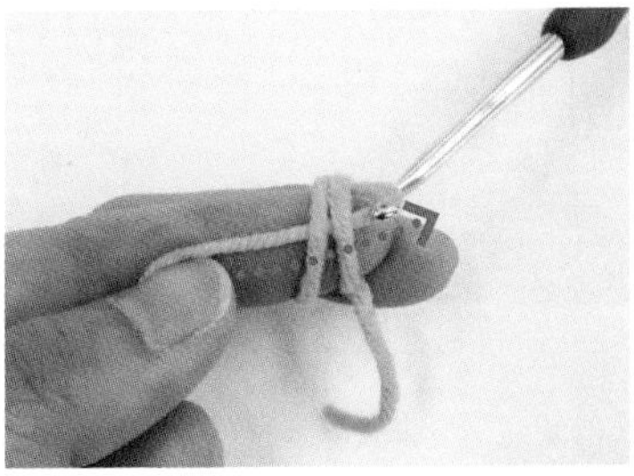

3 Pull the working yarn through, holding the yarn tail between the index and middle finger.

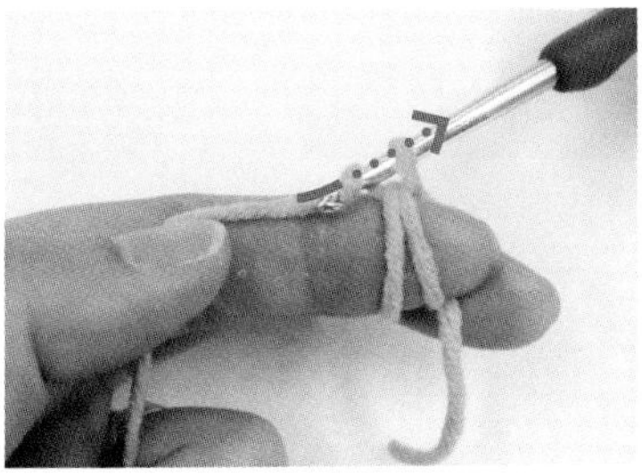

4 Wrap the yarn over the hook and pull it through the loop on hook.

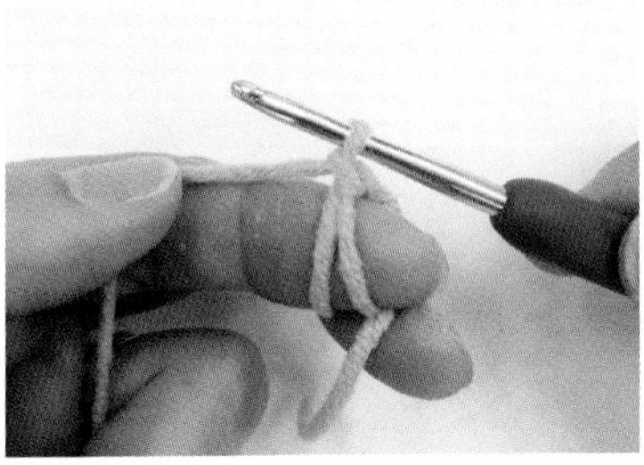

5 The ring is made and you can start crocheting.

» First Round

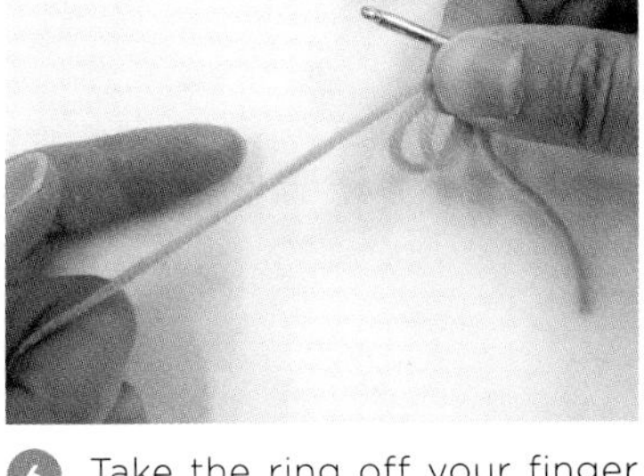

6 Take the ring off your finger carefully.

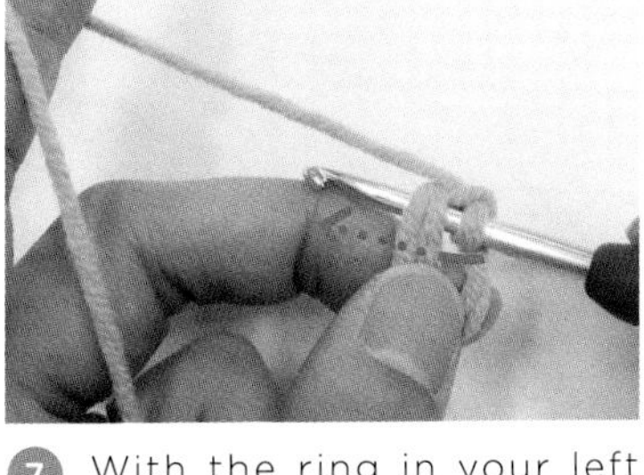

7 With the ring in your left hand, insert the hook into the ring under two strands of yarn.

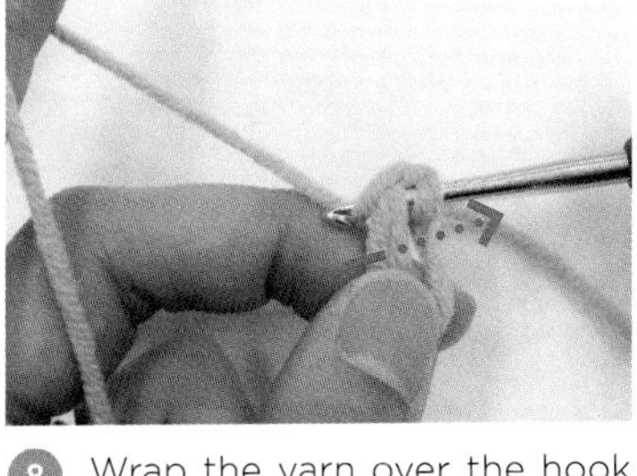

8 Wrap the yarn over the hook and pull it through the ring.

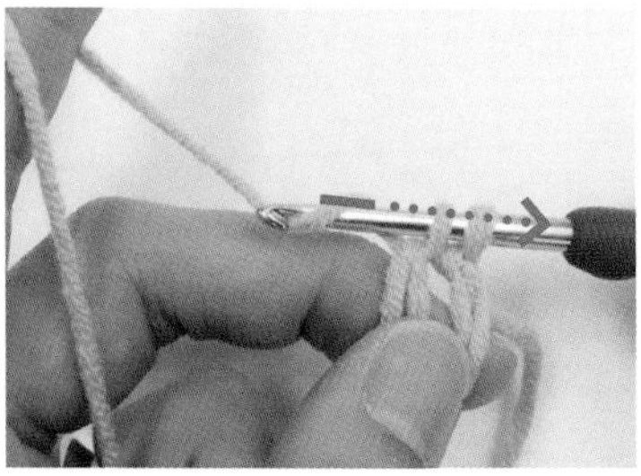

9 Wrap the yarn over the hook again and pull it through both loops on hook to complete a single crochet (X).

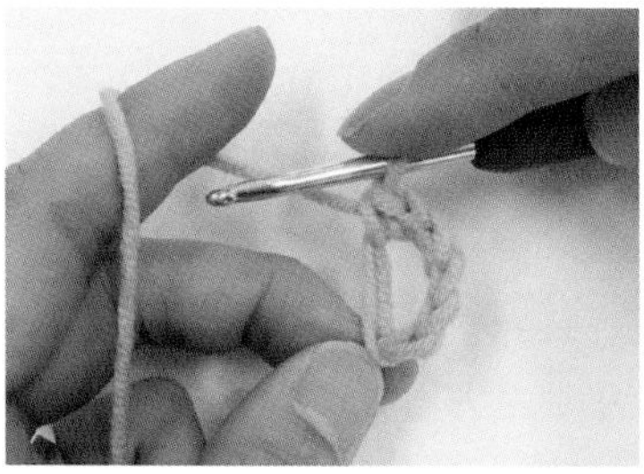

10 Repeat steps 7-9 five times more. You have made 6 single crochets.

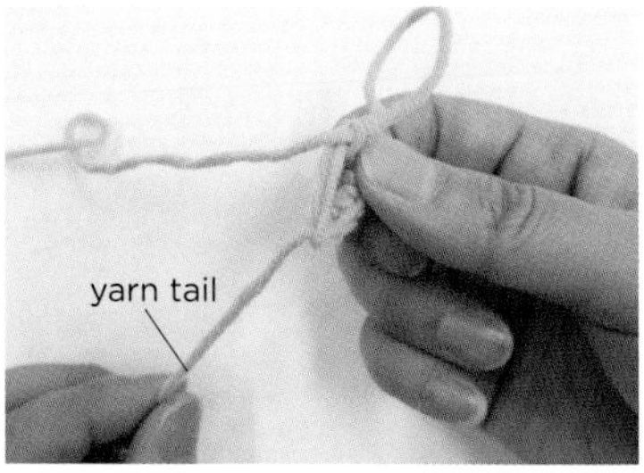

11 Enlarge the working loop on hook and remove hook (taking care not to pull out the stitches). Holding the stitches (with the thumb near the working loop), gently pull the yarn tail to identify which of the two yarn rings is moving.

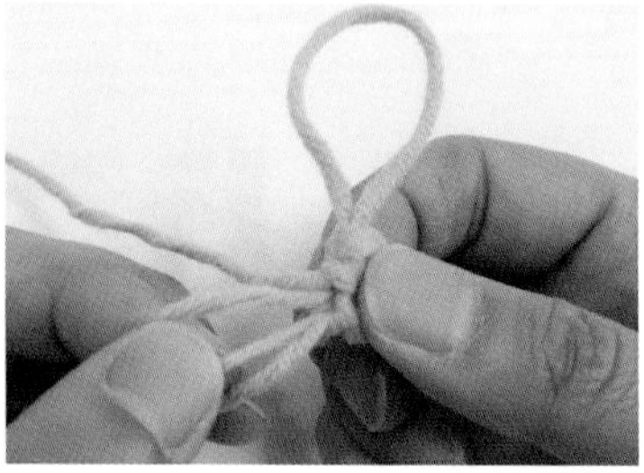

12 Hold that yarn ring and gently tug the bottom of the ring downwards (away from your thumb) to close the other ring.

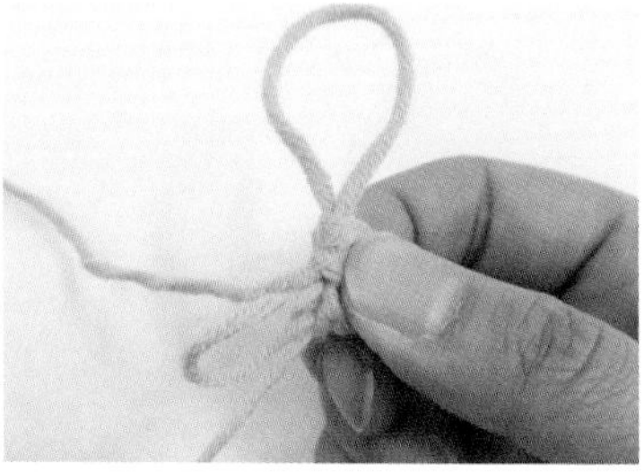

13 When the other ring is tightly closed, tug on the yarn tail to close the first ring.

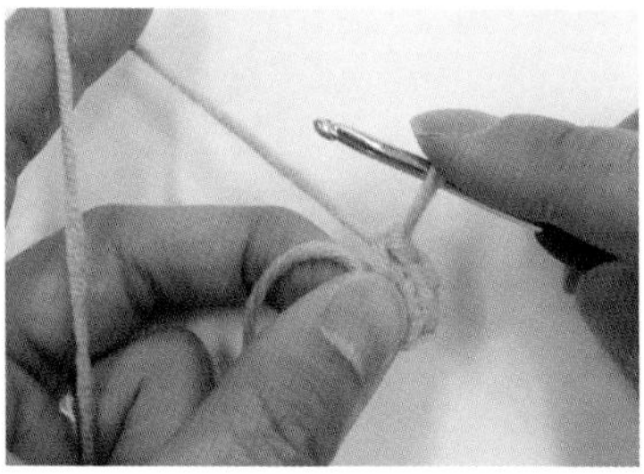

14 Place the hook back in the working loop.

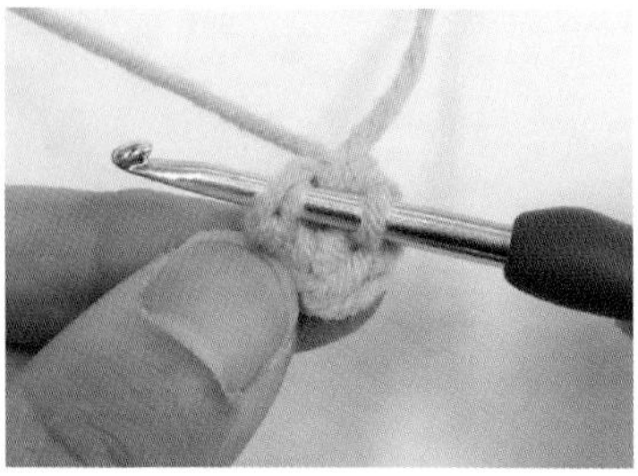

15 Insert the hook in the first single crochet made.

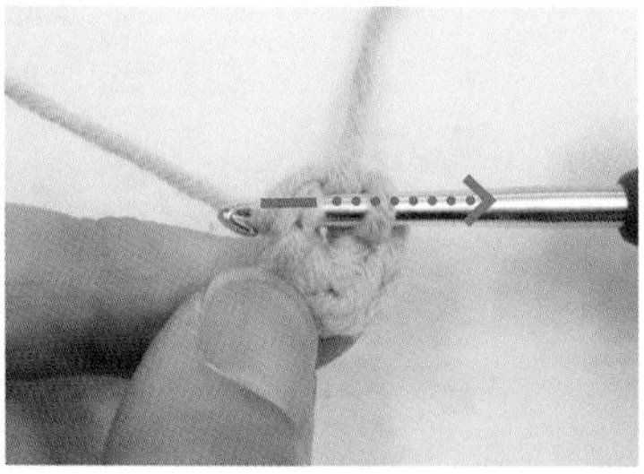

16 Wrap the yarn over the hook and pull the yarn through the stitch and through the loop on the hook to make a slip stitch (•).

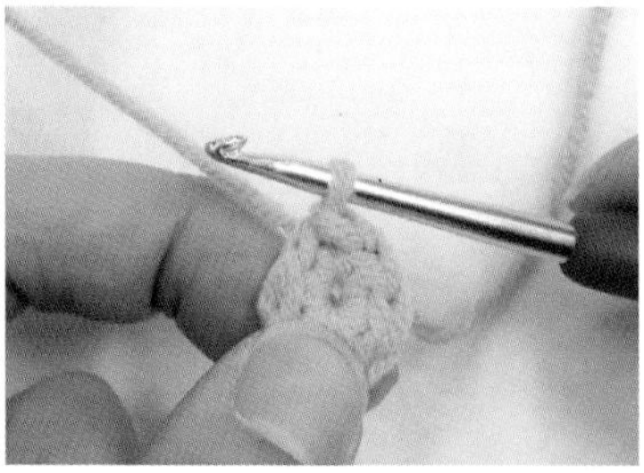

17 You have now joined the first round of single crochet stitches with a slip stitch.

» Second Round

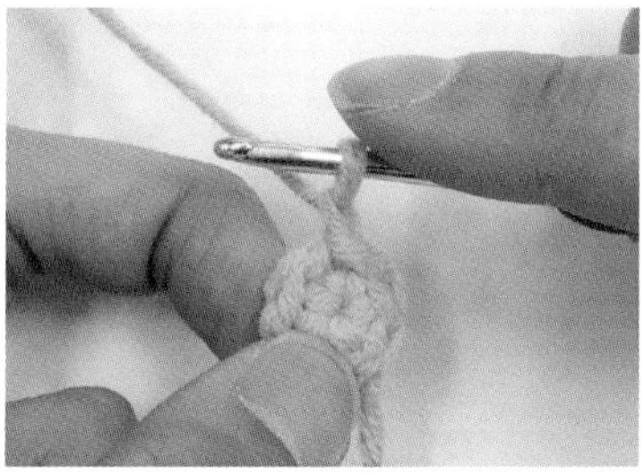

18 To start the round, make one chain stitch, known as the "raising chain" (0), to bring the round up to the height of the stitches.

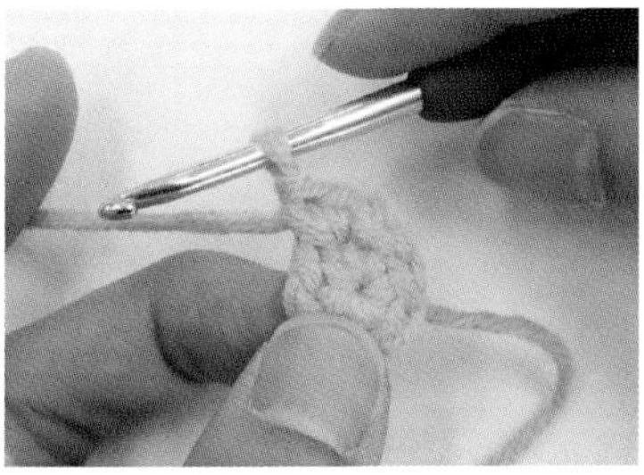

19 Work two single crochet (✕✕) in the first stitch.

tip

Finding the first stitch of a round: At the end of a round, take care not to work in the chain stitch you made, as this stitch is not included in the stitch count of the round. The next stitch is the first single crochet you made.

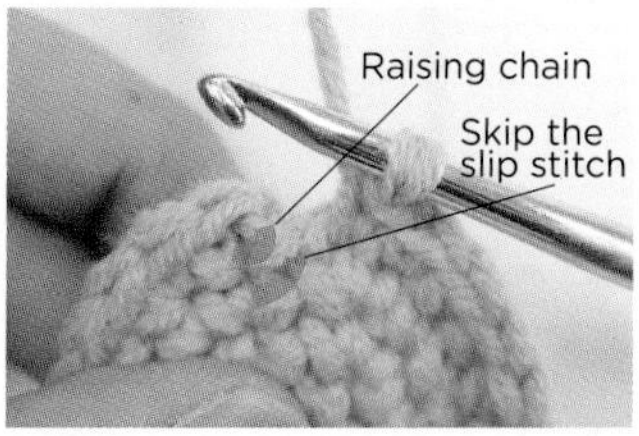

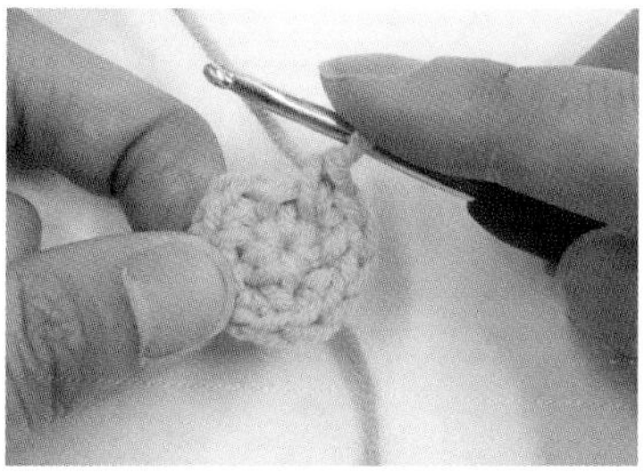

20 Work 2 single crochet stitches in each of the next five stitches - twelve stitches made.

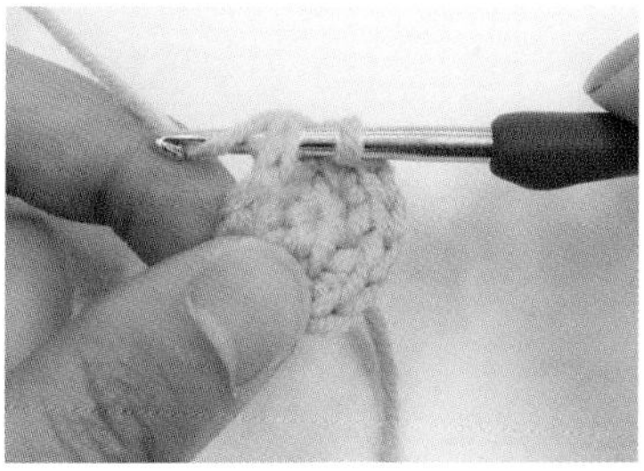

21 Insert the hook in the first single crochet and join with a slip stitch.

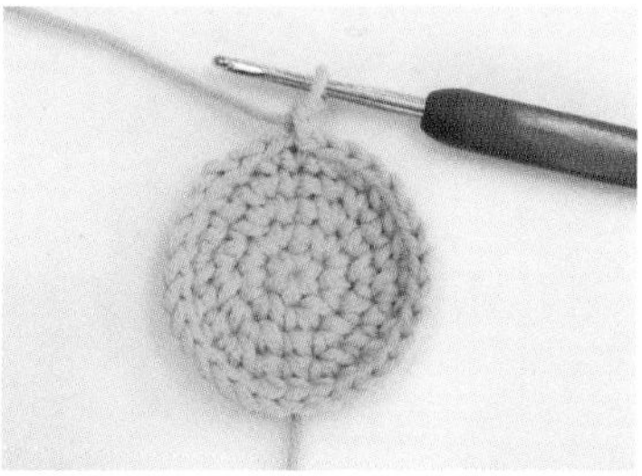

22 The photo shows 5 rounds of stitches complete.

Making Ovals

This method is created by working stitches around both the top and the bottom side of the foundation chain. It is similar to working in rounds, as each oval round is also joined with a slip stitch. We use this method for making soles of shoes, or the base of a bag. In this book, it is used for Benjy's head and Caleb & Clara's shoes.

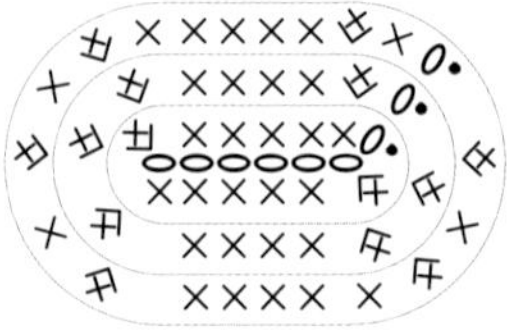

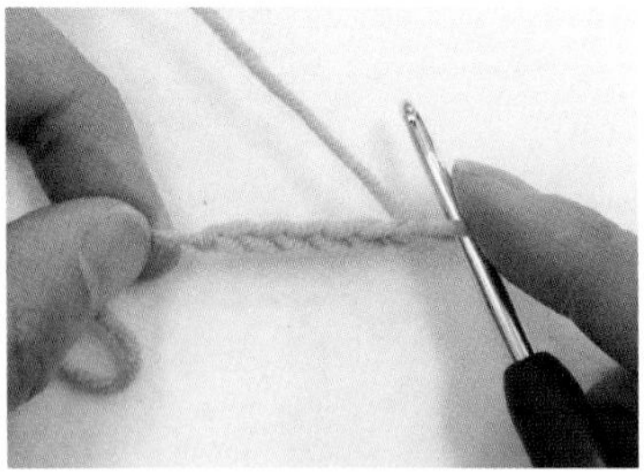

1 Make a foundation chain of 6 stitches (○).

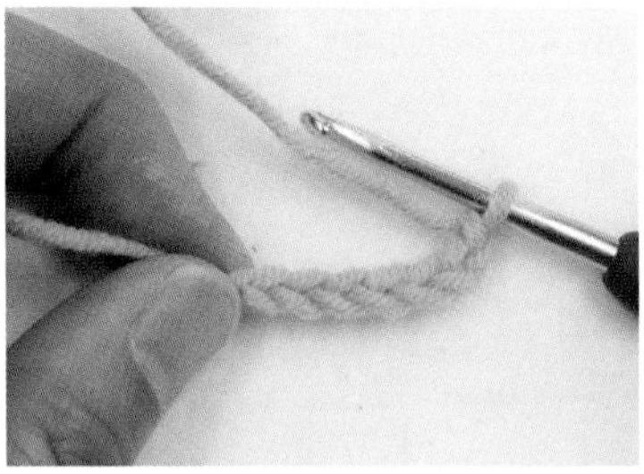

2 Add one raising chain (0) to bring the row up to height.

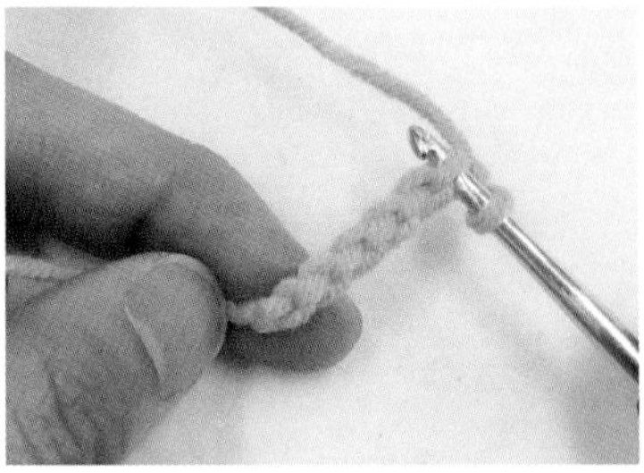

3 Skip the raising chain and insert the hook in the next chain and make a single crochet (×).

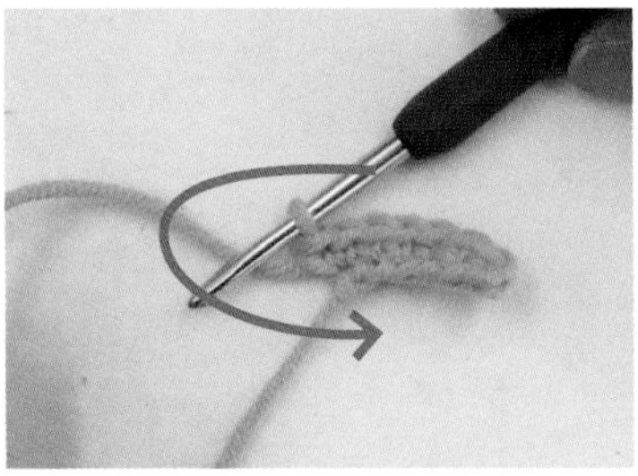

4 Work single crochet stitches in each of the next 4 chains. In the last chain, work 2 single crochets (⩔) in the same stitch. Rotate the piece.

5 With the other side of the foundation chain on top, starting in the first chain, work single crochet (×) stitches in each of the first 5 chains.

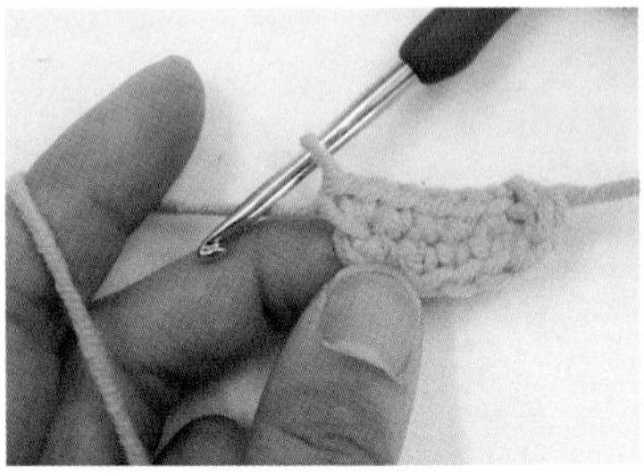

6 In the last chain work 2 single crochets (⩔). On each end of the chain is an increase.

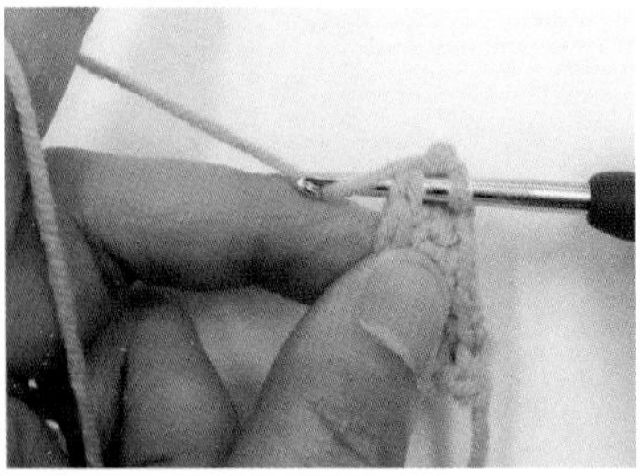

7 Find the first single crochet and join with a slip stitch (•).

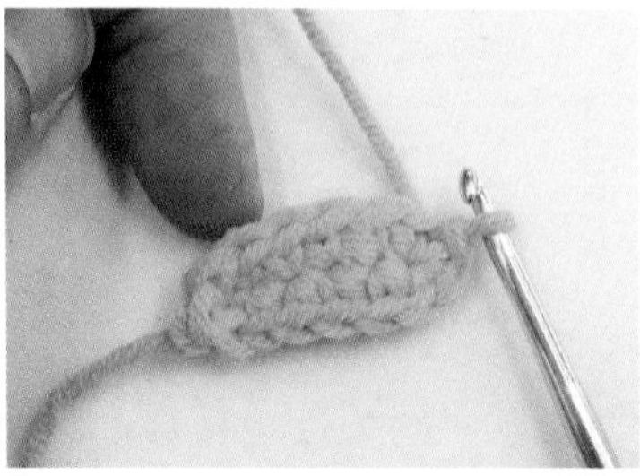

8 The first oval round is finished. The next rounds are similar to working in the round.

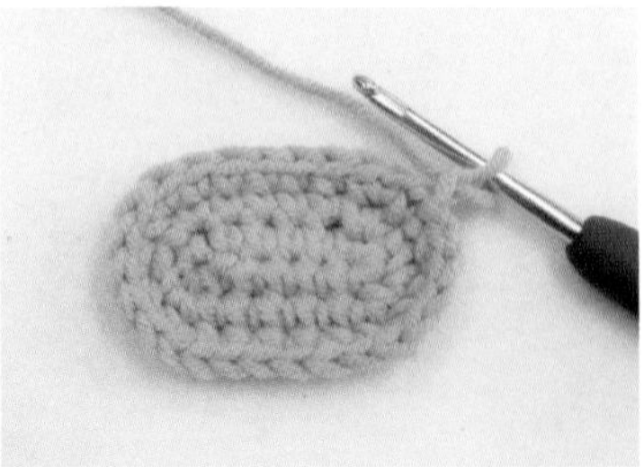

9 The photo shows 3 completed oval rounds.

Making Tubes

This is used to create circular tubes. We use this to make the Caleb & Clara's pants and Jack Lion's mane.

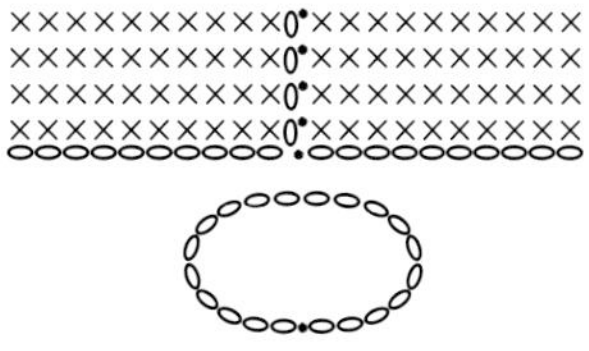

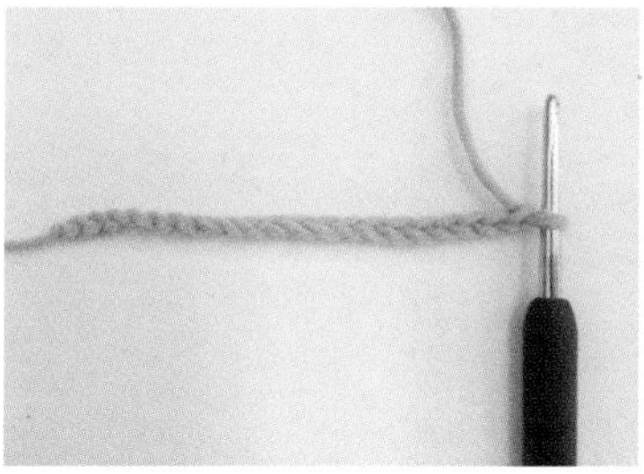

1 Make a foundation chain of 20 stitches (○).

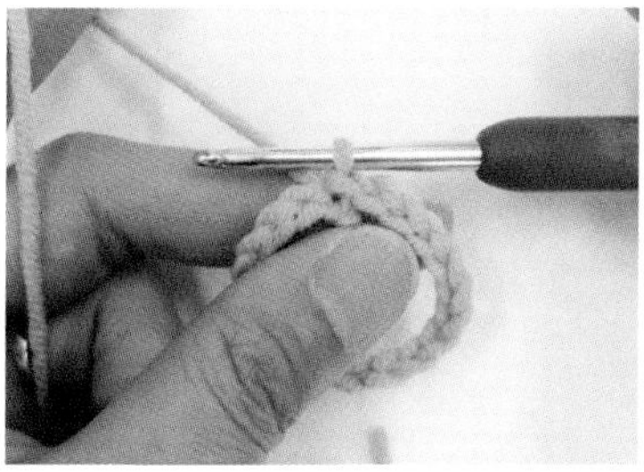

2 Taking care not to twist the stitches, insert the hook in the first chain and make a slip stitch to form a ring. (•).

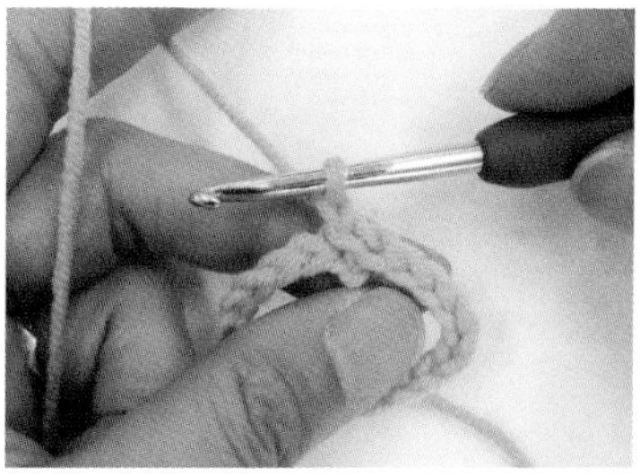

3 Make one raising chain (0). - to bring the round up to height.

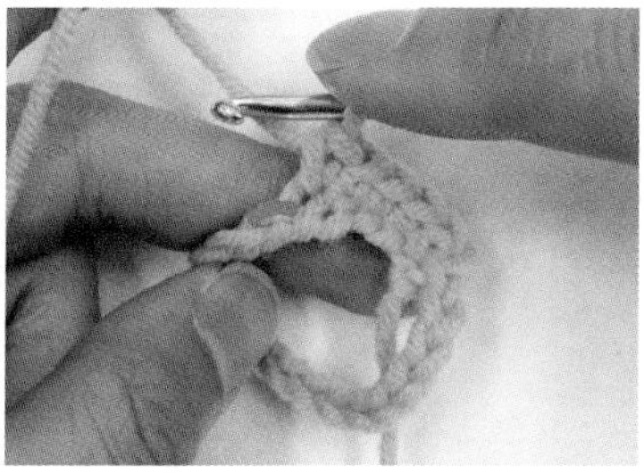

4 Work a single crochet (X) in each stitch around. The photo shows the first 5 stitches of the round.

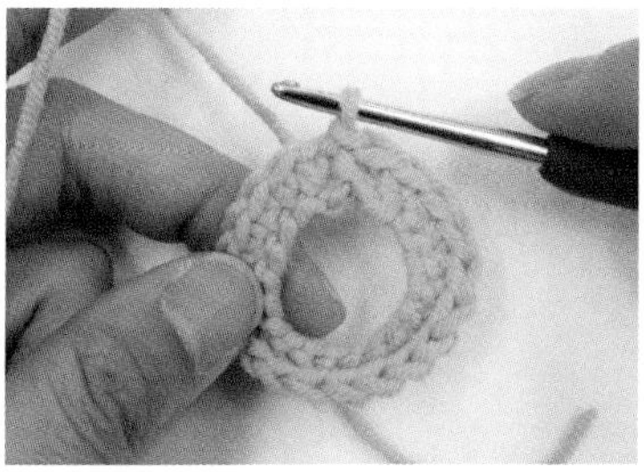

5 After finishing the round, join with a slip stitch to the first single crochet.

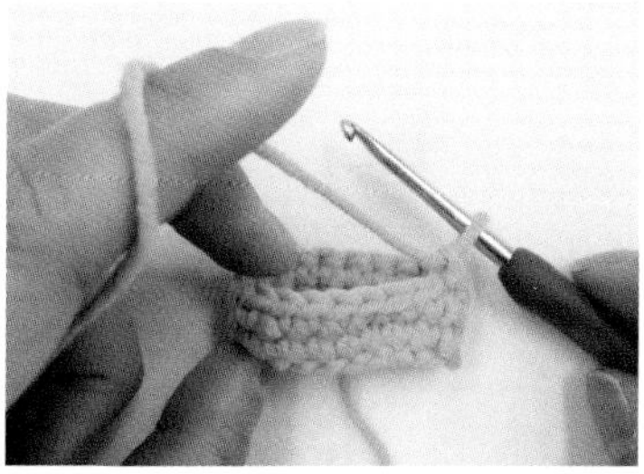

6 Repeat steps 3-5 for as many rounds as needed. The photo shows the first two rounds of a tube.

◦ TECHNIQUES ◦

Changing Colors

This method can also be used to start a new ball of yarn, or when the yarn breaks and you need to rejoin. It is best to change colors at the end of a row or round.

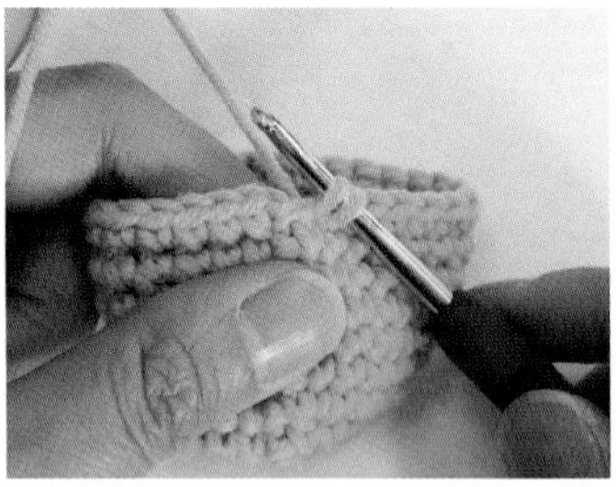

1. Before finishing the last stitch of the round, when there are two loops left on the hook.

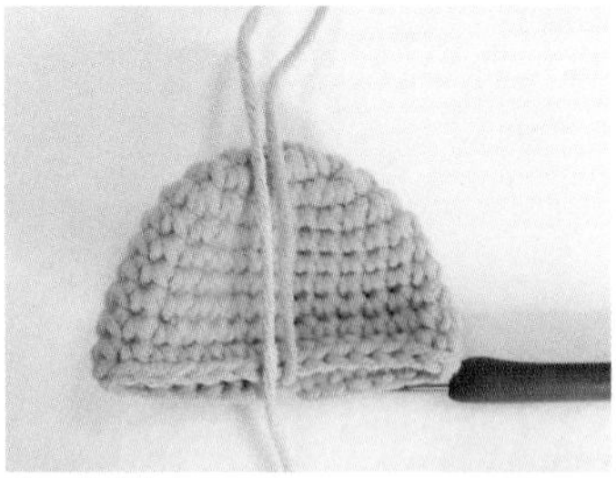

2. Move the yarn to the back of the piece and place the new yarn next to it.

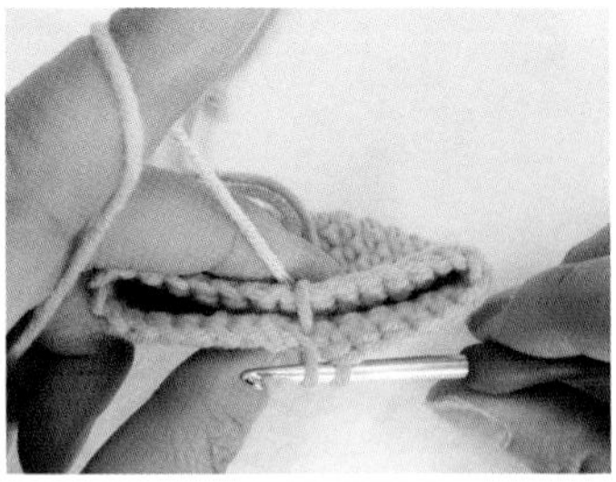

3. Hold the two strands of yarn against the piece with your middle finger and wrap the yarn around the index finger of your left hand, as it is now the working yarn.

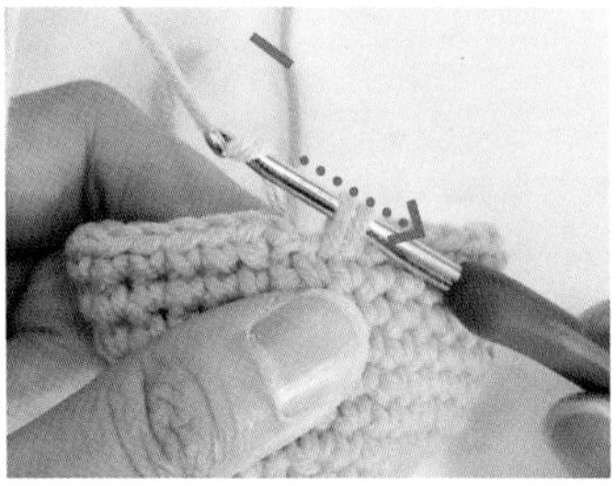

4. Wrap the new yarn over the hook and pull it through the remaining two loops on the hook to complete the stitch.

5. Slip stitch in the first stitch to join and complete the round.

6. Make a raising chain stitch to bring the yarn up to height.

7 Instead of knotting the yarn tails together, work over the two strands with the new yarn for about 4 stitches.

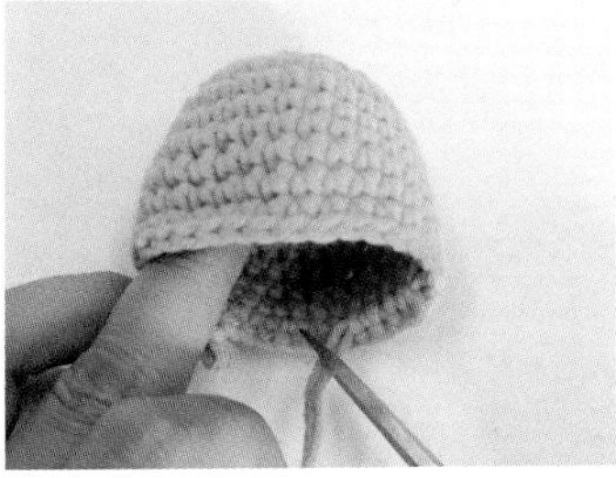

8 After working another 4 stitches without working over the tails, the old tails can be cut and the tail ends neatened.

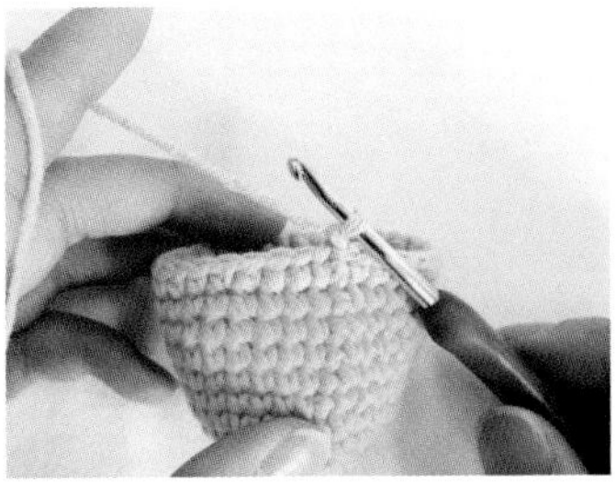

9 The first round in the new color is complete.

tip

When working over the yarn tails, keep them to the inside, making sure they are not visible from the outside.

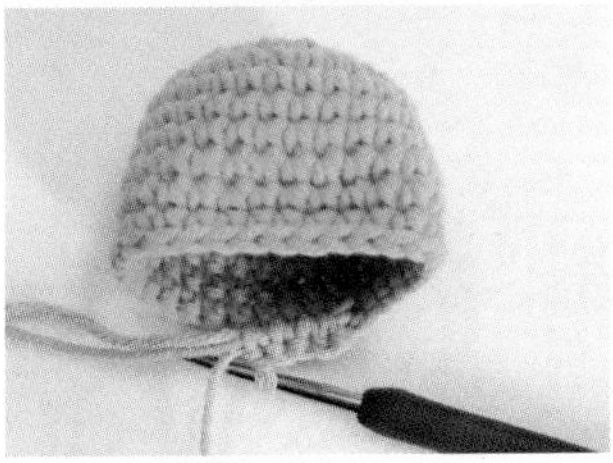

[inside]

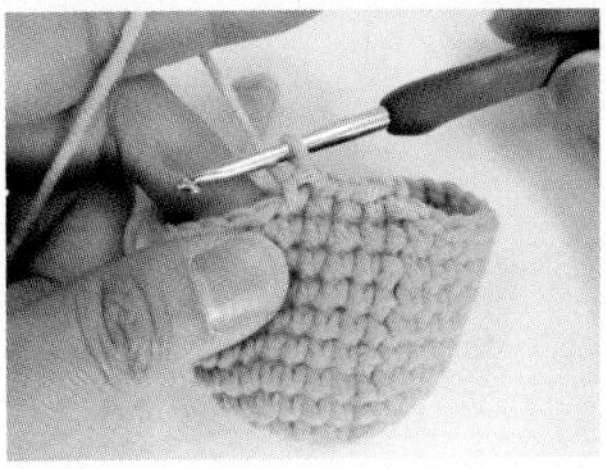

[outside]

Cutting the Yarn and Finishing Off

This is the default method for finishing off all crochet pieces, regardless of the stitch used. It is a way to tie off the work to make sure the stitches don't unravel.

1 When you have finished crocheting, without removing the hook, cut the yarn leaving a tail. Wrap the yarn over the hook again.

2 Pull the wrapped yarn through the stitch and then pull the yarn tail all the way out, removing the hook.

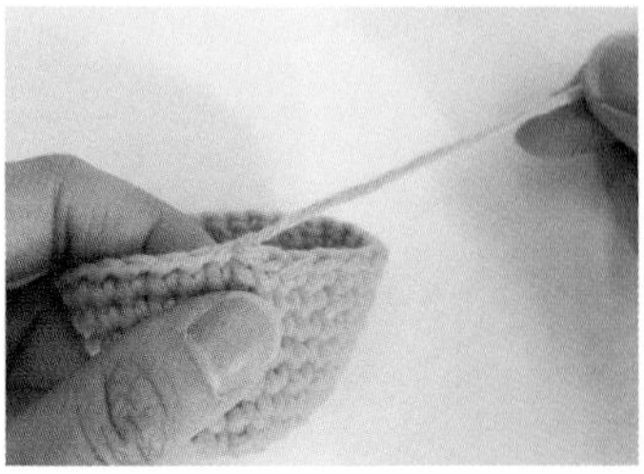

3 Tug the thread to tighten the knot, then trim the yarn, unless you need the yarn tail to assemble the pieces.

Hiding the Yarn Tails

This is a way to neaten up the long tails on pieces where the wrong side is visible or not stuffed. In this book, it is used for the skirt of the Bear Bride and Mister Hottie.

1 Cut the yarn and finish off. Using a yarn needle, sew under a few stitches on the wrong side (inside) of the work to hide the tail.

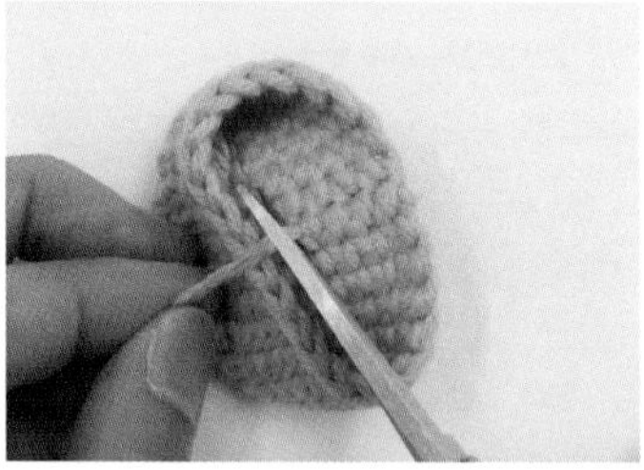

2 When the tail is neatly sewn in, remove the needle and trim the yarn to finish.

Stuffing the Doll

Some stuffing tends to clump together, so tear off small pieces at a time and fluff it out before inserting it to shape the doll. Take care not to overstuff the doll by adding too much stuffing.

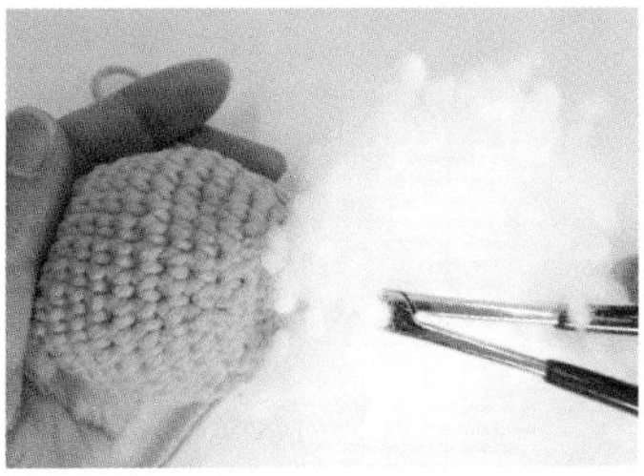

1. Using the forceps, tear off small amounts of stuffing and fill about one-third of the piece.

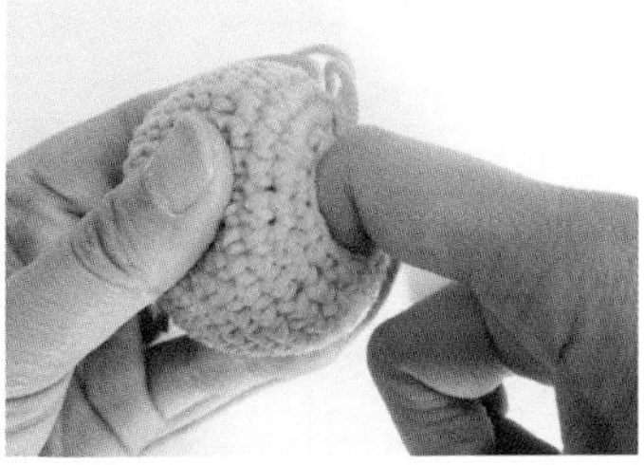

2. Use your fingers to push the stuffing towards the sides before adding more stuffing. Continue adding more stuffing with the forceps until the desired shape is obtained.

Closing the Last Round

This is used to close the hole after completing the last round. It is needed to finish off the dolls' heads and torsos, so practice it well.

1. After following the instructions for "Cutting the Yarn and Finishing Off", thread the tail onto a yarn needle.

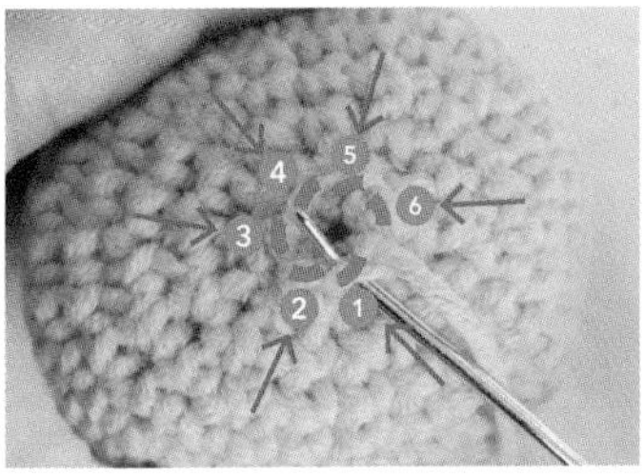

2. Working clockwise, insert the yarn needle (from outside towards center) under the front loop only of each of the six stitches in the last round.

3. Then tug the tail tightly to close the hole.

4. Insert the needle into the center hole, through the stuffing, and bring it out on the other side.

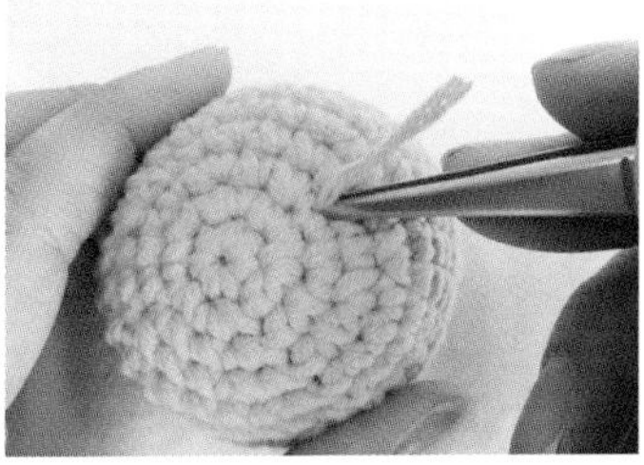

5. Trim the yarn and then using the tweezer, hide the small tail in the stuffed piece.

Sewing Crochet Pieces

Crochet fabrics are more difficult to sew because the surface is more uneven than other fabrics. We'll show you the various ways to sew the different pieces of the doll together.

Straight Stitching

Thread a medium-sized yarn needle with the same type of yarn used to make the doll. To create neat and even sewing stitches, sew in the gaps between the crochet stitches or in the gaps between the crocheted rows or rounds.

① Embroidery

This stitching is mainly used for decoration. Create even stitches by sewing between each crochet stitch and each row or round.

» between the crochet stitches

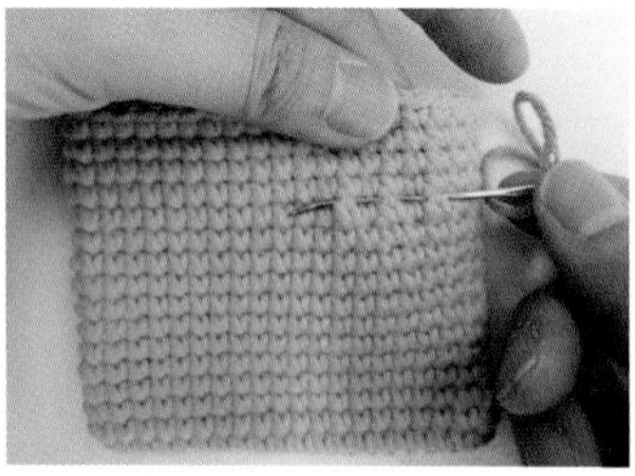

» between the rows or rounds

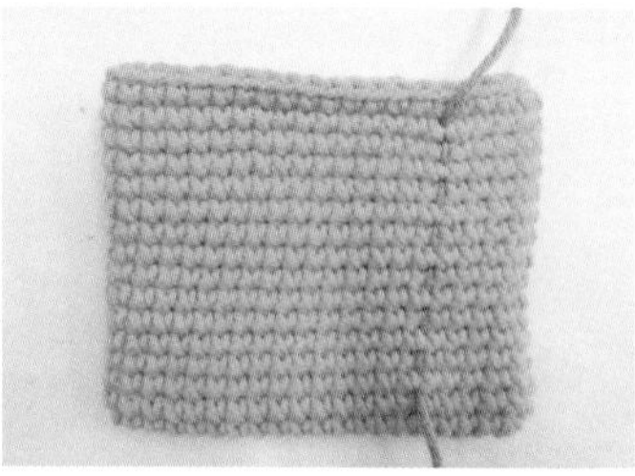

② Whipstitch

This technique leaves the sewing yarn exposed. It is mainly used to attach the arms or ears.

» across edges of fabric

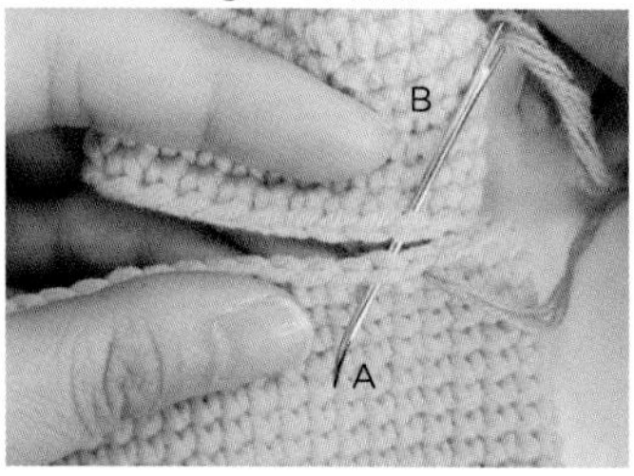

»

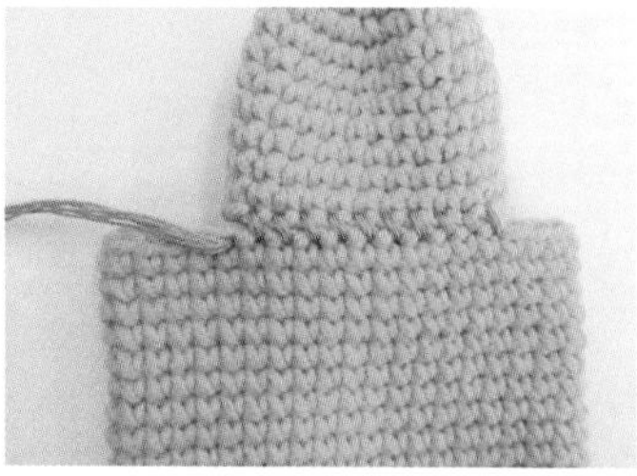

Bring the needle out from the inside in a stitch on crochet piece A. Insert the needle from front to back in a stitch on crochet piece B and bring it out to the front in a stitch on crochet piece A. Continue sewing in each stitch across, alternating A & B crochet pieces.

» horizontally across stitches - attaching arms

»

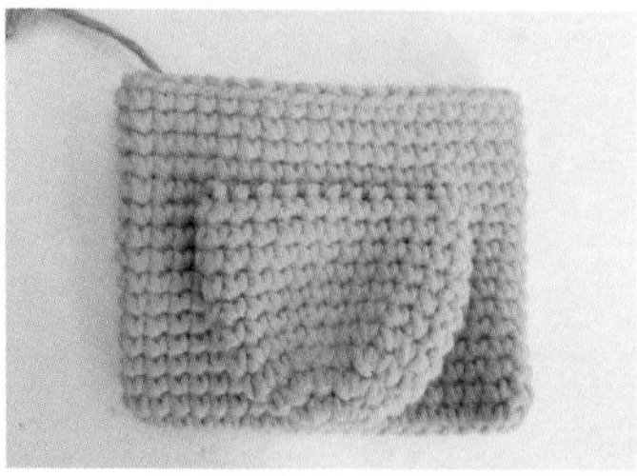

On the folded piece to be attached, insert the needle under both corresponding stitches, then insert needle in and out between the crochet stiches on the main piece. Continue sewing across until piece is attached.

» vertically across rounds - attaching ears

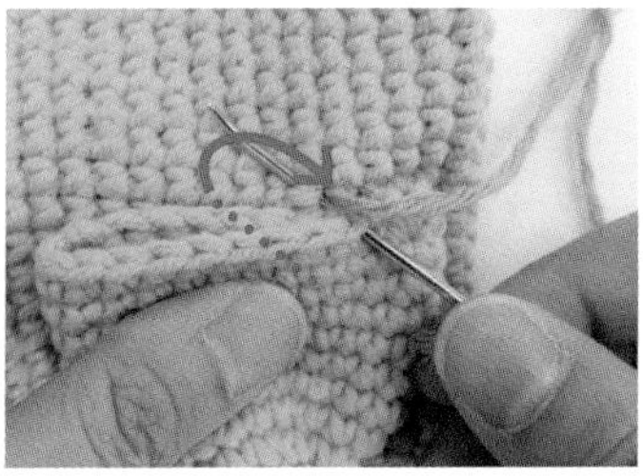

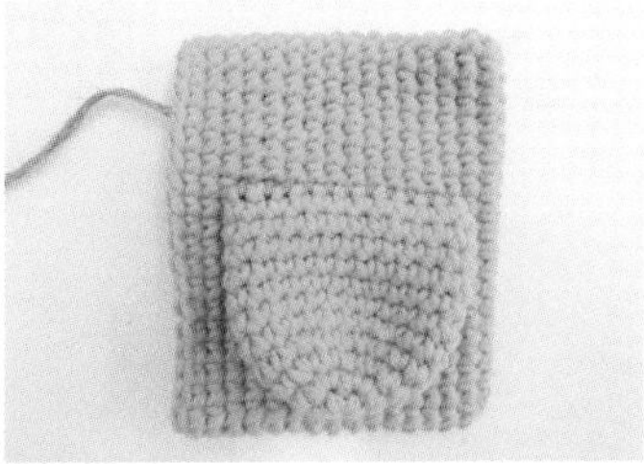

On the folded piece to be attached, insert the needle under both corresponding stitches, then insert needle in and out between crocheted rounds on the main piece. Continue sewing across until piece is attached.

③ Mattress (Invisible) Stitch

The sewing yarn is not visible with this stitch. It connects crochet pieces together firmly and is mainly used to attach the body and head.

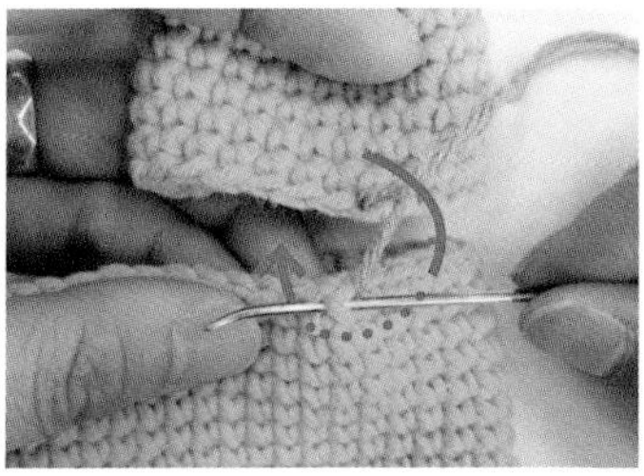

1. Insert the needle in and out between crochet stiches on first one piece and then on the second piece.

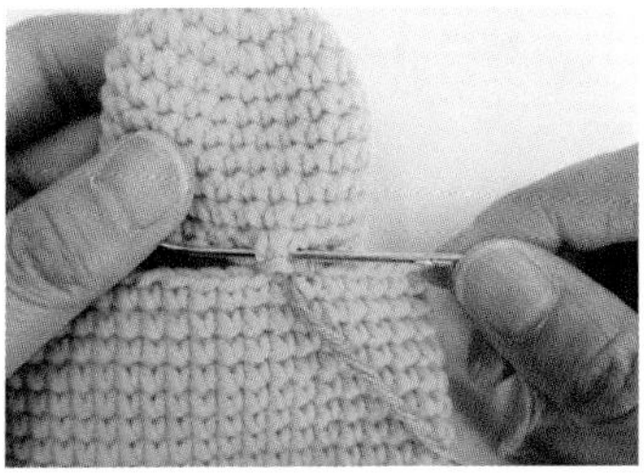

2. Now repeat, inserting the needle back in the same place it came out of on each piece.

3. Repeat this for about 3 to 4 stitches.

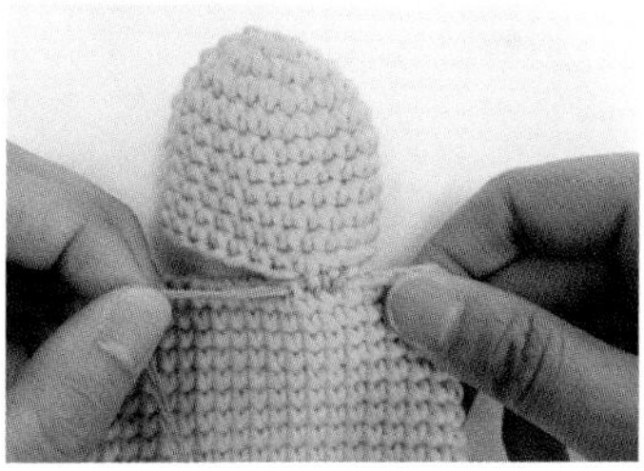

4. Then gently tug the yarn until the stitching disappears.

5. Continue doing this until the two pieces are joined together.

Curved Stitching

Separate the yarn used to make the doll into two strands. Thread one strand onto a smaller yarn needle for sewing, hiding the other strand under the piece. This technique is mainly used for stitching on a snout, cheeks, and other curved pieces.

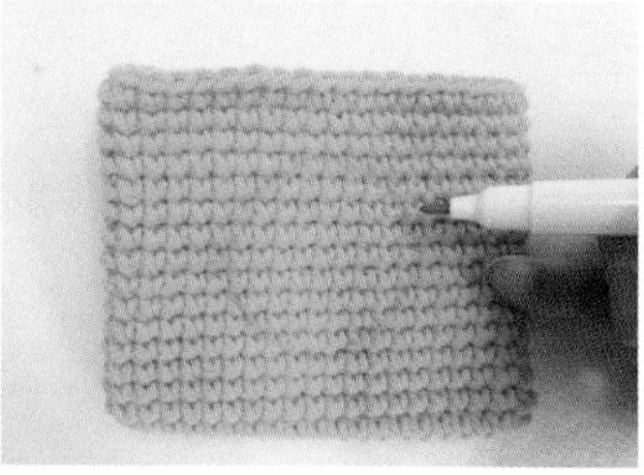

1 Using the water-soluble marking pen, mark the position of the curved piece on the fabric, making sure the shape is not distorted.

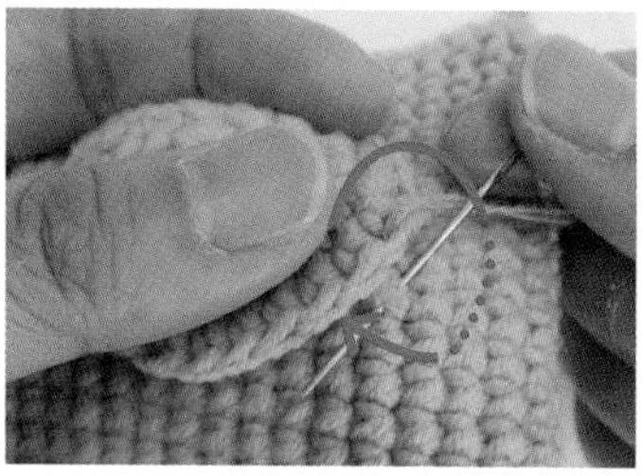

2 With the one strand threaded on the needle, and the other strand tucked under the piece, sew the curved piece onto the fabric, following the marked shape.

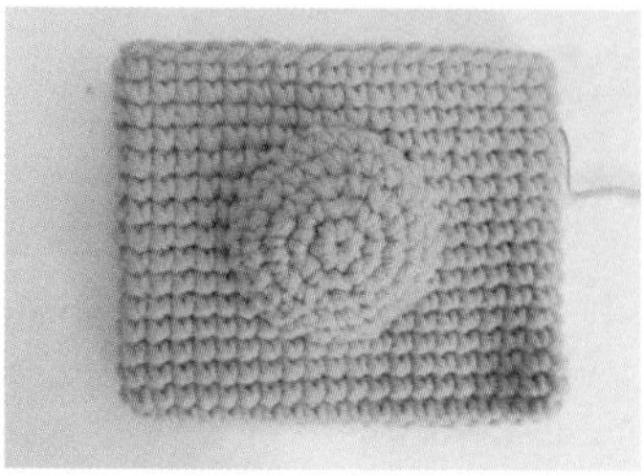

3 The curved piece is attached.

Taking a Break

When you are in the middle of crocheting and need to stop for a while, there is a risk that the stitches will unravel. Here is a tip to prevent that.

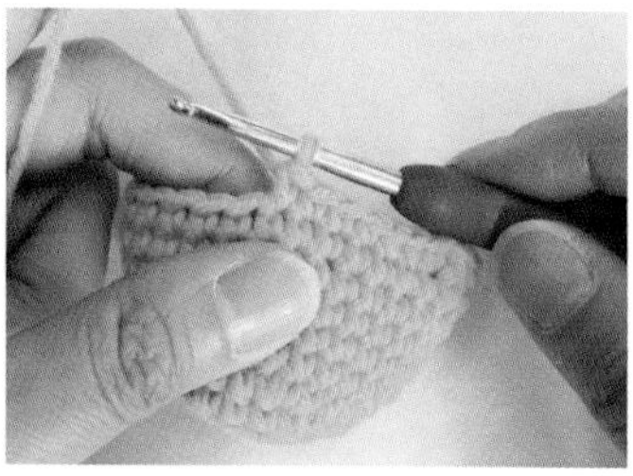

1 When you want to stop, finish the last stitch.

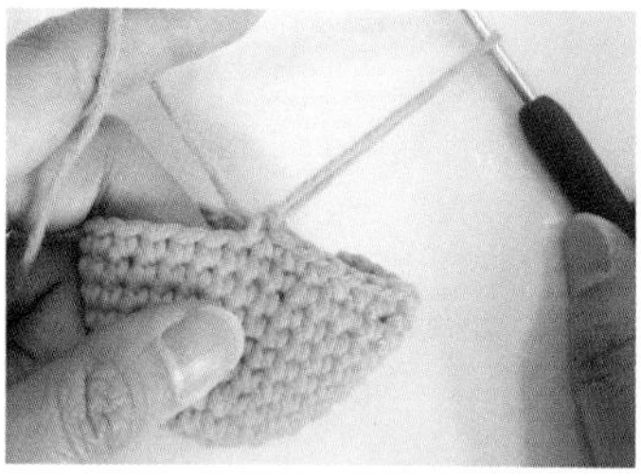

2 Pull the hook to make a large working loop and then remove the hook. Even if the yarn is pulled, the big loop will prevent the stitches from pulling out.

Making Dolls of Different Sizes

By changing the weight of the yarn and the hook size, you can make a variety of different sized dolls using the same pattern.

1. Two strands Medium Weight yarn & 4.00 mm hook
2. Single strand Medium Weight yarn & 3.00 mm hook
3. Single strand Fine Weight yarn & 2.25 mm hook

The photo shows three bears all made with the same pattern, just using different yarns and hooks. The thicker the yarn used (with appropriate hook), the larger the doll, with bigger stitches in the fabric. Please note: When I use one strand of Medium Weight yarn, I use a 3.00 mm hook or US size D-3 (3.25 mm).

◦ Frequently Asked Questions ◦

Q1 Do you need special yarn to crochet the dolls?

You can use any type of yarn for making the dolls. The important thing is to use the appropriate hook for the yarn used. (See page 25 - Finding the Correct Hook for the Yarn.) Feel free to choose any type of yarn to create your dolls, regardless of the fiber content. By using a different yarn, you can create a unique doll using the same pattern. But please bear in mind, using pure cotton yarn is more healthier than any other fiber content for babies and children.

Q2 Why do crochet words confuse me?

If you're new to crochet, the terminology can be confusing at first. But if you look at each of the terms, it's easy to understand why they were so named. In the photo, the different crochet terms are labelled on the swatch, so let's make sure you know them before you start making your doll.

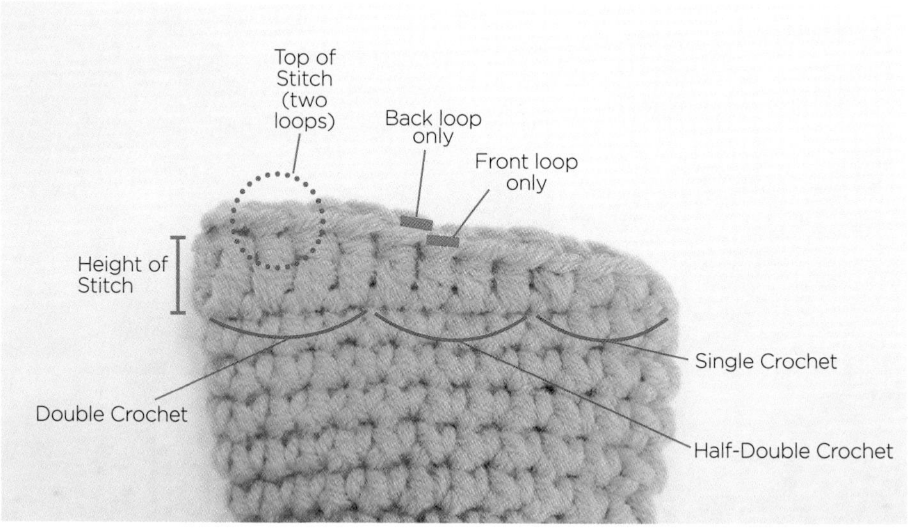

Q3 Do I have to join each round and start the next round with chain stitches?

Even if you decide not to join each round, and work the piece in a spiral, you will still be able to follow the pattern, but there will be a difference in how the pieces look. By joining the ends of rounds and starting the next round with raising chain stitches, makes it easier to count the stitches in the round as well as to count the number of rounds worked. It also makes the lines cleaner when you change colors. Compare the photos to see the difference.

Working in a spiral   Joining rounds + raising chain stitches

Q4 The slip stitch joins slant diagonally. What should I do?

In crochet, when making a stitch, the right hand naturally pulls to the right (or to the left, if you're left-handed). The stitches made tend to lean towards that direction. To prevent this, pull the wrapped yarn upwards when making a new stitch. This is one way to keep the stitches straight.

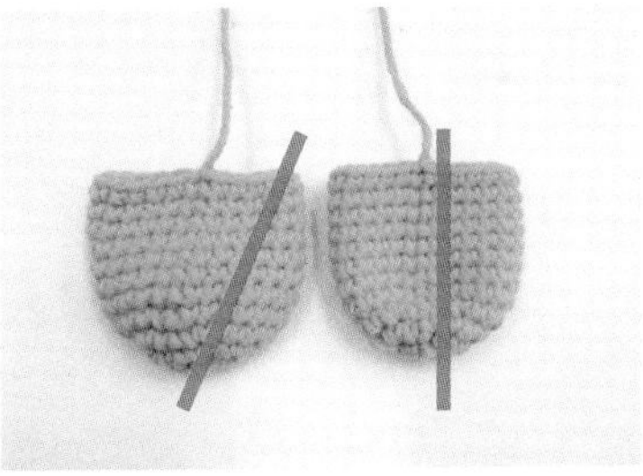

- **Left:** The joins slant to the right
- **Right:** The joins are more straight

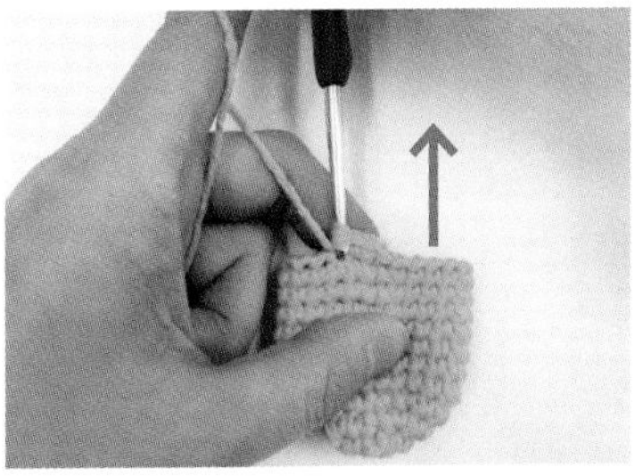

When pulling the wrapped yarn through, consciously pull the yarn upwards. This gives your dolls a neater finish.

Q5 How can I make my stitches tighter?

For a beautifully made doll, it is important to have all your stitches neat and uniform. Knowing the principles and processes of making crochet stitches, helps to improve your doll-making skills.
Let's look at the process of making a single crochet stitch.

» Uneven stitches

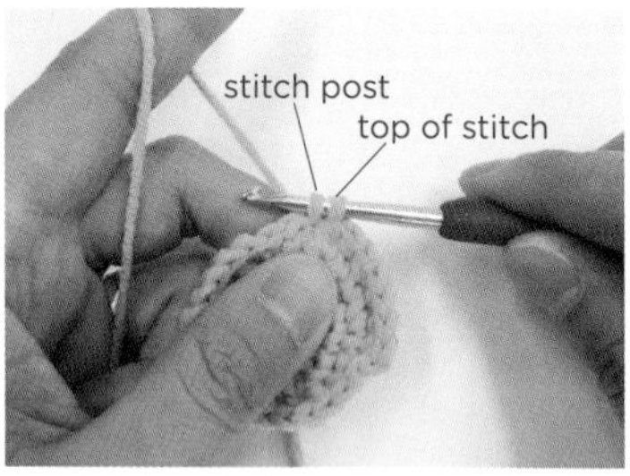

When making a single crochet stitch, the first loop on the hook becomes the post of the stitch, and the second loop becomes the top of the stitch.

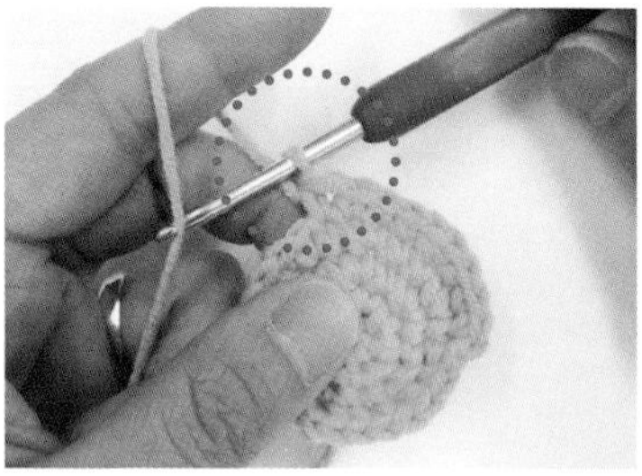

Therefore, if the first loop is loose, and the second loop is tight on the hook, the resulting post of the stitch will be slack and create a hole in the fabric.

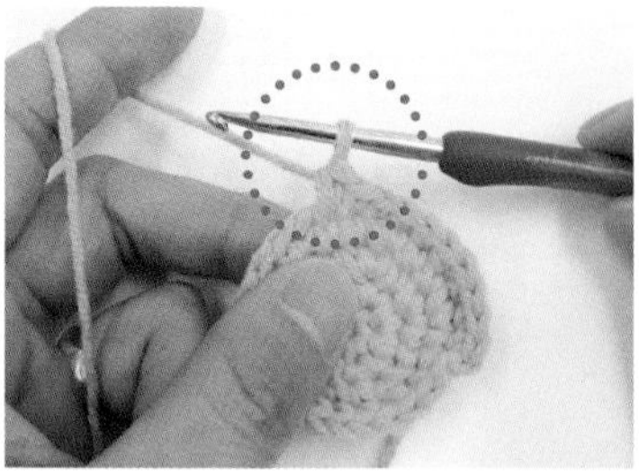

Similarly, when the first loop is tight and the second loop loose, the stitch post is smaller and the tops of the stitches are floppy.

» How to crochet evenly and tightly

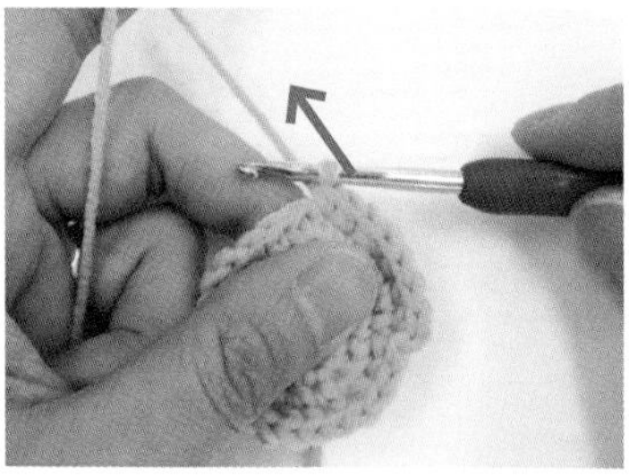

Before starting a single crochet stitch, make sure the loop is tight on the shaft of the hook. Move your index finger in the direction shown, to get tension in the yarn.

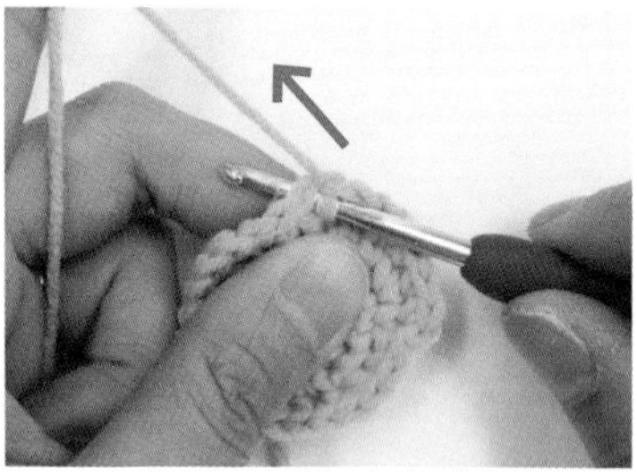

After inserting the hook in the stitch on the previous round, tension the yarn again, before wrapping the yarn over the hook.

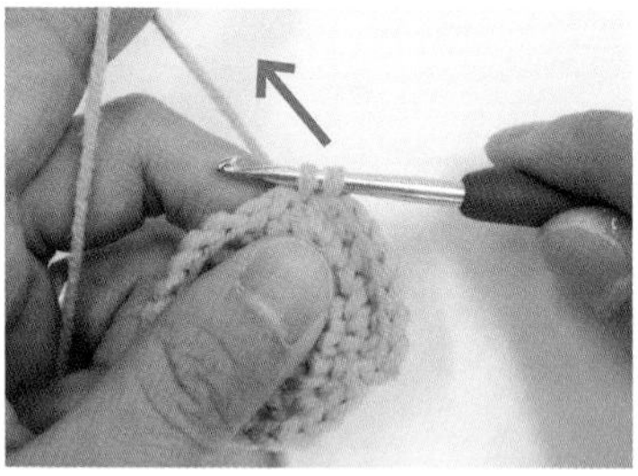

After pulling the wrapped yarn through the stitch, with the two loops on the hook, tension the yarn once more before completing the stitch. Working like this will make your stitches neat and even.

Q6

How do I distinguish between the right and wrong sides of the crochet fabric?

When working in crocheted rows, the direction changes with each row, so the right and wrong sides alternate. However, when working in rounds, ovals and tubes, the direction stays the same and there is a definite right side and wrong side. In the case of single crochet stitches (✕) which are mostly used in this book, the letter V is visible on the right side of the fabric. On the wrong side, one can see small horizontal lines on the stitches. You can decide which side you want to have on the outside of your doll, and then make sure all your doll pieces have the same side showing.

Single Crochet - right side (outside)

Single Crochet - wrong side (inside)

Q7

Q7 How do I wash my dolls?

Basically, we recommend that you follow the laundry instructions on the yarn label. Use a gentle detergent and rinse very thoroughly. If the yarn allows it, place the doll in a laundry net bag before tumble drying. To dry the stuffing, place the doll in a well-ventilated area.

◦ Reading the Patterns ◦

For a beginner, or even someone with experience in crochet, it is easy to miss a row or round, or even miss some stitch instructions when trying to follow written crochet patterns. In this book I use a narrative stitch pattern, so that you can see the instructions at a glance and reduce mistakes.

I also use crochet stitch charts and photo tutorials to help you understand the pattern so you can create your own doll.

1

Part
Identifies which part of the doll you're working on.

Starting Chain & Slip Stitch
The starting chain stitches and the end slip stitches are here, so you don't miss them.

Multiply
Repeat the instructions in the parentheses by the amount of the number.

Feet (Socks) + Legs
*Please see Making ovals on page 46.

Cream

Chain stitch 8

Round 1: (18)	0	(X 7 V 1) * 2 •
Round 2: (24)	0	V 1 X 6 V 3 X 6 V 2 •
Round 3: (30)	0	X 1 V 1 X 6 (X 1 V 1) * 3 X 6 (X 1 V 1) * 2 •
Round 4: (30)	0	X 30 •
Round 5: (24)	0	X 6 (X 1 Λ 1) * 6 X 6 •
Round 6: (18)	0	X 6 Λ 6 X 6 •
Rounds 7-8: (18)	0	X 18 •

Number of Stitches
Repeat the listed stitch by the amount of the number.

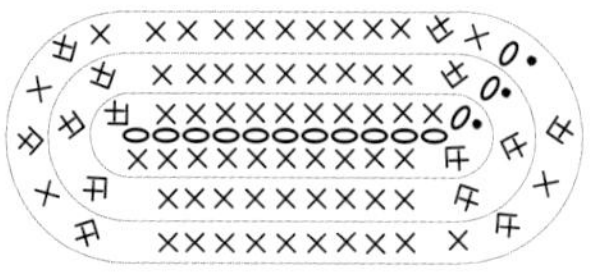

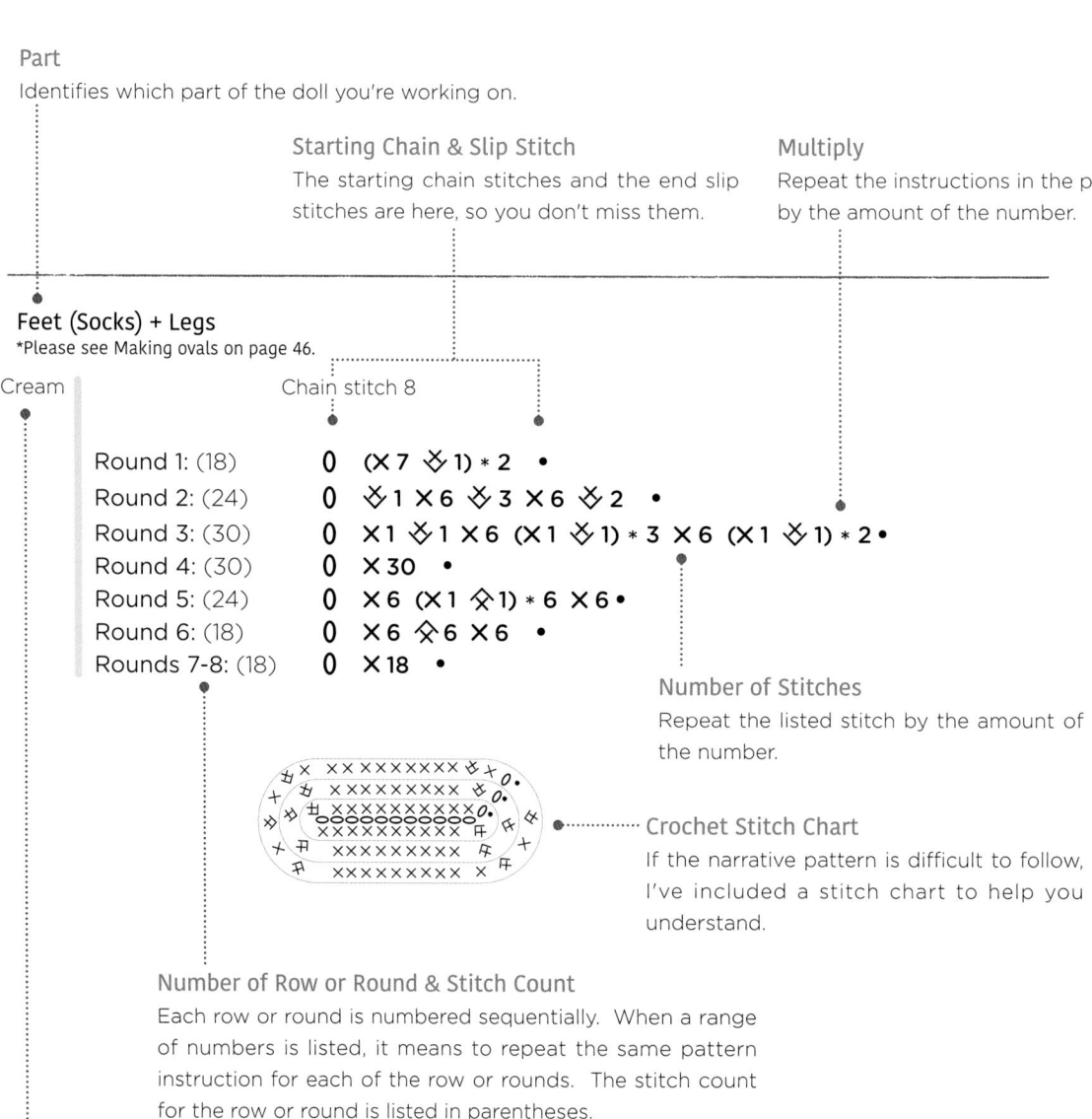

Crochet Stitch Chart
If the narrative pattern is difficult to follow, I've included a stitch chart to help you understand.

Number of Row or Round & Stitch Count
Each row or round is numbered sequentially. When a range of numbers is listed, it means to repeat the same pattern instruction for each of the row or rounds. The stitch count for the row or round is listed in parentheses.

Color
We can also see at a glance the color yarn to use for which rounds.

2

Cream	Round 18: (18)	0 ×18 •	
	Round 19-1: (18)	0 ×18 •	(Don't miss the front loop only!)
	Round 20-1: (18)	0 ×18 •	

Cut the yarn and finish off, hiding the tail on the inside.

Flesh Color		Insert the hook in the back loop of the first stitch on Round 18 and pull the yarn through.	
	Round 19-2: (18)	0 ×18 •	(Don't miss the back loop only)
	Rounds 20-46: (18)	0 ×18 •	

Stuff and shape the foot.

Continue stuffing, referring to Making the Leg Joint on page 163.

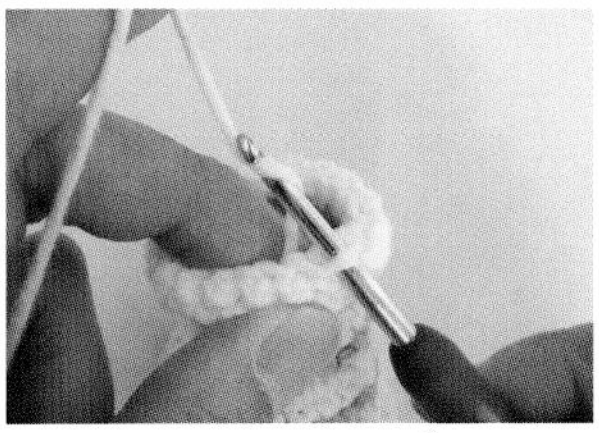

[Starting Caleb's Leg]

Rounds with Back Loops Only and Front Loops Only

Working in either back or front loops only, leaves the other loop available to work in. When a round is first worked in one loop only, that round and the rounds following it are numbered "-1". When going back and working in the remaining loops, that first round and those rounds following are numbered "-2"..

Photo Tutorial

When the pattern instructions are unclear, the photos will illustrate how to proceed.

3

Face + Antenna

Front

- **Eyes:** About 10 rows from bottom, 8 stitches between them.
- **Mouth:** About 5-6 rows from bottom, across 13 stitches.
- **Scar:** Between 3rd and 5th row from top.
- **Antenna:** In the center at top of Head

Placement Description

These photos show the correct positioning of the head, facial features, arms, and body features, when assembling and decorating the doll.

The exact positions can be confirmed by the captions below the photo.

LET'S PLAY!

PART 02

HAVING FUN MAKING YOUR DOLL FRIENDS

WALKING WITH
WACKY BEAR

Allow me to introduce you to Wacky Bear, the first project we will learn to crochet in our doll-making class. From now on, we will complete the doll friends one by one, using the various crochet techniques we learned and practiced earlier.

Don't be nervous. Once you have played with Wacky Bear, you will soon be making lots of other friends. So, let's take a walk with our Wacky Bear.

01 | Wacky Bear (5½" / 14 cm)

Yarn: Medium Weight (Worsted)
- Brown
- Light Beige
- Pink

Hook: Size D-3 (3.25 mm)

Other: Yarn Needle
Stuffing
3⁄16" (5 mm) Bean Buttons - 2 (Eyes)
5⁄16" (8 mm) Button - 1 (Nose)
Sewing Thread & Needle

Legs

[Brown]

Round 1: (6)	In starting ring **X 6** •
Round 2: (9)	**0 (X 1 XV 1) * 3** •
Round 3: (9)	**0 X 9** •
Round 4: (12)	**0 X 1 XV 1 (X 2 XV 1) * 2 X 1** •
Rounds 5~6: (12)	**0 X 12** •

At the end of Leg A, cut the yarn and finish off.
Repeat Rounds 1~6 for Leg B, but do not finish off.

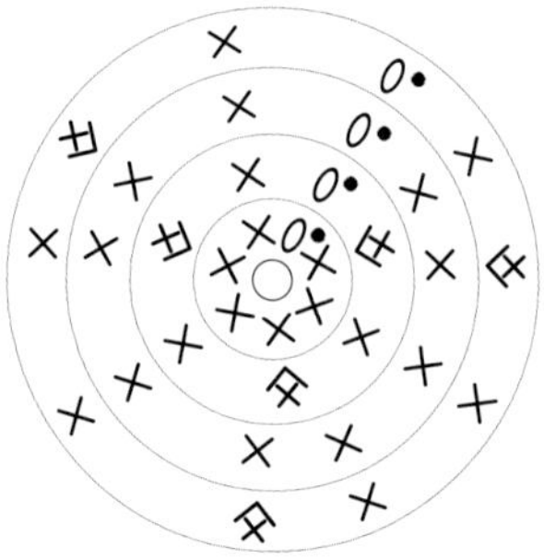

Legs + Body

[Brown]

Round 7: (36)

On Leg B **0 X 11** (Leave last stitch unworked.)

Chain **6** stitches

On Leg A, start in stitch after finish off **X 12**

Working in the chains **X̲ 6** (Don't miss the back loop only!)

On Leg B, in the remaining stitch **X 1** •

Round 8: (36)

On Leg B **0 X 11**

In the chain **X̲ 6** (Don't miss the back loop only!)

On Leg A, and finish round **X 19** •

TIP Joining the Legs

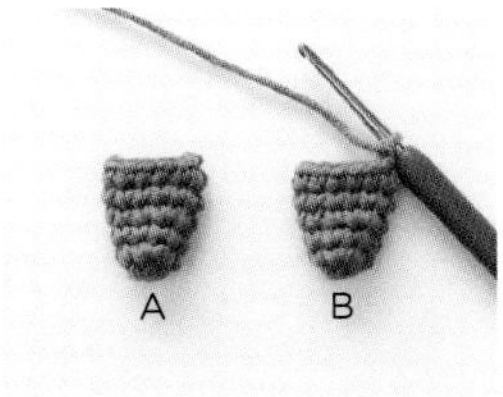

1. At the end of Round 6, finish off for Leg A. For Leg B, do not finish off.

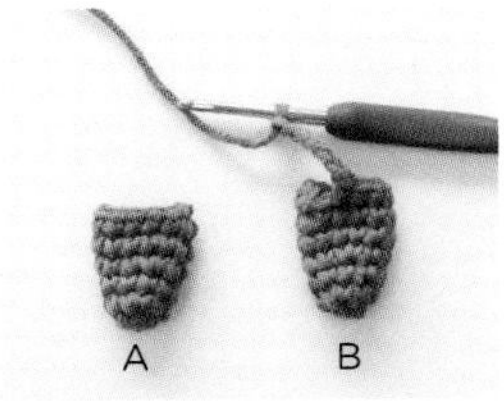

2. Work 11 single crochets (✕) on Leg B, leaving the last stitch unworked. Make 6 chain stitches. (O).

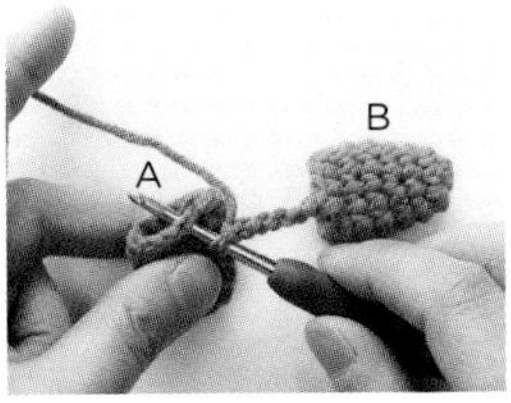

3. On Leg A, starting at the stitch after the finish off (second stitch), work 12 single crochets (✕).

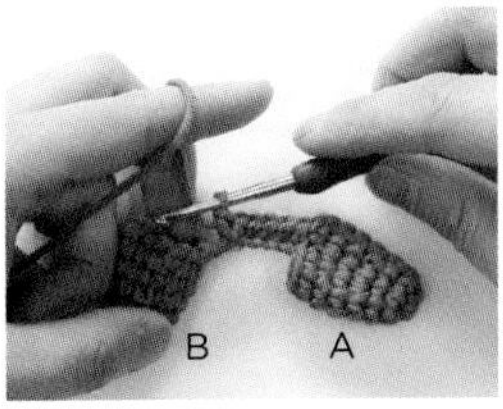

4. Work in the back loop of each of the 6 chains. (✕).

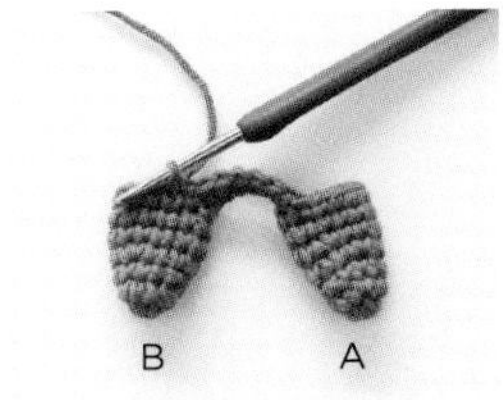

5. To finish the round, work in the remaining stitch on Leg B. (✕) Join with a slip stitch to the first stitch. (•)The stitch count for Round 7 is 36.

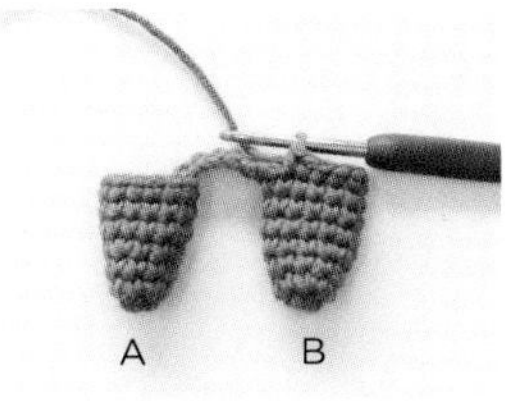

6. Start the next round and work 11 single crochets on Leg B. (✕)

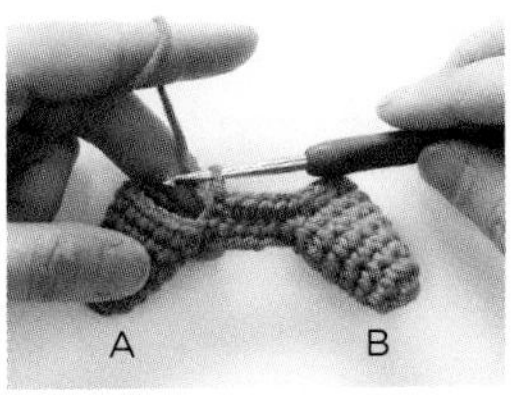

7. In the chains between the legs, work 6 stitches in the back loop only. (✕).

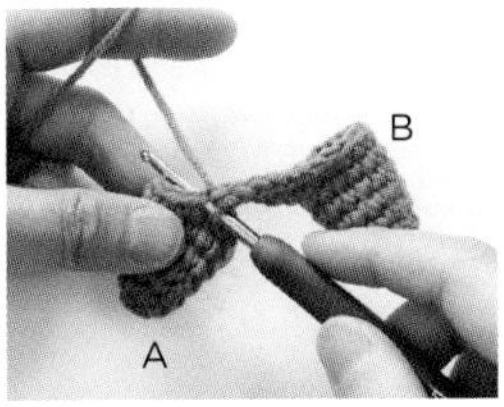

8. Around Leg A and to finish the round, work 19 stitches. (✕) The two legs are now firmly connected. The stitch count for Round 8 is 36.

Body

Continue working on the connected legs

[Brown]

Round 9: (42)	0 (✕5 V1) * 6 •
Rounds 10~11: (42)	0 ✕42 •
Round 12: (48)	0 ✕3 V1 (✕6 V1) * 5 ✕3 •
Rounds 13~16: (48)	0 ✕48 •
Round 17: (45)	0 ✕7 V1 (✕14 Λ1) * 2 ✕7 •
Rounds 18~19: (45)	0 ✕45 •
Round 20: (42)	0 (✕13 Λ1) * 3 •
Round 21: (42)	0 ✕42 •
Round 22: (39)	0 ✕6 Λ1 (✕12 Λ1) * 2 ✕6 •
Round 23: (39)	0 ✕39 •
Round 24: (36)	0 (✕11 Λ1) * 3 •
Rounds 25~30: (36)	0 ✕36 •
Round 31: (30)	0 ✕2 Λ1 (✕4 Λ1) * 5 ✕ 2 •

Round 32: (24)	0 (X 3 ⋀1) * 6 •
	Start stuffing.
Round 33: (18)	0 X 1 ⋀1 (X 2 ⋀1) * 5 X 1 •
Round 34: (12)	0 (X 1 ⋀1) * 6 •
	Continue stuffing until the doll feels like bread dough.
Round 35: (6)	0 ⋀6 •
	Close the last round with a yarn needle.

Arms

[Brown]

Round 1: (6)	In starting ring X 6 •
Round 2: (8)	0 (X 2 ⋁1) * 2 •
Rounds 3~10: (8)	0 X 8 •
	Stuff the Arm about ⅔ full. Leaving a long tail, cut the yarn and finish off.
	Repeat Rounds 1~10 for other Arm.

Ears

[Brown]

Round 1: (6)	In starting ring X 6 •
Round 2: (12)	0 ⋁6 •
Rounds 3~4: (12)	0 X 12 •
	Leaving a 16" (40 cm) long tail, cut the yarn and finish off.
	Repeat Rounds 1~4 for other Ear.

Snout

[Light Beige]

Round 1: (6)	In starting ring X 6 •
Round 2: (12)	0 ⋁6 •
Round 3: (12)	0 X 12 •
	Leaving a 16" (40 cm) long tail, cut the yarn and finish off.

Tail

[Brown]

Round 1: (6)	In starting ring X 6 •
Round 2: (8)	0 (X 2 ⋁1) * 2 •
Round 3: (8)	0 X 8 •
	Leaving a 16" (40 cm) long tail, cut the yarn and finish off.

Face + Ears

Face + Ears

- Ears: Between 4th & 8th round from top of head.
- Snout: Between 7th & 11th round from the crown.
- Eyes: Between the 7th & 8th round down from crown, 1 stitch away from the snout.
- Nose: Two rounds down from tip of snout.
- Cheeks: One round down from eyes, 2 stitches away from snout.

Tail

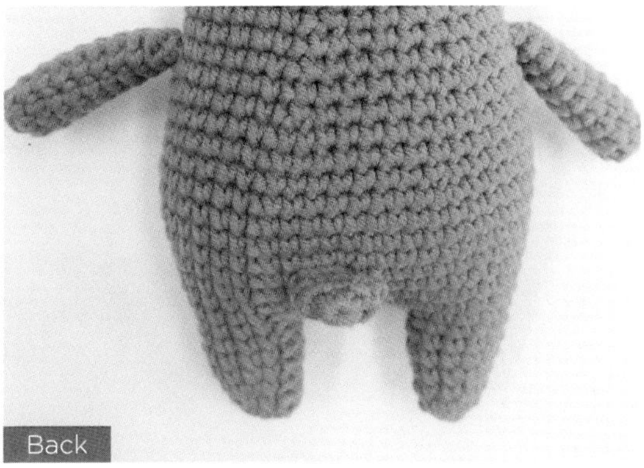
Back

- Tail: Between 12th & 13th round from toes.

Arms + Chest Hair

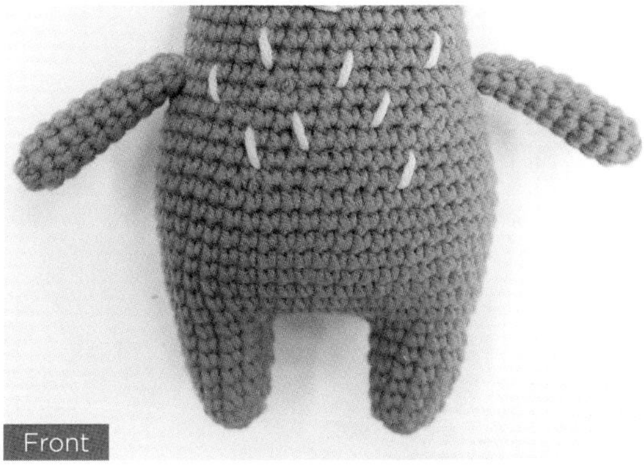
Front

- Arms: Between 21st & 22nd round from toe tip.
- Chest Hair: Random stitches between rounds 17 & 23.

» Body

1. After stuffing, sew the last round closed, using the long tail and yarn needle. The remaining yarn should be hidden in the body. (see Closing the Last Round - page 51)

» Ears

2. Mark the position of both Ears with a water-soluble pen.

3. Fold the Ear in half and flatten it. Thread the yarn tail onto a needle.

4. Starting from the top, working downwards, sew the Ear to the Head. Repeat for the other Ear. (see Whipstitch vertically across rounds - page 53)

5. Bring both the remaining threads out in the same stitch at the back of the bear, and tie them together.

» Snout

6 Mark the position of the Snout with a water-soluble pen.

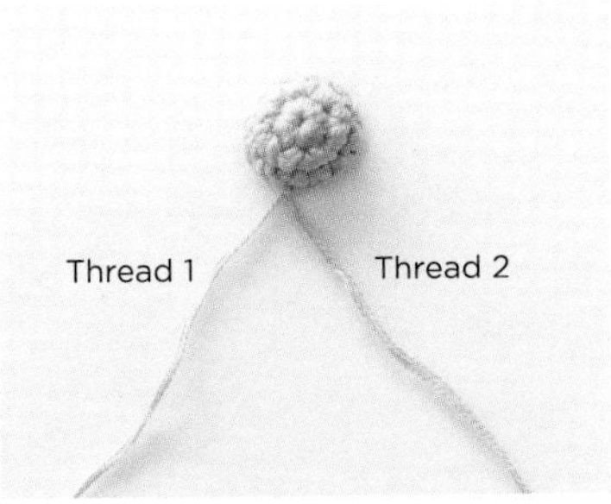

7 Split the yarn tail into two strands. Use one strand for sewing on the Snout, and hide the other strand inside the Snout.

8 Using curved stitching, sew about two thirds of the way around before stuffing the Snout. Continue sewing to secure the Snout firmly. (see Curved Stitching - page 54)

» Arms

9 Mark the arm positions using a water-soluble pen.

10 Thread the yarn tail onto a needle.

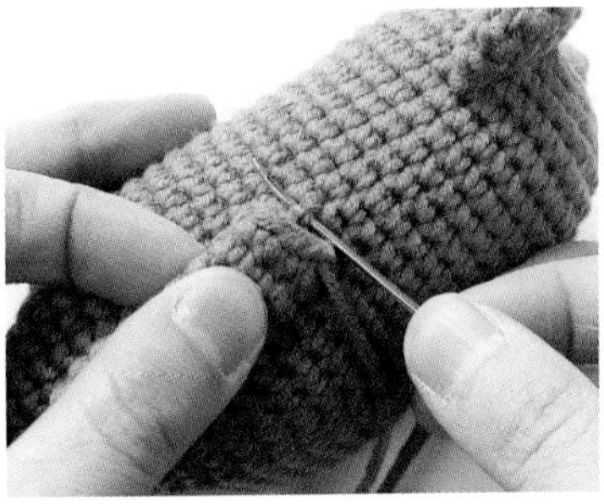

11 Starting from the rear of the torso, working towards the front, sew on each Arm. Hide the remaining yarn. (see Whipstitch horizontally across stitches - page 52)

» Tail

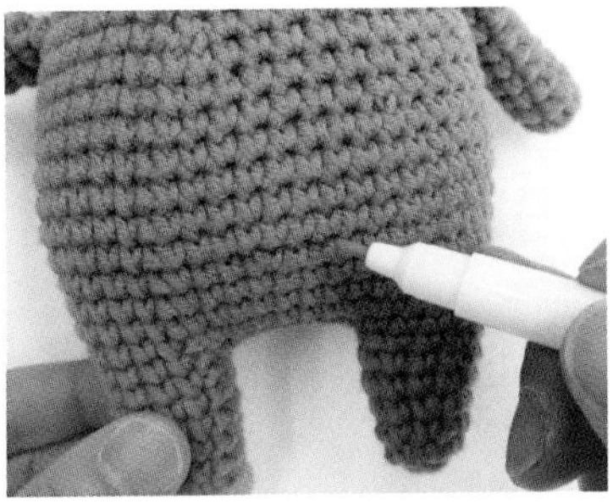

12 Mark the position of the Tail with a water-soluble pen.

13 Shape the Tail, and sew it onto the body. Hide the remaining yarn to complete the bear.

» Eyes

14 Mark the position of the Eyes with straight pins. Place one bean button onto an 8" (20 cm) length of sewing thread.

15 Thread both ends of the sewing thread onto a needle. The sewing thread is not knotted. Insert the needle at the one eye position and out at the other eye position, pulling the thread through until the bean button is locked into place.

16 Remove the straight pins. Take the double strand off the needle and place the second bean button onto one strand.

17 Tie the strands together and pull tightly until the back of the bean button enters the body. Secure the knot and hide the ends inside the body.

» Mouth + Nose

18 Knot a length of dark brown thread on a needle, and insert the needle from behind the face and out near the top of the Snout. Tug the thread gently until the knot is hidden in the head.

19 Embroider the mouth onto the snout following the sewing diagrams.

» Cheeks

20 Finish by sewing a nose button at the top of the embroidered mouth.

21 Knot a length of pink yarn on a needle, and insert the needle from behind the face and out at the position of the Cheek under the Eye.

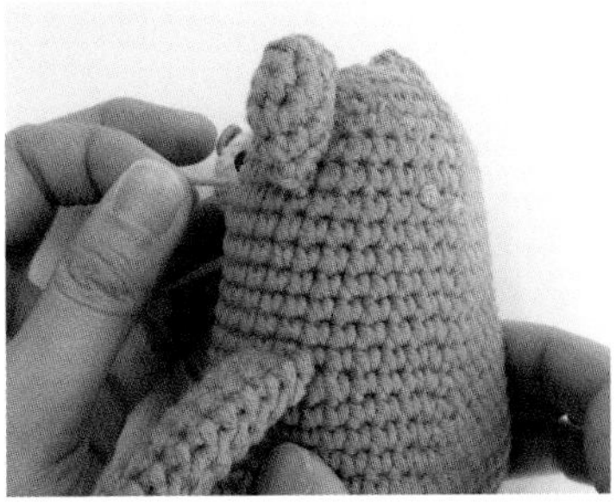

22 Gently tug the yarn to hide the knot in the body.

23 Insert the needle two stitches outwards and then out at the same spot. Repeat this once more to complete the Cheek.

24 Insert the needle again two stitches outwards, and bring it out at the other Cheek position.

25 Sew the other Cheek in the same way, and then bring the needle out at the back of the body.

» Chest Hair

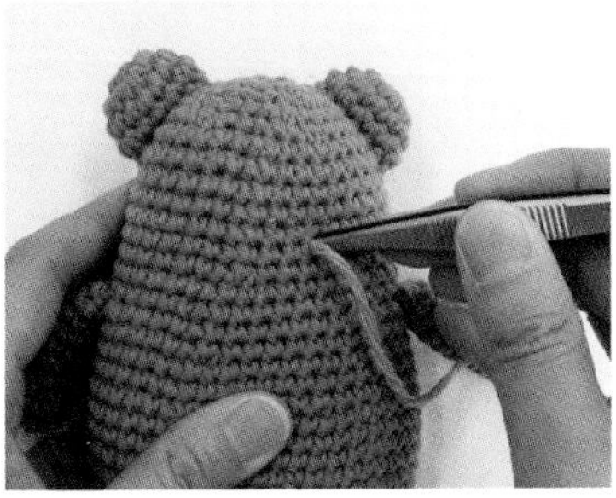

26 Using the tweezers, hide the yarn inside the torso.

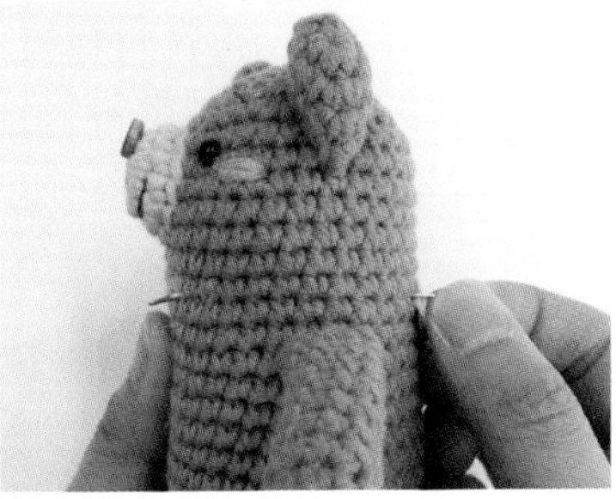

27 Knot a length of light beige yarn onto a needle and insert it from the back of the torso to a position at the front of the chest. Tug the yarn to hide the knot.

28 Randomly sew the Chest Hairs. Each hair is stitched vertically across two rounds.

CLASSIC
PIANO

INVITATION TO A
WEDDING PARTY

Today is the day that a pair of loving bears are finally getting married!
Isn't the Bear Bride so pretty in her white dress? And doesn't
the Bear Groom look handsome in his smart bow tie?

Let's gather together and celebrate the beautiful couple's new beginning!

02 | Bear Groom (6" / 15 cm)

Yarn: Medium Weight (Worsted)
- Brown
- Cream
- Light Beige
- Dark Gray
- Light Pink
- Light Gray

Hook: Size D-3 (3.25 mm)

Other: Yarn Needle
Stuffing
3⁄16" (5 mm) Bean Buttons - 2 (Eyes)
5⁄16" (8 mm) Button - 1 (Nose)
5⁄16" (8 mm) Buttons - 2 (Suspenders)
Sewing Thread & Needle

03 | Bear Bride (6" / 15 cm)

Yarn: Medium Weight (Worsted)
- Brown
- Cream
- Light Beige
- Light Pink

Hook: Size D-3 (3.25 mm)

Other: Yarn Needle
Stuffing
3⁄16" (5 mm) Bean Buttons - 2 (Eyes)
5⁄16" (8 mm) Button - 1 (Nose)
Sewing Thread & Needle

Legs + Body + Face

[Light Gray]

Round 1: (6)	In starting ring X **6** •
Round 2: (9)	**0** (X **1** ⋎ **1**) * **3** •
Round 3: (9)	**0** X **9** •

[Dark Gray]

Round 4: (12)	**0** X **1** ⋎ **1** (X **2** ⋎ **1**) * **2** X **1** •
Rounds 5~6: (12)	**0** X **12** •
	At the end of Leg A, cut the yarn and finish off. Repeat Rounds 1~6 for Leg B, but do not finish off.
Round 7: (36)	On Leg B **0** X **11** (Leave last stitch unworked.)
	Chain Stitch **6**
	On Leg A, start in the second stitch X **12**
	Working in the chains X̲ **6** (Don't miss the back loop only!)
	On Leg B, in the remainig stitch X **1** •
Round 8: (36)	Leg B **0** X **11**
	Working in the chains X̲ **6** (Don't miss the back loop only!)
	On Leg A, and finish round X **19** •
Round 9: (42)	**0** (X **5** ⋎ **1**) * **6** •
Rounds 10~11: (42)	**0** X **42** •
Round 12: (48)	**0** X **3** ⋎ **1** (X **6** ⋎ **1**) * **5** X **3** •
Rounds 13~14: (48)	**0** X **48** •

[Cream]

Rounds 15-16: (48)	**0** X **48** •
Round 17: (45)	**0** X **7** ⋏ **1** (X **14** ⋏ **1**) * **2** X **7** •
Rounds 18-19: (45)	**0** X **45** •
Round 20: (42)	**0** (X **13** ⋏ **1**) * **3** •
Round 21: (42)	**0** X **42** •
Round 22: (39)	**0** X **6** ⋏ **1** (X **12** ⋏ **1**) * **2** X **6** •
Round 23: (39)	**0** X **39** •

[Brown]	Round 24: (36)	0 (X 11 ⋀ 1) * 3 •
	Rounds 25-30: (36)	0 X 36 •
	Round 31: (30)	0 X 2 ⋀ 1 (X 4 ⋀ 1) * 5 X 2 •
	Round 32: (24)	0 (X 3 ⋀ 1) * 6 •
		Start stuffing.
	Round 33: (18)	0 X 1 ⋀ 1 (X 2 ⋀ 1) * 5 X •
	Round 34: (12)	0 (X 1 ⋀ 1) * 6 •
		Continue stuffing to fill the doll.
	Round 35: (6)	0 ⋀ 6 •
		Close the last round with a yarn needle.

Arms

[Brown]	Round 1: (6)	In starting ring X 6 •
	Round 2: (8)	0 (X 2 ⋁ 1) * 2 •
	Round 3: (8)	0 X 8 •
[Cream]	Rounds 4-10: (8)	0 X 8 •
		Stuff the Arm about ⅔ full. Leaving a 16″ (40 cm) long tail, cut the yarn and finish off.
		Repeat Rounds 1-10 for other Arm.

Ears

[Brown]	Round 1: (6)	In starting ring X 6 •
	Round 2: (12)	0 ⋁ 6 •
	Rounds 3-4: (12)	0 X 12 •
		Leaving a 16″ (40 cm) long tail, cut the yarn and finish off.
		Repeat Rounds 1-4 for other Ear.

Snout

[Light Beige]	Round 1: (6)	In starting ring X 6 •
	Round 2: (12)	0 ⋁ 6 •
	Round 3: (12)	0 X 12 •
		Leaving a 16″ (40 cm) long tail, cut the yarn and finish off.

Hat

[Dark Gray]

Round 1: (6) — In starting ring X 6 •

Round 2: (12) — 0 ⋁ 6 •

Rounds 3-4: (12) — 0 X 12 •

[Light Gray]

Round 5: (12) — 0 X 12 •

[Dark Gray]

Round 6: (18) — 0 (X̄ 1 ⋁̄ 1) * 6 • (Don't miss the front loop only.)

Leaving a 16" (40 cm) long tail, cut the yarn and finish off.

Bow Tie

[Light Pink]

* Please see Working in Rows on page 42.

Chain Stitch **12**

Row 1: (12) — Add one turning chain, start in second chain from hook X 12

Rows 2-5: (12) — Start each row with a turning chain and work across. X 12

At the end of Row 5, finish off leaving a 16" (40 cm) long tail

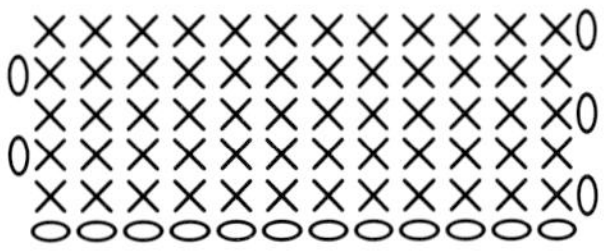

Suspenders

[Light Gray]

* Please see Working in Rows on page 42.

Chain Stitch **30**

Row 1: (30) — Add 4 turning chains (buttonhole), start in 5th ch from hook X30

Finish off, leaving a 4" (10 cm) tail.

Repeat for second suspender.

Note :The Face and Ears are the same as Wacky Bear on page 69.

Bow Tie + Suspender Buttons

◦ **Bow tie:** About 7 to 8 rounds up from waist.
◦ **Suspender Buttons:** Between rounds 13 & 14 from toe tip, and about 15 stitches between them.

Suspenders

◦ **Suspenders:** Between rounds 13 & 14 from toe tip, and about 15 stitches between them.

» Face + Ears + Arms

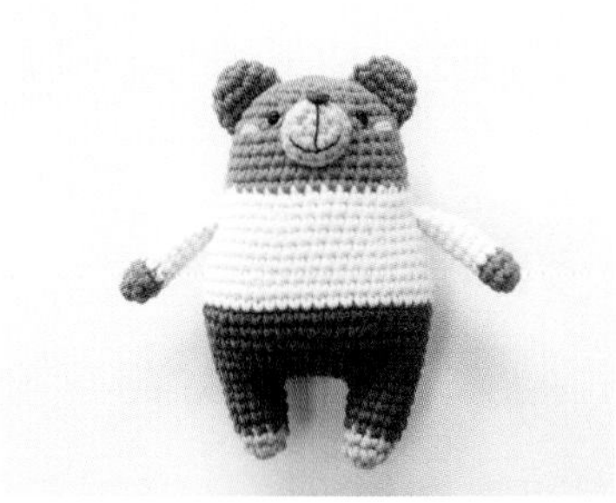

1 For the Groom Bear, follow the Wacky Bear photo tutorials #1 through #26 (except for the Tail) on page 70.

» Buttons

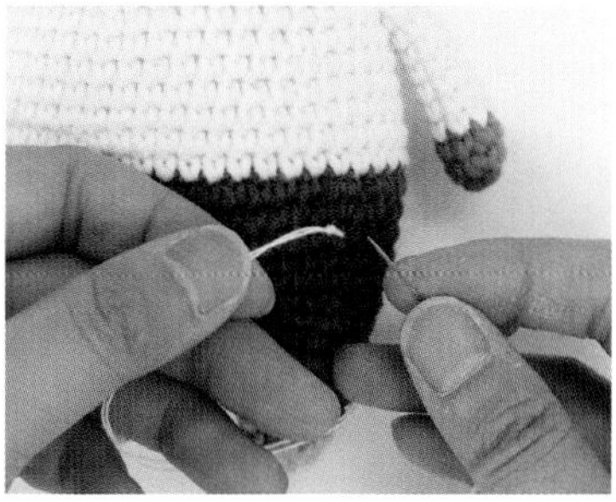

2 Sew on the buttons using a double strand of thread. Thread the needle and tie the two ends together in a knot.

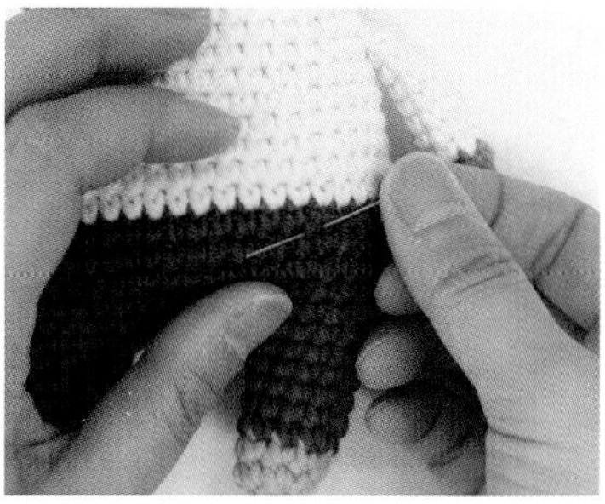

3 Insert the needle at the position for the button, and bring it out in the next stitch.

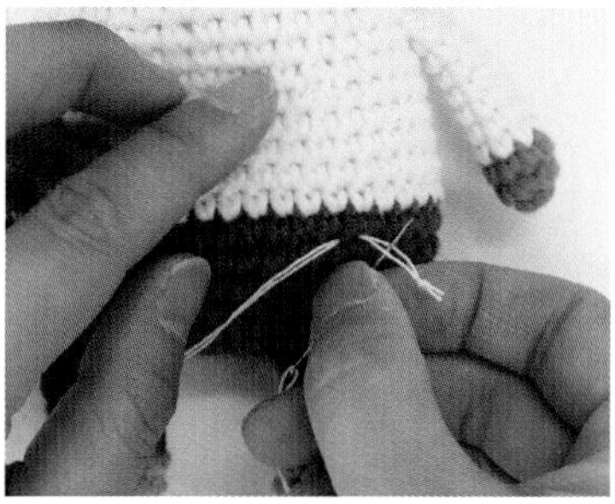

4 Insert the needle between the two strands of thread at the knot and pull gently to tighten.

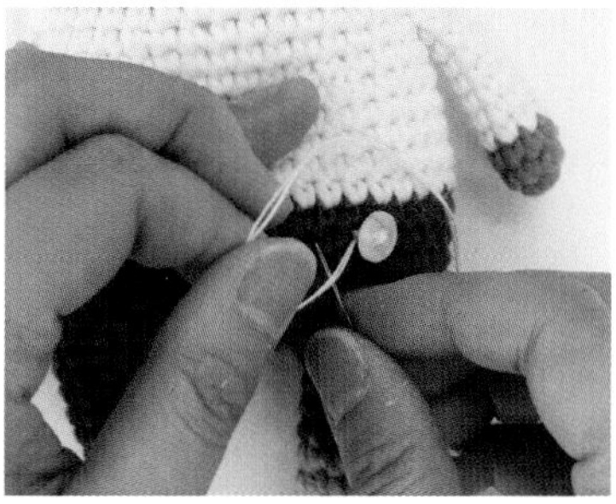

5 Sew on the button and hide the remaining thread in the body. Repeat for other button.

» **Suspenders**

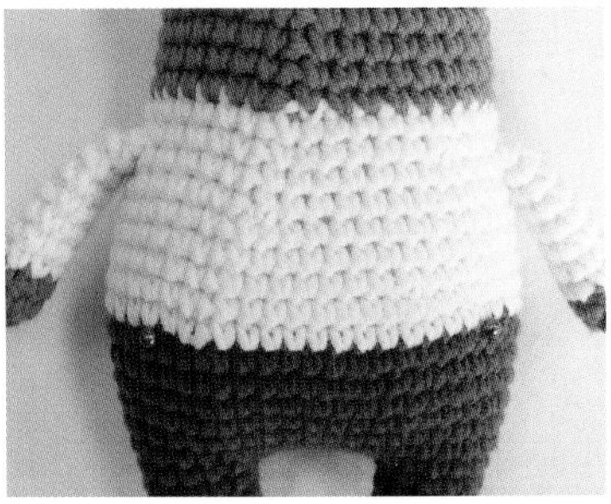

6 At the back of the Groom, mark the position of the suspenders with straight pins.

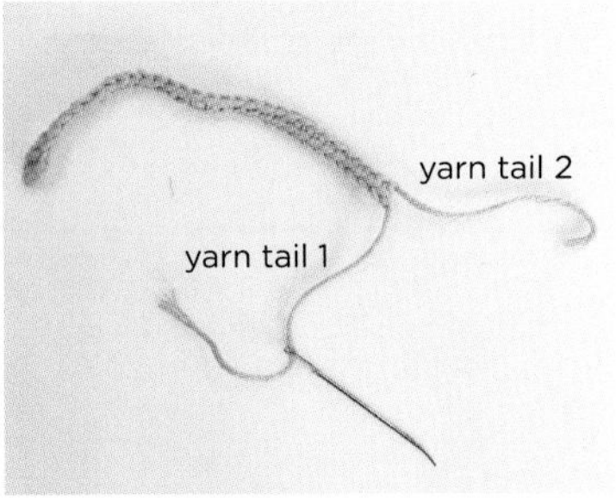

7 With the right side of one strap facing, thread yarn tail 1 onto a needle.

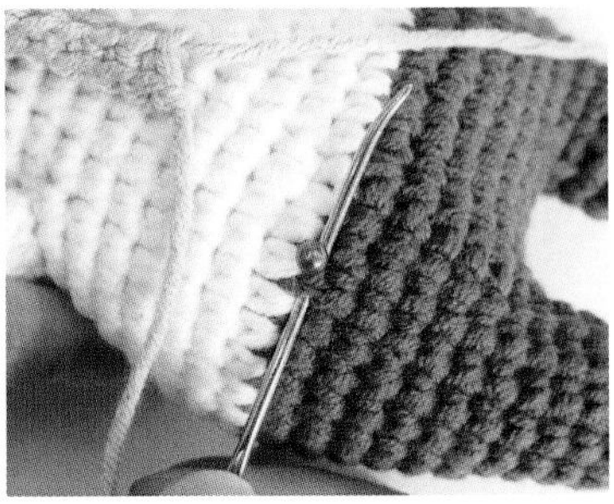

8 Insert the needle, one stitch to the left on the pin, and bring it out at the marked position.

9 Thread yarn tail 2 onto a needle and insert it one stitch to the right of the same pin, bringing it out at the same marked position.

10 Yarn tails 1 & 2 come out of the same stitch. Remove the straight pin. Tie the two tails together in a knot.

11 Thread both tails onto the needle. Insert the needle where the tails came out, and hide the tails in the body. Repeat for other strap.

12 Cross the two suspenders at the back.

13 At the front of the bear, fasten the suspenders to the buttons.

» Hat

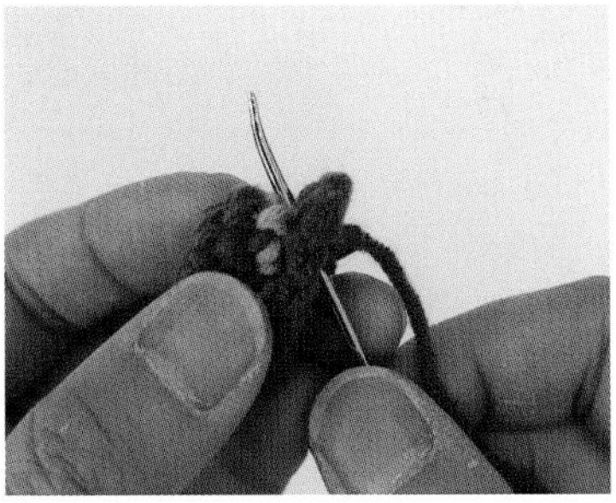

14 Thread the yarn tail onto a needle and insert the needle between the 4th and 5th round of the hat.

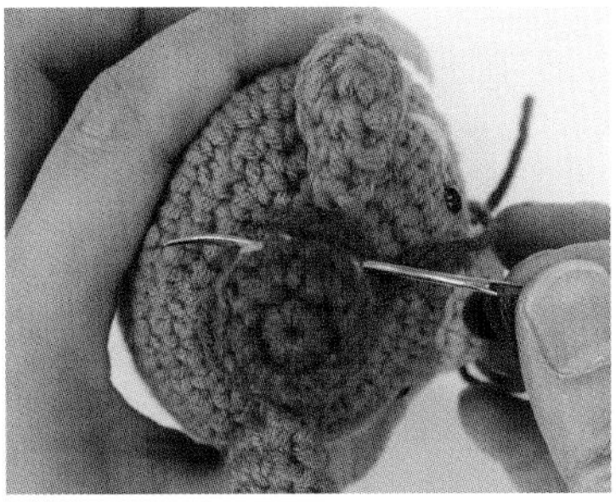

15 Position the hat at the top of the head between the ears. Sew the hat in place using curved stitching between rounds 4 & 5, keeping the hat's shape.

» Bow Tie

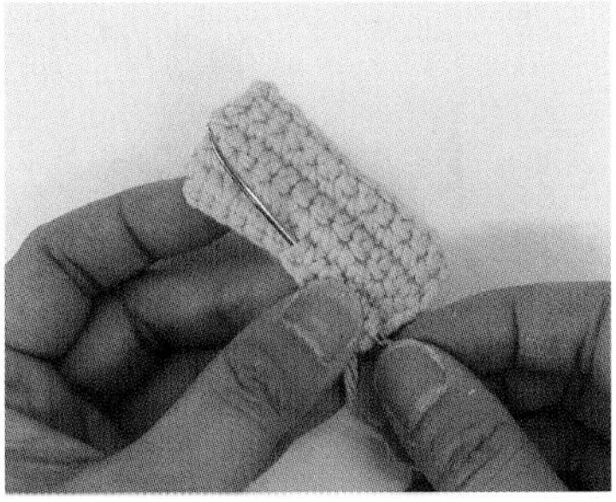

16 Hide the one yarn tail on the wrong side. Thread the other tail onto a needle and weave it under the first 6 stitches, bringing it out in the center.

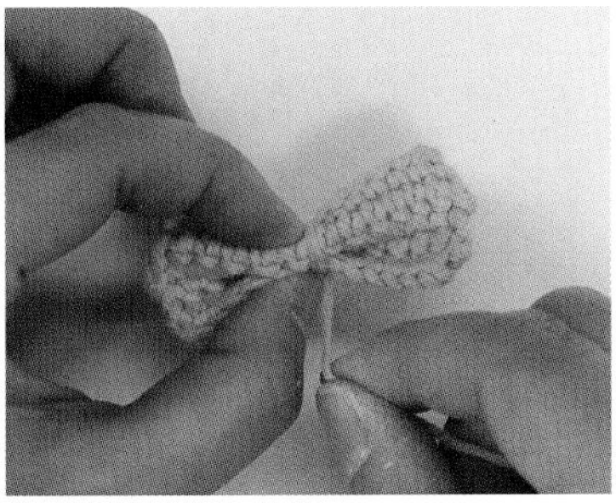

17 Wind the yarn about 4 times around the center, to form a bow tie shape.

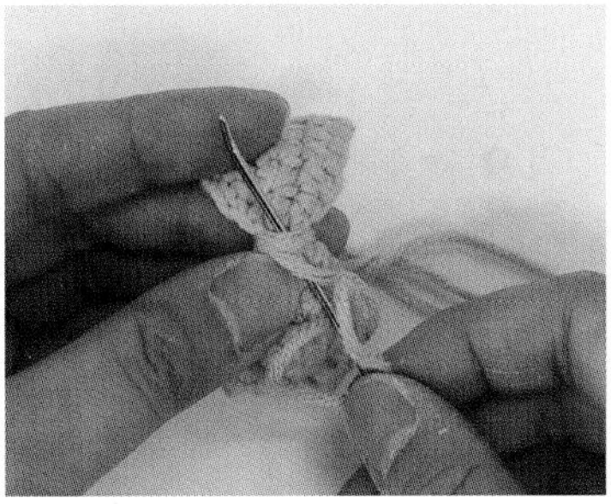

18 Insert the needle under the winds, and secure it firmly.

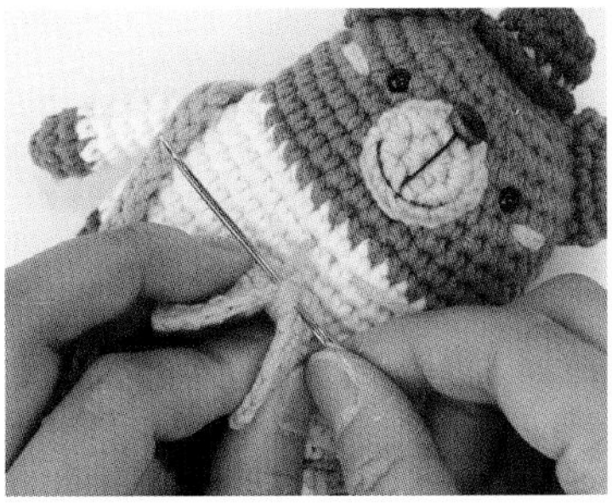

19 Position the bow tie and sew it in place, to finish the Groom Bear.

Legs + Body + Face

[Cream]	Round 1: (6)	In starting ring **X 6**
	Round 2: (9)	**0 (X 1 ⋁ 1) * 3 •**
	Round 3: (9)	**0 X 9 •**
[Brown]	Round 4: (12)	**0 X 1 ⋁ 1 (X 2 ⋁ 1) * 2 X 1 •**
	Rounds 5-6: (12)	**0 X 12 •** At the end of Leg A, cut the yarn and finish off. Repeat Rounds 1~6 for Leg B, but do not finish off.
[Cream]	Round 7: (36)	On Leg B **0 X 11** (Leave last stitch unworked.) Chain stitches **6** On Leg A, start in the second stitch **X 12** Working in the chains **X̲ 6** (Don't miss the back loop only!) On Leg B **X 1 •**
	Round 8: (36)	Leg B **0 X 11** From chain **X̲ 6** (Don't miss the back loop only!) On Leg A, and finish round **X 19 •**
	Round 9: (42)	**0 (X 5 ⋁ 1) * 6 •**
	Rounds 10-11: (42)	**0 X 42 •**
	Round 12: (48)	**0 X 3 ⋁ 1 (X 6 ⋁ 1) * 5 X 3 •**
	Rounds 13-15: (48)	**0 X 48 •**
	Round 16: (48)	**0 X̲ 48 •** (Don't miss the back loop only!)
	Round 17: (45)	**0 X̲ 7 ⋀̲ 1 (X̲ 14 ⋀̲ 1) * 2 X̲ 7 •** (Don't miss the back loop only!)
	Rounds 18-19: (45)	**0 X 45 •**
	Round 20: (42)	**0 (X 13 ⋀ 1) * 3 •**
	Round 21: (42)	**0 X 42 •**
	Round 22: (39)	**0 X 6 ⋀ 1 (X 12 ⋀ 1) * 2 X 6 •**
	Round 23: (39)	**0 X 39 •**

[Brown]	Round 24: (36)	0 (X 11 ⋀ 1) * 3 •
	Rounds 25-30: (36)	0 X 36 •
	Round 31: (30)	0 X 2 ⋀ 1 (X 4 ⋀ 1) * 5 X 2 •
	Round 32: (24)	0 (X 3 ⋀ 1) * 6 •
		Start stuffing.
	Round 33: (18)	0 X 1 ⋀ 1 (X 2 ⋀ 1) * 5 X 1 •
	Round 34: (12)	0 (X 1 ⋀ 1) * 6 •
		Continue stuffing to fill the doll.
	Round 35: (6)	0 ⋀ 6 •
		Close the last round with a yarn needle.

Arms

[Brown]	Round 1: (6)	In starting ring X 6 •
	Round 2: (8)	0 (X 2 ⋁ 1) * 2 •
	Rounds 3-6: (8)	0 X 8 •
[Cream]	Rounds 7-10: (8)	0 X 8 •
		Stuff the Arm about ⅔ full. Leaving a 16" (40 cm) long tail, cut the yarn and finish off.
		Repeat Rounds 1-10 for other Arm.

Ears

[Brown]	Round 1: (6)	In starting ring X 6 •
	Round 2: (12)	0 ⋁ 6 •
	Rounds 3-4: (12)	0 X 12 •
		Leaving a 16" (40 cm) long tail, cut the yarn and finish off.
		Repeat Rounds 1-4 for other Ear.

Snout

[Light Beige]	Round 1: (6)	In starting ring X 6 •
	Round 2: (12)	0 ⋁ 6 •
	Round 3: (12)	0 X 12 •
		Leaving a 16" (40 cm) long tail, cut the yarn and finish off.

Hair Ribbon [Cream]

*Please see Working in Rows on page 42.

Chain Stitch **12**

Row 1: (12) — Add one turning chain, start in second chain from hook **X 12**

Rows 2-5: (12) — Start each row with a turning chain and work across. **X 12**

At the end of Row 5, finish off leaving a 16" (40 cm) long tail

Skirt

[Cream]

Skirt Frill 1 — With the bear's head facing down, working in the unused front loops on Round 15, attach the yarn at back of the body.

Rounds 1-3: (48) — 0 **X 48** •

Round 4: (48) — 0 (**X 1**  **1) * 8** •

When done, cut the yarn and finish off, hiding the yarn tail in the body.

[Cream]

Skirt Frill 2 — Starting at back of the body, working in the unused front loops on Round 16, attach the yarn at back of body.

Rounds 1-2: (48) — 0 **X 48** •

Round 3: (48) — 0 (**X 1**  **1) * 8** •

When done, cut the yarn and finish off, hiding the yarn tail in the body

TIP Making the Skirt Frills

1. Here you can see the unused front loops of Rounds 15 & 16 which were made when Rounds 16 & 17 were worked in back loops only.

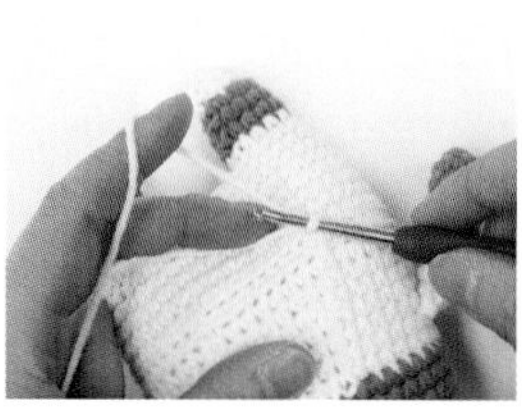

2. Turn the bear upside down and working in Round 15, work 3 rounds of single crochet, (**X**) then work a round of shell stitches.

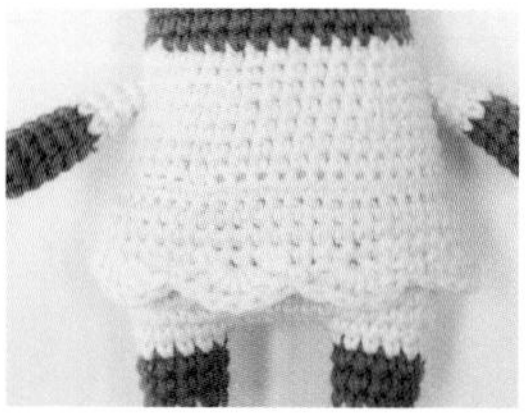

3. This is what the first skirt frill looks like.

4. Similarly, make the other frill in the unused loops on Round 16, working two rounds of single crochet, then a round of shell stitches, to complete the Skirt.

» Face + Ears + Arms

1. For the Bear Bride, before completing the skirt, follow the Wacky Bear photo tutorials #1 through #26 (except for the Tail) on page 70.

» Waist Tie

2. Thread a strand of Pink yarn on a needle. Weave the yarn between the stitches of Round 15 around the body.

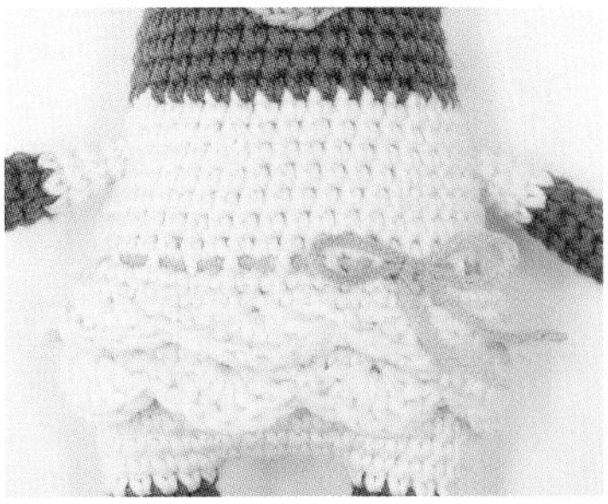

3. Tie the ends of the yarn into a bow to finish.

» Eyelashes

4. With black thread on a needle, insert the needle from behind the face and out above the eye.

5. Insert the needle above the eye and bring it out one stitch away.

6. Insert the needle in the same place and bring it out above the other eye.

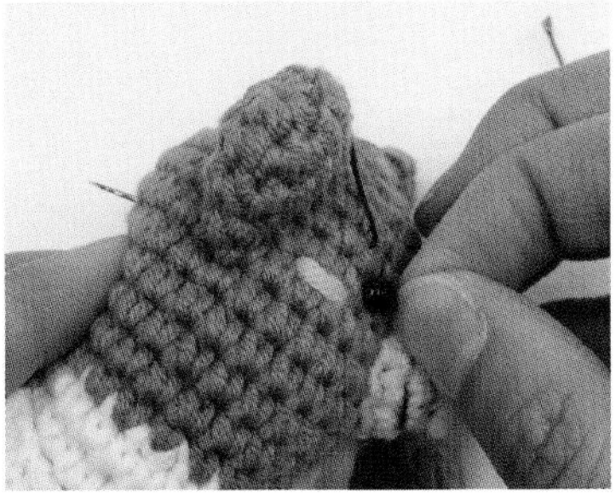

7. Repeat step 5 for the other eye, and then insert the needle in the same place and bring it out behind the head. Hide the ends.

» Hair Ribbon

8. Follow the photo tutorials of the Groom's bow tie - #16 to #18 on page 81.

   Position the Ribbon on the head between the ears and sew in place, to finish the Bear Bride.

HOMESICK **AMIGOS**

Rodriguez and Sanchez are handsome amigos from Mexico! However, they really miss their hometown, where the neighbors were passionate about the music they played. Now they just dream of home. Welcome them as your new friends.

04 | Rodriguez (10" / 26 cm)

Yarn: Medium Weight (Worsted)

- Green
- Brown
- Dark Brown
- Beige
- Yellow
- Red
- Dark Green

Hook: Size D-3 (3.25 mm)

Other: Yarn Needle
Stuffing
½" (13 mm) Buttons – 2 (Suspenders)
Dark Brown Felt - 2" (5 cm) x 5" (12 cm)
Craft Wire - 20" (50 cm)
Sewing Thread & Needle

05 | Sanchez (9" / 23 cm)

Yarn: Medium Weight (Worsted)

- Green
- Brown
- Dark Brown
- Beige
- Yellow
- Red
- Dark Green

Hook: Size D-3 (3.25 mm)

Other: Yarn Needle
Stuffing
½" (13 mm) Buttons – 2 (Suspenders)
Dark Brown Felt - 2" (5 cm) x 5" (12 cm)
Sewing Thread & Needle

Legs

[Dark Brown]	Round 1: (6)	In starting ring × 6 •
	Round 2: (12)	0 V 6 •
	Round 3: (18)	0 (× 1 V 1) ∗ 6 •
	Round 4: (24)	0 × 6 V 6 × 6 •
	Round 5: (24)	0 × 24 •
	Round 6: (18)	0 × 6 Λ 6 × 6 •
	Round 7: (14)	0 × 5 Λ 4 × 5 •
	Rounds 8-10: (14)	0 × 14 •
[Brown]	Rounds 11-13: (14)	0 × 14 • At the end of Leg A, cut the yarn and finish off. Repeat Rounds 1~13 for Leg B, but do not finish off.
	Round 14: (42)	On Leg B 0 × 12 (Leave the last 2 stitches unworked.) Chain Stitch **7** On Leg A, start in the fifth stitch × 14 Working in the chains X̲ 7 (Don't miss the back loop only!) In remaining stitches on Leg B × 2 •
	Round 15: (42)	On Leg B 0 × 12 On chain X̲ 7 (Don't miss the back loop only!) On Leg A and finish round × 23 •
	Round 16: (45)	0 (× 13 V 1) ∗ 3 •
	Rounds 17-20: (45)	0 × 45 •
	Round 21: (48)	0 × 7 V 1 (× 14 V 1) ∗ 2 × 7 •
	Round 22-1: (48)	0 X̄ 48 (Don't miss the front loop only!)
	Round 23-1: (48)	0 × 48 • Cut the yarn and finish off, hiding the tails on the inside. Start stuffing each leg, shaping the boots.

Body + Face

[Green]

Join the yarn to the back loop of the first stitch on Round 21.

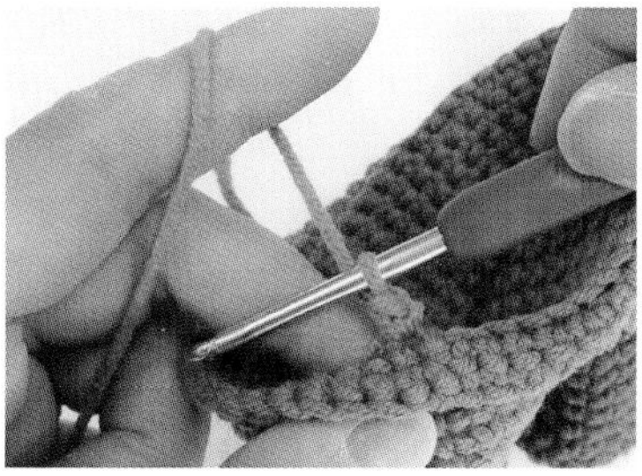

[Starting the Body]

Round 22-2: (48)	0 X 48 •
Round 23-2: (48)	0 X 48 •
Rounds 24-30: (48)	0 X 48 •
Round 31: (51)	0 (X 15 V 1) * 3 •
Rounds 32-40: (51)	0 X 51 •
Round 41: (54)	0 X 8 V 1 (X 16 V 1) * 2 X 8 •
Rounds 42-50: (54)	0 X 54 •
Round 51: (48)	0 (X 7 Λ 1) * 6 •
Round 52: (42)	0 X 3 Λ 1 (X 6 Λ 1) * 5 X 3 •
Round 53: (36)	0 (X 5 Λ 1) * 6 •
Round 54: (30)	0 X 2 Λ 1 (X 4 Λ 1) * 5 X 2 •
	Start stuffing.
Round 55: (24)	0 (X 3 Λ 1) * 6 •
Round 56: (18)	0 X 1 Λ 1 (X 2 Λ 1) * 5 X 1 •
Round 57: (12)	0 (X 1 Λ 1) * 6 •
	Continue stuffing to fill the doll.
Round 58: (6)	0 Λ 6 •
	Close the last round with a yarn needle.

Arms

[Green]

Round 1: (6)	In starting ring X 6 •
Round 2: (9)	0 (X 1 V 1) * 3 •
Rounds 3-15: (9)	0 X 9 •
	Stuff the Arms. Leaving a 16" (40 cm) long tail, cut the yarn and finish off. Repeat Rounds 1-15 for other Arm.

Suspenders [Dark Brown]

Row 1: (40)

Chain Stitch **40**

Add 4 turning chains (buttonhole), start in 5th ch from hook **X 40**

Finish off, leaving a 4" (10 cm) tail.

Repeat for second suspender.

* Please see Working in Rows on page 42.

Sombrero

[Beige]	Round 1: (6)	In starting ring **X 6 •**
	Round 2: (8)	**0 (X̲ 2 V̲ 1) * 2 •** (Don't miss the back loop only!)
	Round 3: (10)	**0 (X 3 V 1) * 2 •**
	Round 4: (12)	**0 X 2 V 1 X 4 V 1 X 2 •**
	Round 5: (14)	**0 (X 5 V 1) * 2 •**
	Round 6: (16)	**0 X 3 V 1 X 6 V 1 X 3 •**
	Round 7: (18)	**0 (X 7 V 1) * 2 •**
	Round 8: (24)	**0 X̄ 1 V̄ 1 (X̄ 2 V̄ 1) * 5 X̄ 1 •** (Don't miss the front loop only!)
	Round 9: (30)	**0 (X 3 V 1) * 6 •**
[Red]	Round 10: (36)	**0 X 2 V 1 (X 4 V 1) * 5 X 2 •**
[Yellow]	Round 11: (42)	**0 (X 5 V 1) * 6 •**
[Dark Green]	Round 12: (48)	**0 X 3 V 1 (X 6 V 1) * 5 X 3 •**
[Beige]	Round 13: (54)	**0 (X 7 V 1) * 6 •** Leaving a 16" (40 cm) long tail, cut the yarn and finish off.

Mustache Template

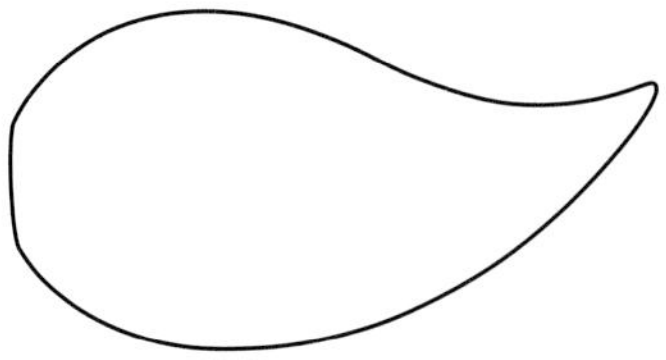

Face

- **Eyes:** Between 16th & 18th round down from crown, with 10 stitches between them.
- **Eyebrow:** About 3 rounds above eye and 2 stitches away on same round as eye.
- **Mustache:** Between 21st & 23rd round down from crown.

Suspenders

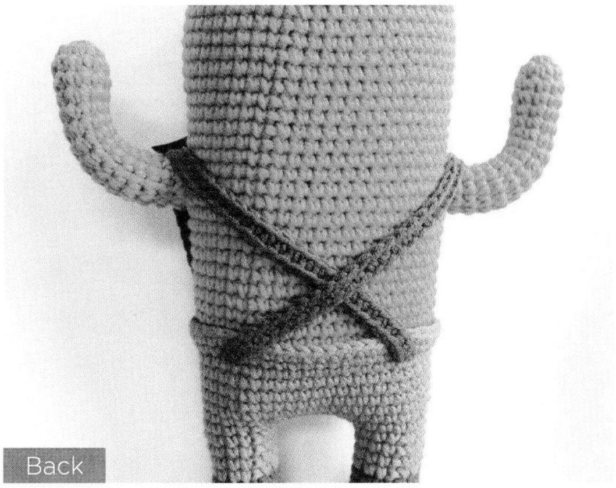

- **Straps:** Between rounds 21 & 22 from toe tip, and about 14 stitches between them.

Arms + Chest Hair + Buttons

- **Arms:** Between 12th & 14th rounds from waistline.
- **Chest Hair:** Between 6th & 12th rounds from waist.
- **Buttons:** Round 21 from toe tip, 14 stitches between them.

» Body

1 After stuffing, sew the last round closed, using the long tail and yarn needle. The remaining yarn should be hidden in the body. (see Closing the Last Round - page 51).

» Arms

2 Mark the arm positions using a water-soluble pen.

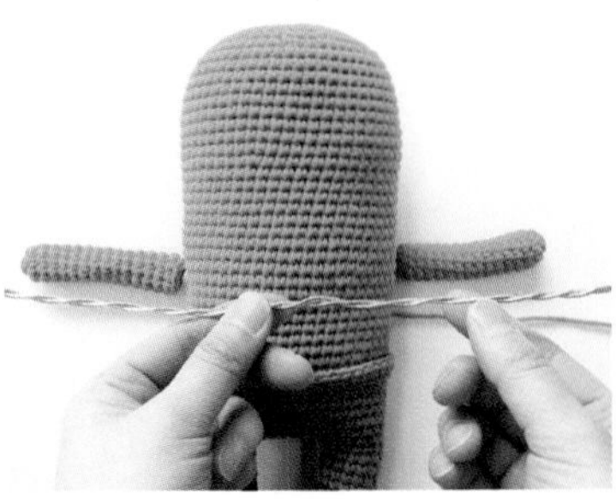

3 Align both arms in the correct position. Prepare the craft wire by folding in half and twisting together. With the twisted piece, measure across the length of both arms and trim the wire to fit.

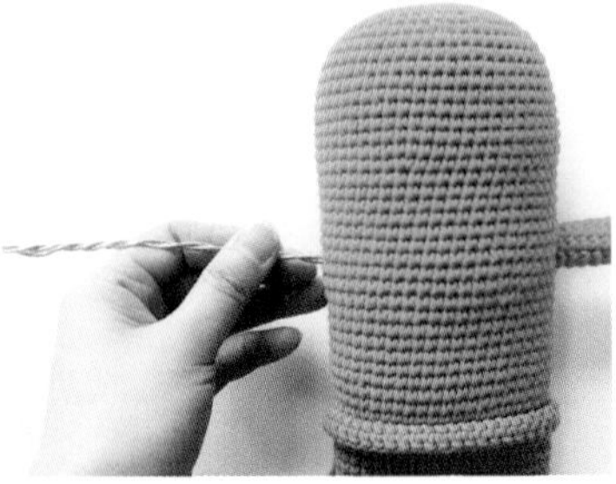

4 Push the wire through the center of both marked positions on the body. Insert one end of the wire into the middle of an arm, and sew the arm in place.

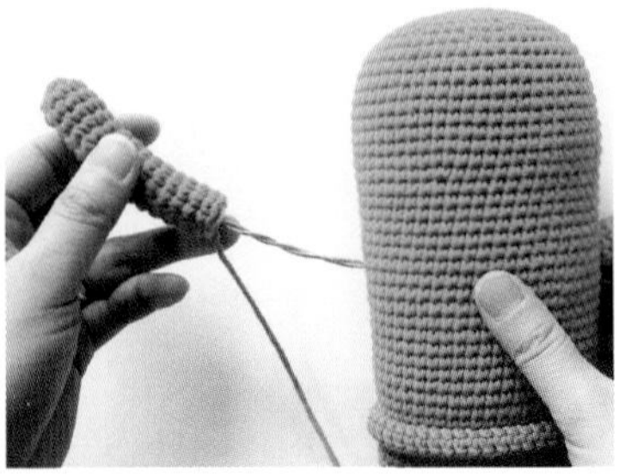

5 Insert the other end of the wire into the other arm, and sew in place.

» Buttons + Suspenders

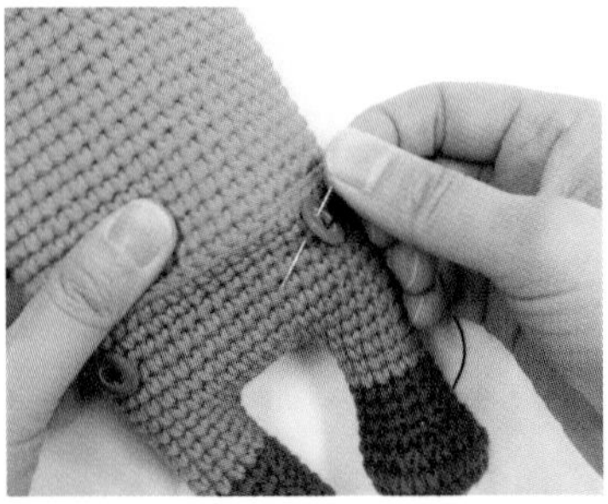

6 Attach the buttons in position, following Bear Groom photo tutorial #2-5 on page 79.

7 With the back facing, attach both straps following Bear Groom photo tutorial #6-13 on page 80.

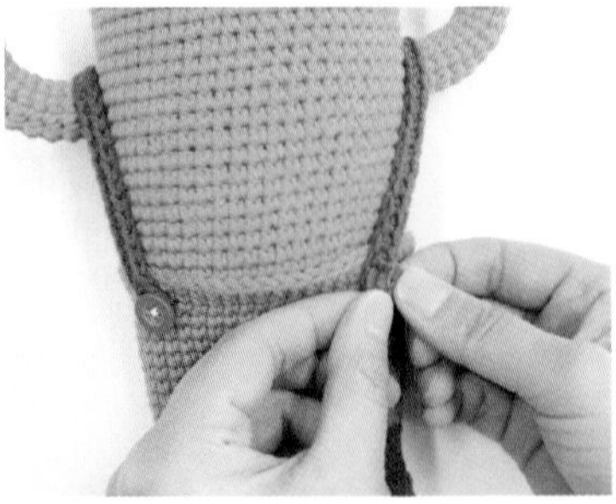

8 With the front facing, fasten the suspenders on the buttons.

» Eyes + Eyebrows

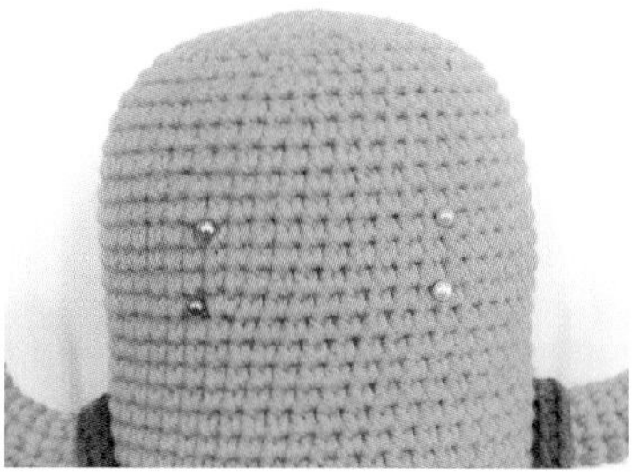

9 Mark the top and bottom position of each eye with straight pins.

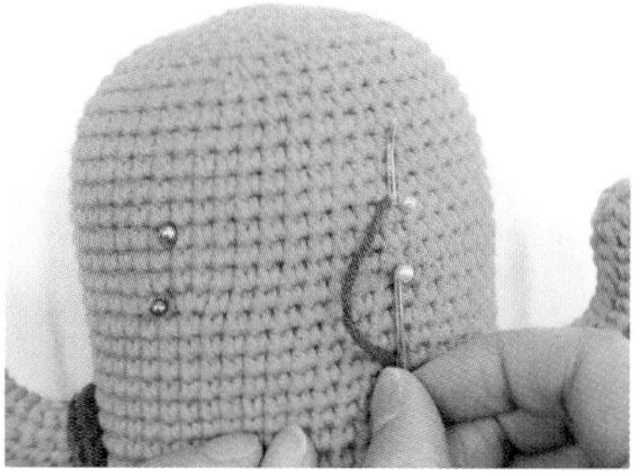

10 With dark brown yarn on a needle, embroider the eye using 3 straight stitches in the same place (for 3-D effect). Follow Cheeks photo tutorial #21-26 on page 73.

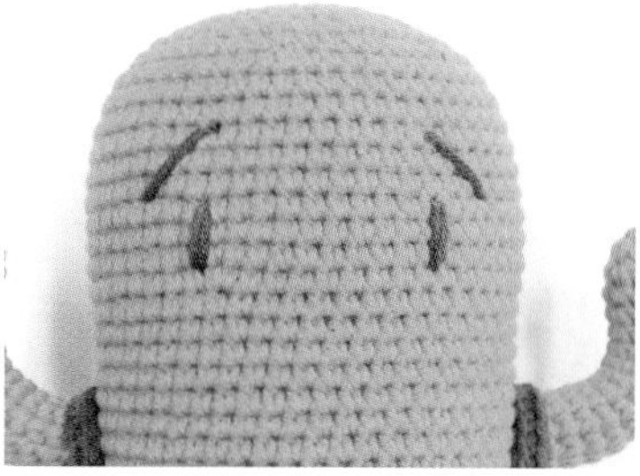

11 Mark the position of the eyebrows and embroider using one straight stitch each.

» Mustache

12 Fold the Brown felt in half and using the Mustache template, cut out the shape.

13 With dark brown thread on the needle, position and sew the center part of the mustache to the face.

» Chest Hair

14 Using beige yarn, embroider Chest Hairs following Wacky Bear's photo tutorial #27-28 on page 73.

» Sombrero

15 Thread the yarn tail onto a needle and bring it out between rounds 7 & 8.

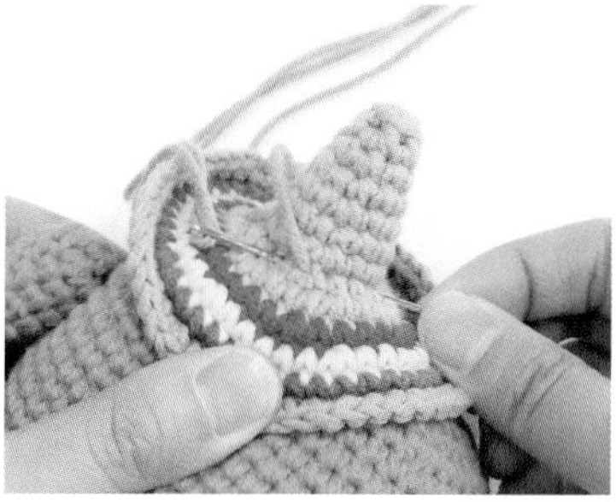

16 Stuff the hat with a small amount of stuffing. Position it at an angle on the head and sew it in place.

Leg

[Dark Brown]

Round 1: (6)	In starting ring X 6 •
Round 2: (12)	0 V 6 •
Round 3: (18)	0 (X 1 V 1) * 6 •
Round 4: (24)	0 X 6 V 6 X 6 •
Round 5: (24)	0 X 24 •
Round 6: (18)	0 X 6 Λ 6 X 6 •
Round 7: (14)	0 X 5 Λ 4 X 5 •
Rounds 8-10: (14)	0 X 14 •

[Brown]

Rounds 11-12: (14)	0 X 14 • <u>At the end of Leg A, cut the yarn and finish off. Repeat Rounds 1-12 for Leg B, but do not finish off.</u>
Round 13: (42)	On Leg B 0 X 12 (Leave the last 2 stitches unworked.) Chain Stitch 7 On Leg A, start in the fifth stitch X 14 Working in the chains X̲ 7 (Don't miss the back loop only!) In remaining stitches on Leg B X 2 •
Round 14: (42)	On Leg B 0 X 12 On chain X̲ 7 (Don't miss the back loop only!) On Leg A and finish round X 23 •
Round 15: (42)	0 X 42 •
Round 16: (48)	0 X 3 V 1 (X 6 V 1) * 5 X 3 •
Round 17: (54)	0 (X 7 V 1) * 6 •
Rounds 18-19: (54)	0 X 54 •
Round 20-1: (54)	0 X̅ 54 • (Don't miss the front loop only!)
Round 21-1: (54)	0 X 54 • <u>Cut the yarn and finish off, hiding the tails on the inside. Start stuffing each leg, shaping the boots.</u>

Body + Face	[Green]	Join the yarn to the back loop of the first stitch on Round 19.
	Round 20-2: (54)	0 X 54 •
	Round 21-2: (54)	0 X 54 •
	Round 22: (57)	0 (X 17 V 1) * 3 •
	Round 23: (60)	0 X 9 V 1 (X 18 V 1) * 2 X 9 •
	Round 24: (63)	0 (X 19 V 1) * 3 •
	Round 25: (66)	0 X 10 V 1 (X 20 V 1) * 2 X 10 •
	Rounds 26-35: (66)	0 X 66 •
	Round 36: (63)	0 X 10 Λ 1 (X 20 Λ 1) * 2 X 10 •
	Round 37: (60)	0 (X 19 Λ 1) * 3 •
	Round 38: (57)	0 X 9 Λ 1 (X 18 Λ 1) * 2 X 9 •
	Round 39: (54)	0 (X 17 Λ 1) * 3 •
	Round 40: (51)	0 X 8 Λ 1 (X 16 Λ 1) * 2 X 8 •
	Round 41: (48)	0 (X 15 Λ 1) * 3 •
	Round 42: (42)	0 X 3 Λ 1 (X 6 Λ 1) * 5 X 3 •
	Round 43: (36)	0 (X 5 Λ 1) * 6 •
	Round 44: (30)	0 X 2 Λ 1 (X 4 Λ 1) * 5 X 2 •
		Start stuffing.
	Round 45: (24)	0 (X 3 Λ 1) * 6 •
	Round 46: (18)	0 X 1 Λ 1 (X 2 Λ 1) * 5 X 1 •
	Round 47: (12)	0 (X 1 Λ 1) * 6 •
		Continue stuffing to fill the doll.
	Round 48: (6)	0 Λ 6 •
		Close the last round with a yarn needle.

Arms	[Green]	
	Round 1: (6)	In starting ring X 6 •
	Round 2: (9)	0 (X 1 V 1) * 3 •
	Round 3: (12)	0 X 1 V 1 (X 2 V 1) * 2 X 1 •
	Round 4: (15)	0 (X 3 V 1) * 3 •
	Round 5: (18)	0 X 24 V 1 (X 4 V 1) * 2 X 2 •
	Rounds 6-8: (18)	0 X 18 •
	Round 9: (15)	0 X 2 Λ 1 (X 4 Λ 1) * 2 X 2 •
	Round 10: (12)	0 (X 3 Λ 1) * 3 •
	Round 11: (9)	0 X 1 Λ 1 (X 2 Λ 1) * 2 X 1 •
		Stuff the Arm about ⅔ full. Leaving a 16" (40 cm) long tail, cut the yarn and finish off.
		Repeat Rounds 1~15 for other Arm.

Suspenders

[Dark Brown]

* Please see Working in Rows on page 42.

Row 1: (45) — Chain stitch **45**

Add 4 turning chains (buttonhole), start in 5th ch from hook **X 45**

Finish off, leaving a 4" (10 cm) tail.

Repeat for second suspender.

Sombrero

[Beige]

Round 1: (6)	In starting ring **X 6 •**
Round 2: (8)	**0 (X̲ 2 V̲ 1) * 2 •** (Don't miss the back loop only!)
Round 3: (8)	**0 X 8 •**
Round 4: (10)	**0 (X 3 V 1) * 2 •**
Round 5: (10)	**0 X 10 •**
Round 6: (12)	**0 X 2 V 1 X 4 V 1 X 2 •**
Round 7: (12)	**0 X 12 •**
Round 8: (14)	**0 (X 5 V 1) * 2 •**
Round 9: (14)	**0 X 14 •**
Round 10: (16)	**0 X 3 V 1 X 6 V 1 X 3 •**
Round 11: (16)	**0 X 16 •**
Round 12: (18)	**0 (X 7 V 1) * 2 •**
Round 13: (24)	**0 X̄ 1 V̄ 1 (X̄ 2 V̄ 1) * 5 X̄ 1 •** (Don't miss the front loop only!)
Round 14: (30)	**0 (X 3 V 1) * 6 •**
Round 15: (36)	**0 X 2 V 1 (X 4 V 1) * 5 X 2 •**
Round 16: (42)	**0 (X 5 V 1) * 6 •**
Round 17: (48)	**0 X 3 V 1 (X 6 V 1) * 5 X 3 •**

[Red] Round 18: (54) **0 (X 7 V 1) * 6 •**

[Yellow] Round 19: (60) **0 X 4 V 1 (X 8 V 1) * 5 X 4 •**

[Dark Green] Round 20: (66) **0 (X 9 V 1) * 6 •**

[Beige] Round 21: (72) **0 X 5 V 1 (X 10 V 1) * 5 X 5 •**

Leaving a 16" (40 cm) long tail, cut the yarn and finish off.

Face

- **Eyes:** Over 2 stitches, about 13-14 rounds down from crown, with 5 stitches between them.
- **Eyebrows:** About 3 rounds above eye.
- **Mustache:** Between 17th & 18th round down from crown.

Arms + Chest Hair + Buttons

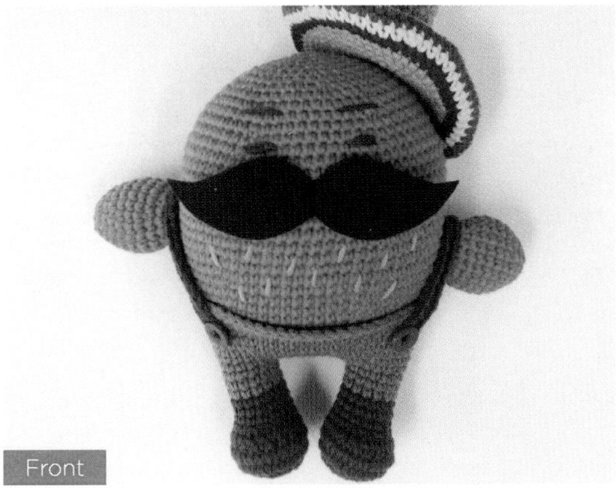

- **Arms:** Between 5th & 8th round up from waistline.
- **Chest Hair:** Between 4th & 9th round from waist.
- **Buttons:** Round 19 from toe tip, 16 stitches between them.

Suspenders

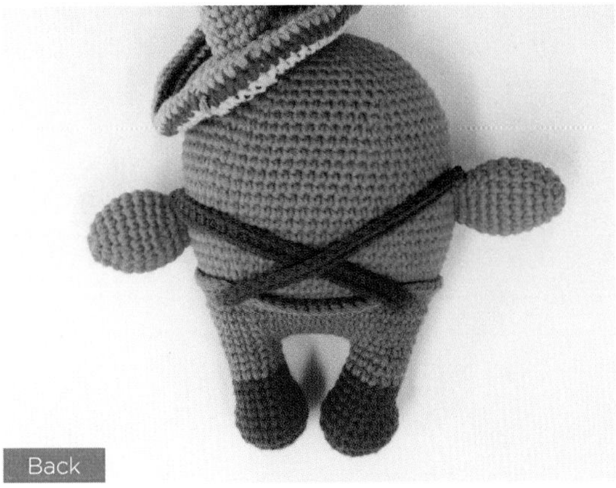

- **Straps:** Round 19 from toe tip, and 16 stitches between them.

» Body

1. After stuffing, sew the last round closed, using the long tail and yarn needle. The remaining yarn should be hidden in the body. (see Closing the Last Round - page 51)

» Arms

2. Mark the arms at an angle using a water-soluble pen.

3. Sew each arm onto the body, following the markings.

» Buttons + Suspenders

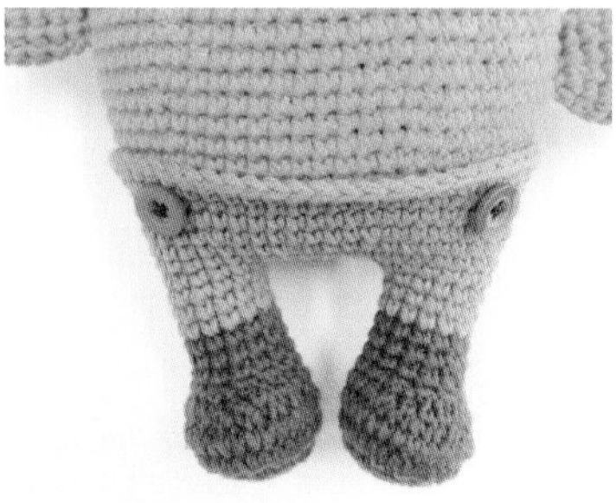

4. Attach the buttons in position, following Bear Groom photo tutorial #2-5 on page 79.

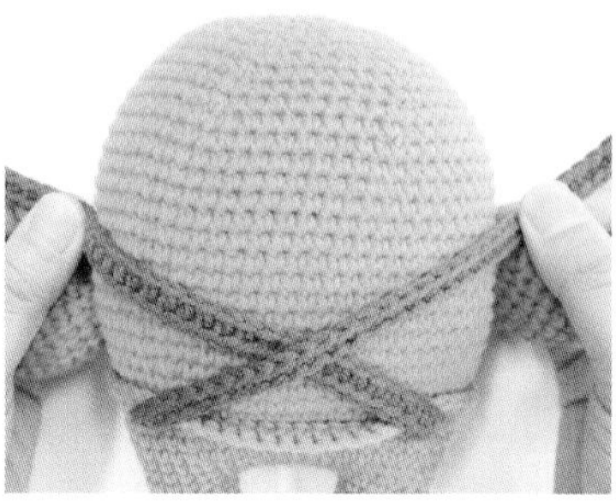

5. With the back facing, attach both straps following Bear Groom photo tutorial #6-13 on page 80.

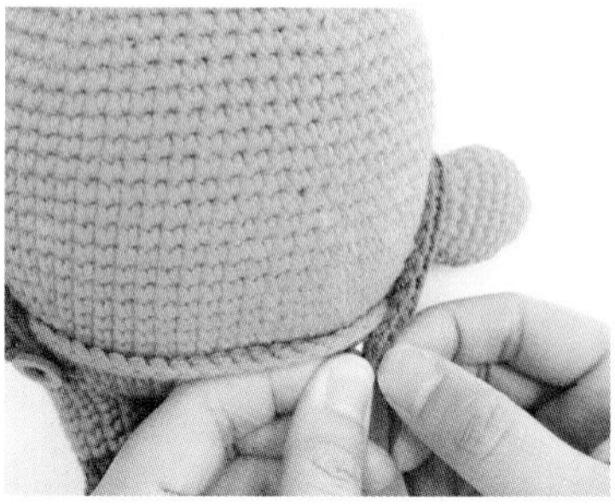

6. With the front facing, fasten the suspenders on the buttons.

» Eyes + Eyebrows

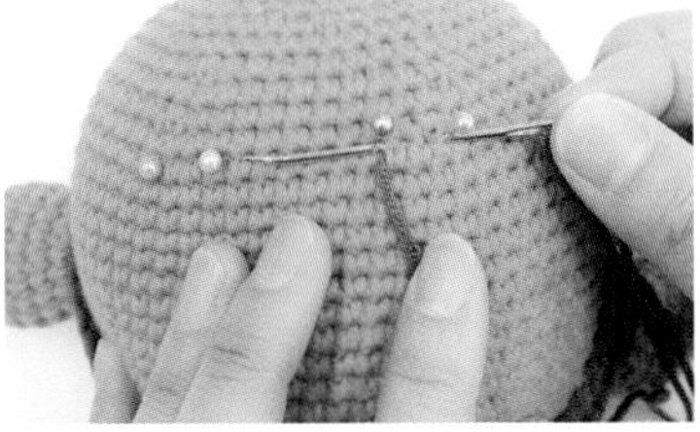

7 Mark the position of each eye with straight pins. With dark brown yarn on a needle, embroider the eye using 3 straight stitches in the same place (for 3-D effect). Follow Cheeks photo tutorial #21-26 on page 73.

8 Mark the position of the eyebrows and embroider using one straight stitch each.

» Mustache

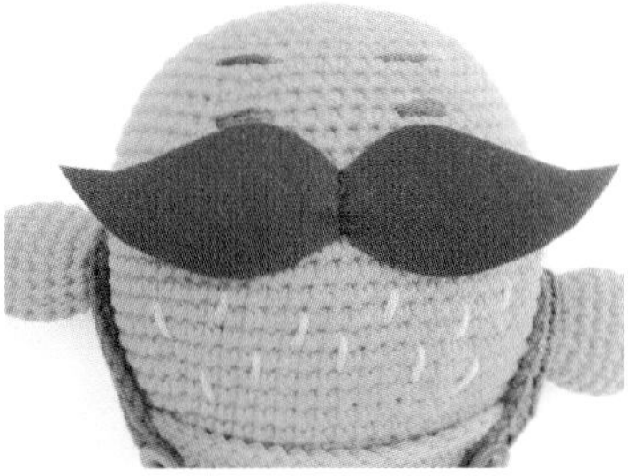

9 Using the template, cut out the felt shape, and sew the center part of the mustache to the face.

» Sombrero

10 Thread the yarn tail onto a needle and bring it out between Rounds 12 & 13.

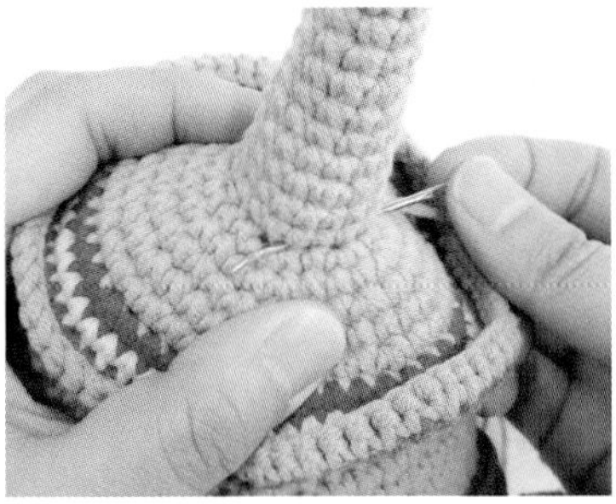

11 Stuff the hat with a small amount of stuffing. Position it at an angle on the head and sew it in place.

» Chest Hair

12 Using light beige yarn, embroider Chest Hairs following Wacky Bear's photo tutorial #27-28 on page 73.

Jack Lion is of African royalty and wants to be friends with more animals. He left his kingdom and crossed the ocean to visit Elliott. The first new friend Elliott introduced him to, was William.

William Bear, a friendly chap, is a descendant of European aristocracy. Because of this, he has a lot in common with Jack. Today, the three new friends are sitting down to share a pot of hot tea together. What they will talk about?

Elliott Elephant came to England to study how to become a gentleman. He is used to the warm weather of Africa, so the ever-changing European climate makes it easy for him to catch colds. Because of this, you'll never see him without his scarf.

TEATIME WITH
THE PEACEFUL ANIMALS

06 | William Bear (7½" / 19 cm)

Yarn: Medium Weight (Worsted)
- Beige
- Cyan
- Dark Gray
- Cream
- Light Pink

Hook: Size D-3 (3.25 mm)

Other: Yarn Needle
Stuffing
¼" (6 mm) Bean Buttons - 2 (Eyes)
5⁄16" (8 mm) Button - 1 (Nose)
Sewing Thread & Needle

07 | Jack Lion (7½" / 19 cm)

Yarn: Medium Weight (Worsted)
- Mustard
- Light Gray
- Claret Red
- Dark Brown
- Cream

Hook: Size D-3 (3.25 mm)

Other: Yarn Needle
Stuffing
¼" (6 mm) Bean Buttons - 2 (Eyes)
5⁄16" (8 mm) Button - 1 (Nose)
Sewing Thread & Needle

08 | Elliott Elephant (7½" / 19 cm)

Yarn: Medium Weight (Worsted)
- Light Gray
- Cream
- Red
- Black
- Light Green
- Light Pink

Hook: Size D-3 (3.25 mm)

Other: Yarn Needle
Stuffing
¼" (6 mm) Bean Buttons - 2 (Eyes)
Sewing Thread & Needle

Legs + Body

[Beige]

Round 1: (6)	In starting ring X 6 •
Round 2: (12)	0 ⋎6 •
Round 3: (16)	0 X 4 ⋎4 X 4 •
Round 4: (20)	0 X 6 ⋎4 X 6 •
Round 5: (20)	0 X 20 •
Round 6: (16)	0 X 6 ⋏4 X 6 •
Round 7: (12)	0 X 4 ⋏4 X 4 •
Round 8: (10)	0 X 4 ⋏2 X 4 •
Rounds 9-14: (12)	0 X 10 •
	At the end of Leg A, cut the yarn and finish off. Repeat Rounds 1-14 for Leg B, but do not finish off.
	Start stuffing each leg, shaping the feet.
Round 15: (30)	On Leg B 0 X 8 (Leave the last 2 stitches unworked.)
	Chain Stitch 5
	On Leg A, start in the fourth stitch X 10
	Working in the chains X̲ 5 (Don't miss the back loop only!)
	In remaining stitches on Leg B X 2 •
Round 16: (30)	On Leg B 0 X 8
	On chain X̲ 5 (Don't miss the back loop only!)
	On Leg A and finish round X 17 •
Round 17: (36)	0 X 2 ⋎1 (X 4 ⋎ 1) * 5 X 2 •
Rounds 18-20: (36)	0 X 36 •

[Turquoise, Dark Gray]

For Rounds 21-32, alternate the colors, working 2 rounds in each color.

Rounds 21-22: (36)	0 X 36 •
Round 23: (33)	0 X 5 ⋏1 (X 10 ⋏ 1) * 2 X 5 •
Round 24: (33)	0 X 33 •
Round 25: (30)	0 (X 9 ⋏ 1) * 3 •
Round 26: (30)	0 X 30 •
Round 27: (27)	0 X 4 ⋏1 (X 8 ⋏ 1) * 2 X 4 •
Round 28: (27)	0 X 27 •
	Start stuffing.
Round 29: (24)	0 (X 7 ⋏ 1) * 3 •
Round 30: (24)	0 X 24 •
Round 31: (21)	0 X 3 ⋏1 (X 6 ⋏1) * 2 X 3 •
Round 32: (18)	0 (X 5 ⋏ 1) * 3 •
	Continue stuffing to fill the doll. Cut the yarn and finish off, hiding the tail on the inside.

Head

[Beige)

Round 1: (6)	In starting ring ✕6 •
Round 2: (12)	0 ⋁6 •
Round 3: (18)	0 (✕1 ⋁ 1) * 6 •
Round 4: (24)	0 ✕1 ⋁1 (✕2 ⋁1) * 5 ✕1 •
Round 5: (30)	0 (✕3 ⋁1) * 6 •
Round 6: (36)	0 ✕2 ⋁1 (✕4 ⋁1) * 5 ✕2 •
Round 7: (42)	0 (✕5 ⋁1) * 6 •
Round 8: (48)	0 ✕3 ⋁1 (✕6 ⋁ 1) * 5 ✕3 •
Rounds 9-16: (48)	0 ✕48 •
Round 17: (42)	0 ✕3 ⋀1 (✕6 ⋀1) * 5 ✕3 •
Round 18: (36)	0 (✕5 ⋀1) * 6 •
Round 19: (30)	0 ✕2 ⋀1 (✕4 ⋀1) * 5 ✕2 •
Round 20: (24)	0 (✕3 ⋀1) * 6 •
Round 21: (18)	0 ✕1 ⋀1 (✕2 ⋀1) * 5 ✕1 •
	Stuff the Head. Leaving a 16" (40 cm) long tail, cut the yarn and finish off.

Ears

[Beige]

Round 1: (6)	In starting ring ✕6 •
Round 2: (12)	0 ⋁6 •
Rounds 3-4: (12)	0 ✕12 •
	Leaving a 16" (40 cm) long tail, cut the yarn and finish off. Repeat Rounds 1-4 for other Ear.

Snout

[Cream]

Round 1: (6)	In starting ring ✕6 •
Round 2: (12)	0 ⋁6 •
Round 3: (18)	0 (✕1 ⋁1) * 6 •
Round 4: (18)	0 ✕18 •
	Leaving a 16" (40 cm) long tail, cut the yarn and finish off.

Arms

[Beige]

Round 1: (6) — In starting ring ×6 •

Round 2: (12) — 0 ⩔6 •

Rounds 3-4: (12) — 0 ×12 •

Round 5: (8) — 0 (×1 ⩕1) * 4 •

[Turquoise
Dark Gray]

For Rounds 6-17, alternate the colors, working 2 rounds in each color.

Rounds 6-17: (8) — 0 ×8 •

Stuff the Arm about ⅔ full. Leaving a 16" (40 cm) long tail, cut the yarn and finish off.

Repeat Rounds 1~17 for other Arm.

Face

- **Eyes:** Between 9th & 10th Round down from crown, with 7 stitches between them.
- **Eyebrows:** About 3 Rounds above eyes.
- **Snout:** Between 10th & 16th Round down from crown
- **Cheeks:** Over 2 stitches, starting 1 Round below eye and 1 stitch across.

Ears

- **Ears:** Between 5th & 9th Round down from crown.

Arms

- **Arms:** Between 1st & 2nd Round from the neck join.

» Head+Body

1 Sew the Head to the Body, and after about 2/3 of the way around, add more stuffing to the neck before finishing. See Mattress (Invisible) Stitch on page 53.

» Arms

2 Mark the position of the Arms with a water-soluble pen. Sew the arms in place, working from the back to the front. Repeat for other arm.

» Ears

3 Mark the position of the Ears with a water-soluble pen. Fold the ear in half to flatten. Using the yarn tail, sew on the ear following the marking. Repeat for other ear.

» Snout

4 Mark the position with a water-soluble pen. Split the yarn into 2 strands. Roll up the one strand and hide under the snout.

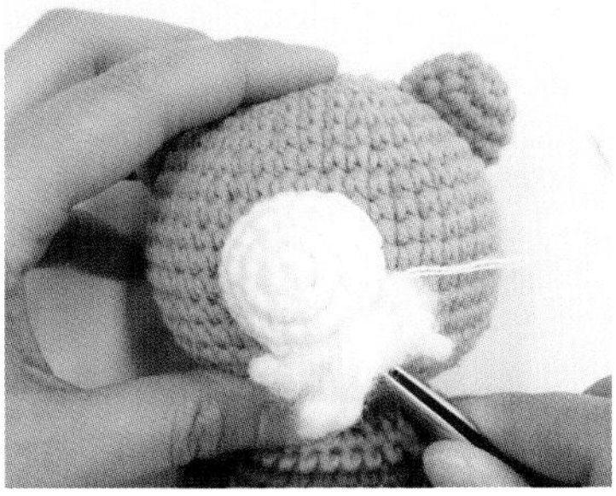

5 Position the snout and using the other strand, sew about 2/3 of the way, adding more stuffing before finishing. Follow photo tutorial #6-8 of Wacky Bear on page 71.

» Eyes

6 Mark the position of the Eyes with straight pins. Place one bean button onto a length of sewing thread. Follow photo tutorial #14-17 of Wacky Bear on page 72.

» Mouth + Nose

7 Using dark brown thread, embroider the mouth following photo tutorial #18-20 of Wacky Bear on page 72-73.

» Eyebrows

8 Identify the position of the eyebrows, and embroider them using dark brown thread, and angling the stitch downwards.

» Cheeks

9 Using the pink yarn, embroider each cheek, following photo tutorial #21-26 on page 73.

Legs + Body

[Mustard]

Round 1: (6)	In starting ring X 6 •
Round 2: (12)	0 ⩛6 •
Round 3: (16)	0 X 4 ⩛4 X 4 •
Round 4: (20)	0 X 6 ⩛4 X 6 •
Round 5: (20)	0 X 20 •
Round 6: (16)	0 X 6 ⩚4 X 6 •
Round 7: (12)	0 X 4 ⩚4 X 4 •
Round 8: (10)	0 X 4 ⩚2 X 4 •
Rounds 9-14: (10)	0 X 10 •
	At the end of Leg A, cut the yarn and finish off. Repeat Rounds 1~14 for Leg B, but do not finish off.
	Start stuffing each leg, shaping the feet.
Round 15: (30)	On Leg B 0 X 8 (Leave the last 2 stitches unworked.)
	Chain Stitch 5
	On Leg A, start in the fourth stitch X 10
	Working in the chains X̲ 5 (Don't miss the back loop only!)
	In remaining stitches on Leg B X 2 •
Round 16: (30)	On Leg B 0 X 8
	On chain X̲ 5 (Don't miss the back loop only!)
	On Leg A and finish round X 17 •
Round 17: (36)	0 X 2 ⩛1 (X 4 ⩛1) ∗ 5 X 2 •
Rounds 18-20: (36)	0 X 36 •

[Purple Light Gray]

	For Rounds 21-32, alternate the colors, working 2 rounds in each color.
Rounds 21-22: (36)	0 X 36 •
Round 23: (33)	0 X 5 ⩚1 (X 10 ⩚1) ∗ 2 X 5 •
Round 24: (33)	0 X 33 •
Round 25: (30)	0 (X 9 ⩚1) ∗ 3 •
Round 26: (30)	0 X 30 •
Round 27: (27)	0 X 4 ⩚1 (X 8 ⩚1) ∗ 2 X 4 •
Round 28: (27)	0 X 27 •
	Start stuffing.
Round 29: (24)	0 (X 7 ⩚1) ∗ 3 •
Round 30: (24)	0 X 24 •
Round 31: (21)	0 X 3 ⩚1 (X 6 ⩚1) ∗ 2 X 3 •
Round 32: (18)	0 (X 5 ⩚1) ∗ 3 •
	Continue stuffing to fill the doll. Cut the yarn and finish off, hiding the tail on the inside.

Head

[Mustard]

Round 1: (6) In starting ring × 6 •
Round 2: (12) 0 ⋁ 6 •
Round 3: (18) 0 (× 1 ⋁ 1) * 6 •
Round 4: (24) 0 × 1 ⋁ 1 (× 2 ⋁ 1) * 5 × 1 •
Round 5: (30) 0 (× 3 ⋁ 1) * 6 •
Round 6: (36) 0 × 2 ⋁ 1 (× 4 ⋁ 1) * 5 × 2 •
Round 7: (42) 0 (× 5 ⋁ 1) * 6 •
Round 8: (48) 0 × 3 ⋁ 1 (× 6 ⋁ 1) * 5 × 3 •
Rounds 9-16: (48) 0 × 48 •
Round 17: (42) 0 × 3 ⋀ 1 (× 6 ⋀ 1) * 5 × 3 •
Round 18: (36) 0 (× 5 ⋀ 1) * 6 •
Round 19: (30) 0 × 2 ⋀ 1 (× 4 ⋀ 1) * 5 × 2 •
Round 20: (24) 0 (× 3 ⋀ 1) * 6 •
Round 21: (18) 0 × 1 ⋀ 1 (× 2 ⋀ 1) * 5 × 1 •

Stuff the Head. Leaving a 16" (40 cm) long tail, cut the yarn and finish off.

Ears

[Mustard]

Round 1: (6) In starting ring × 6 •
Round 2: (8) 0 (× 2 ⋁ 1) * 2 •
Round 3: (10) 0 (× 3 ⋁ 1) * 2 •
Round 4: (12) 0 (× 4 ⋁ 1) * 2 •
Round 5: (14) 0 (× 5 ⋁ 1) * 2 •
Round 6: (16) 0 (× 6 ⋁ 1) * 2 •

Leaving a 16" (40 cm) long tail, cut the yarn and finish off.
Repeat Rounds 1~6 for other Ear.

Muzzle

[Cream]

Round 1: (6) In starting ring × 6 •
Round 2: (12) 0 ⋁ 6 •
Round 3: (18) 0 (× 1 ⋁ 1) * 6 •
Round 4: (18) 0 × 18 •

Leaving a 16" (40 cm) long tail, cut the yarn and finish off. Repeat Rounds 1-4 for other piece.

Arms

[Mustard]

Round 1: (6) In starting ring X 6 •

Round 2: (12) 0 ⩡ 6 •

Rounds 3-4: (12) 0 X 12 •

Round 5: (8) 0 (X 1 ⩢ 1) * 4 •

[Purple
Light Gray]

For Rounds 6-17, alternate the colors, working 2 rounds in each color.

Rounds 6-17: (8) 0 X 8 •

Stuff the Arm about 2/3 full. Leaving a 16" (40 cm) long tail, cut the yarn and finish off.

Repeat Rounds 1-17 for other Arm.

Mane

[Dark Brown]

* Please see Making Tubes on page 42.

Chain stitch 50

Join with a slip stitch to the first chain.

Round 1: (50) 0 X 50 •

Round 2: (50) 0 (X 1 ○ 10) * 50 •

Leaving a 16" (40 cm) long tail, cut the yarn and finish off.

*Please note the position of the Arms is the same as William Bear on page 104.

Face

- **Eyes:** Between 9th & 10th round down from crown, with 5 stitches between them.
- **Eyebrows:** About 2-3 rounds above eyes.
- **Muzzle:** Between 11th & 15th round down from crown

Ears

- **Ears:** Between 4th & 10th Round down from crown.

» Head + Body + Arms + Ears + Muzzle

1 Follow the photo tutorial #1-5 for William Bear - page 105 - to attach head, arms and ears. Use the same method as the snout for attaching the two pieces of the muzzle.

» Eyes

2 Mark the position of the Eyes with straight pins. Place one bean button onto a length of sewing thread. Follow photo tutorial #14-17 of Wacky Bear on page 72.

» Nose

3 Sew a button nose in the space between the two muzzle pieces.

» Eyebrows

4 Identify the position of the eyebrows, and embroider them using dark brown thread, and angling the end of the stitch downwards.

» Mane

5 Place the mane over the head, and sew it in place.

Legs + Body

[Light Gray]

Round 1: (6) In starting ring X 6 •

Round 2: (12) 0 ⋎ 6 •

Round 3: (16) 0 X 4 ⋎ 4 X 4 •

Round 4: (20) 0 X 6 ⋎ 4 X 6 •

Round 5: (20) 0 X 20 •

Round 6: (16) 0 X 6 ⋏ 4 X 6 •

Round 7: (12) 0 X 4 ⋏ 4 X 4 •

Round 8: (10) 0 X 4 ⋏ 2 X 4 •

Rounds 9-14: (10) 0 X 10 •

<u>At the end of Leg A, cut the yarn and finish off. Repeat Rounds 1~14 for Leg B, but do not finish off.</u>

<u>Start stuffing each leg, shaping the feet.</u>

Round 15: (30) On Leg B 0 X 8 (Leave the last 2 stitches unworked.)

Chain Stitch 5

On Leg A, start in the fourth stitch X 10

Working in the chains X̲ 5 (Don't miss the back loop only!)

In remaining stitches on Leg B X 2 •

Round 16: (30) On Leg B 0 X 8

On Chain X̲ 5 (Don't miss the back loop only!)

On Leg A and finish round X 17 •

Round 17: (36) 0 X 2 ⋎ 1 (X 4 ⋎ 1) * 5 X 2 •

Rounds 18-20: (36) 0 X 36 •

[Red Cream]

<u>For rounds 21-32, alternate the colors, working 2 rounds in each color.</u>

Rounds 21-22: (36) 0 X 36 •

Round 23: (33) 0 X 5 ⋏ 1 (X 10 ⋏ 1) * 2 X 5 •

Round 24: (33) 0 X 33 •

Round 25: (30) 0 (X 9 ⋏ 1) * 3 •

Round 26: (30) 0 X 30 •

Round 27: (27) 0 X 4 ⋏ 1 (X 8 ⋏ 1) * 2 X 4 •

Round 28: (27) 0 X 27 •

<u>Start stuffing.</u>

Round 29: (24) 0 (X 7 ⋏ 1) * 3 •

Round 30: (24) 0 X 24 •

Round 31: (21) 0 X 3 ⋏ 1 (X 6 ⋏ 1) * 2 X 3 •

Round 32: (18) 0 (X 5 ⋏ 1) * 3 •

<u>Continue stuffing to fill the doll. Cut the yarn and finish off, hiding the tail on the inside.</u>

Head

[Light Gray]

Round 1: (6) In starting ring X 6 •

Round 2: (12) 0 V 6 •

Round 3: (18) 0 (X 1 V 1) * 6 •

Round 4: (24) 0 X 1 V 1 (X 2 V 1) * 5 X 1 •

Round 5: (30) 0 (X 3 V 1) * 6 •

Round 6: (36) 0 X 2 V 1 (X 4 V 1) * 5 X 2 •

Round 7: (42) 0 (X 5 V 1) * 6 •

Round 8: (48) 0 X 3 V 1 (X 6 V 1) * 5 X 3 •

Rounds 9-16: (48) 0 X 48 •

Round 17: (42) 0 X 3 Λ 1 (X 6 Λ 1) * 5 X 3 •

Round 18: (36) 0 (X 5 Λ 1) * 6 •

Round 19: (30) 0 X 2 Λ 1 (X 4 Λ 1) * 5 X 2 •

Round 20: (24) 0 (X 3 Λ 1) * 6 •

Round 21: (18) 0 X 1 Λ 1 (X 2 Λ 1) * 5 X 1 •

Stuff the Head. Leaving a 16" (40 cm) long tail, cut the yarn and finish off.

Ears

[Light Gray]

Round 1: (6) In starting ring X 6 •

Round 2: (12) 0 V 6 •

Round 3: (18) 0 (X 1 V 1) * 6 •

Round 4: (24) 0 X 1 V 1 (X 2 V 1) * 5 X 1 •

Round 5: (25) 0 (X 3 V 1) * 5 •

Leaving the last 4 stitches unworked, cut the yarn leaving a 16" (40 cm) long tail and finish off.
Repeat Rounds 1~5 for other Ear.

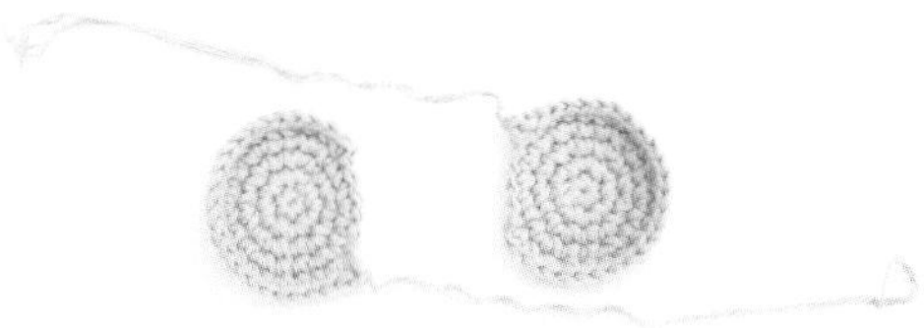

[Elliott's Ears]

Trunk

[Light Gray]

Round 1: (6) In starting ring X 6 •

Rounds 2-8: (6) 0 X 6 •

Leaving a 16" (40 cm) long tail, cut the yarn and finish off.

Arms

[Light Gray]

Round 1: (6) In starting ring X 6 •

Round 2: (12) 0 ⋎ 6 •

Rounds 3-4: (12) 0 X 12 •

Round 5: (8) 0 (X 1 ⋏ 1) * 4 •

[Red Cream]

For rounds 6-17, alternate the colors, working 2 rounds in each color.

Rounds 6-17: (8) 0 X 8 •

Stuff the Arm about ⅔ full. Leaving a 16" (40 cm) long tail, cut the yarn and finish off.
Repeat Rounds 1-17 for other Arm.

Hat

[Black]

Round 1: (6) In starting ring X 6 •

Round 2: (12) 0 ⋎ 6 •

Rounds 3-4: (12) 0 X 12 •

[Red]

Round 5-6: (12) 0 X 12 •

[Black]

Round 7: (18) 0 (X̄ 1 ⋎̄ 1) * 6 • (Don't miss the front loop only!)

Leaving a 16" (40 cm) long tail, cut the yarn and finish off.

Scarf

* Please see Working in Rows on page 42.

[Light Green]

Row 1: (60) Chain Stitch **60**
Add 1 turning chain, start in 2nd ch from hook X 60
Finish off, leaving a 4" (10 cm) tail.

* Please note the position of the Arms is the same as William Bear on page 104.

Face

- **Eyes:** Between 10th & 11th round down from crown, with 8 stitches between them.
- **Eyebrows:** About 5 rounds above eyes.
- **Trunk:** Between 11th & 12th round down from crown
- **Mouth:** About 15 rounds down from crown.
- **Cheeks:** Over 2 stitches, starting 1 round below eye and 1 stitch across.

Ears

- **Ears:** Between 9th & 15th round down from crown.

»Head + Body + Arms

1. Follow the photo tutorial #1-2 for William - page 105 - to attach head and arms.

» Ears

2. Mark the position of the Ears with a water-soluble pen. Using the yarn tail, with the right side facing forward, sew on the ear following the marking and shaping the ear to fit. Repeat for other ear.

» Trunk

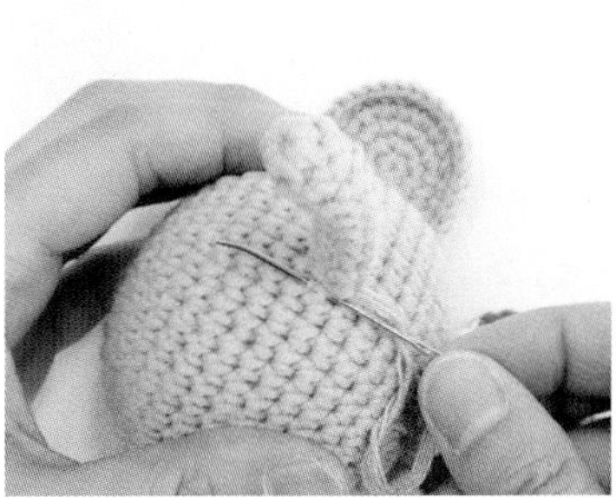

3. Mark the position of the Trunk with a water-soluble pen. Using the yarn tail, sew the trunk in position.

» Eyes

4 Mark the position of the Eyes with straight pins. Place one bean button onto a length of sewing thread. Follow photo tutorial #14-17 of Wacky Bear on page 72.

» Eyebrows + Mouth

5 Identify the position of the eyebrows and mouth, and using dark brown thread embroider them, angling the eyebrows downwards.

» Cheeks

6 Using the pink yarn, embroider each cheek, following photo tutorial #21-26 on page 73.

» Hat

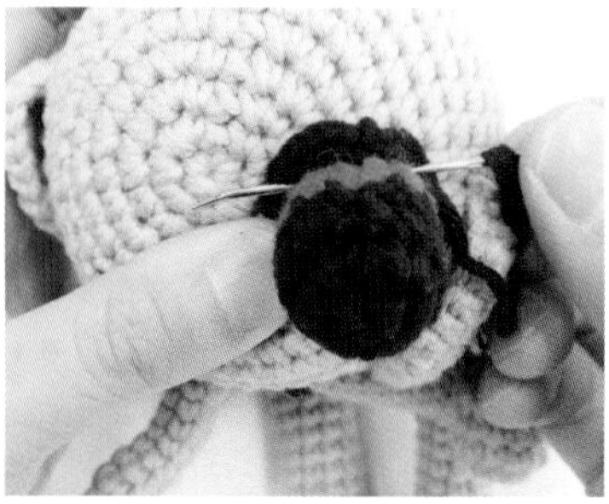

7 Thread the yarn tail onto a needle and bring it out between rounds 6 & 7. Stuff the hat with a small amount of stuffing. Position it at an angle on the head and sew it in place.

» Scarf

8 Tie the scarf around Elliott's neck.

BEST FRIENDS
FOREVER

Here are two friends who are so close they do everything together. When Benjy first got Wiener, the little puppy was so small he fitted in Benjy's hand. Wiener is now all grown up and he's filled out, making it difficult for Benjy to carry him. But these best friends still enjoy lots of cuddles together.

09 | Benjy (13½ " / 34 cm)

Yarn: Medium Weight (Worsted)
- Brown
- Purple
- Blue
- Light Gray
- Dark Pink
- Pink
- Flesh Color
- Dark Gray
- Cream
- Light Green

Hook: Size D-3 (3.25 mm)

Other: Yarn Needle
Stuffing
¼" (6 mm) Buttons - 2 (Eyes)
½" (13 mm) Buttons - 2 (Suspenders)
Dark Yellow Felt - 1¼" (3 cm) x 2½ (6 cm)
Sewing Thread & Needle

10 | Wiener (9¾" / 25 cm)

Yarn: Medium Weight (Worsted)
- Brown
- Dark Brown
- Dark Pink
- Light Green

Hook: Size D-3 (3.25 mm)

Other: Yarn Needle
Stuffing
5⁄16" (8 mm) Bean Buttons - 2 (Eyes)
⅜" (10 mm) Button - 1 (Collar)
Sewing Thread & Needle

Legs + Body

[Dark Gray]

Round 1: (6)	In starting ring **X 6** •
Round 2: (12)	**0** **⋎ 6** •
Round 3: (18)	**0** **(X 1 ⋎ 1) * 6** •
Round 4: (24)	**0** **X 6 ⋎ 6 X 6** •
Rounds 5-6: (24)	**0** **X 24** •
Round 7: (18)	**0** **X 6 ⋏ 6 X 6** •
Round 8: (14)	**0** **X 5 ⋏ 4 X 5** •
Rounds 9-11: (14)	**0** **X 14** •

[Purple]

Rounds 12-19: (14)	In starting ring **X 14** •
	<u>At the end of Leg A, cut the yarn and finish off. Repeat Rounds 1~19 for Leg B, but do not finish off.</u>
	<u>Start stuffing each leg, shaping the feet.</u>
Round 20: (48)	On Leg B **0** **X 12** (Leave the last 2 stitches unworked.)
	Chain Stitch **10**
	On Leg A, start in the second stitch **X 14**
	Working in the chains **X̲ 10** (Don't miss the back loop only!)
	In remaining stitches on Leg B **X 2** •
Round 21: (48)	On Leg B **0** **X 12**
	On chain **X̲ 10** (Don't miss the back loop only!)
	On Leg A and finish round **X 26**
Round 22: (54)	**0** **(X 7 ⋎ 1) * 6** •
Rounds 23-27: (54)	**0** **X 54** •

[Blue, Light Gray, Light Green, Cream]

	<u>For Rounds 28-46, alternate the 4 colors, working 1 round in each color.</u>
Rounds 28-34: (54)	**0** **X 54** •
Round 35: (51)	**0** **X 8 ⋏ 1 (X 16 ⋏ 1) * 2 X 8** •
Round 36: (51)	**0** **X 51** •
Round 37: (48)	**0** **(X 15 ⋏ 1) * 3** •
Round 38: (48)	**0** **X 48** •
Round 39: (45)	**0** **X 7 ⋏ 1 (X 14 ⋏ 1) * 2 X 7** •
Round 40: (45)	**0** **X 45** •
Round 41: (42)	**0** **(X 13 ⋏ 1) * 3** •
Round 42: (42)	**0** **X 42** •
	<u>Start stuffing.</u>

Round 43: (39) 0 X 6 ⋏ 1 (X 12 ⋏ 1) * 2 X 6 •
Round 44: (39) 0 X 39 •
Round 45: (36) 0 (X 11 ⋏ 1) * 3 •
Round 46: (36) 0 X 36 •
Continue stuffing to fill the doll. Cut the yarn and finish off, hiding the tail on the inside.

Arms

[Flesh Color]

Round 1: (6) In starting ring X 6 •
Round 2: (12) 0 ⋎ 6 •
Rounds 3-4: (12) 0 X 12 •
Round 5: (14) 0 X 5 Ѷ 2 X 5 •
Round 6: (12) 0 X 5 ⋏ 2 X 5 •
Round 7: (10) 0 X 4 ⋏ 2 X 4 •

[Green, Light Gray , Blue, Cream]

For rounds 8-25, alternate the 4 colors, working 1 round in each color.
Rounds 8-25: (10) 0 X 10 •
Stuff the Arm about ⅔ full. Leaving a 16" (40 cm) long tail, cut the yarn and finish off.
Repeat Rounds 1~25 for other Arm.

Mouth

[Dark Pink]

Round 1: (6) In starting ring X 6 •
Round 2: (12) 0 ⋎ 6 •
Leaving a 16" (40 cm) long tail, cut the yarn and finish off.

Cheeks

[Pink]

Round 1: (6) In starting ring X 6 •
Round 2: (12) 0 ⋎ 6 •
Leaving a 16" (40 cm) long tail, cut the yarn and finish off.
Repeat Rounds 1~2 for other Cheek.

Head

* Please see Making Ovals on page 46.

[Flesh Color]

	Chain stitch **11**
Round 1: (24)	0 (X 10 V 1) * 2 •
Round 2: (30)	0 V 1 X 9 V 3 X 9 V 2 •
Round 3: (36)	0 X 1 V 1 X 9 (X 1 V 1) * 3 X 9 (X 1 V 1) * 2 •
Round 4: (42)	0 X 1 V 1 X 10 (X 1 V 1 X 1) * 3 X 9 (X 1 V 1 X 1) * 2
Round 5: (48)	0 X 3 V 1 X 9 (X 3 V 1) * 3 X 9 (X 3 V 1) * 2 •
Round 6: (54)	0 X 2 V 1 X 11 (X 2 V 1 X 2) * 3 X 9 (X 2 V 1 X 2) * 2 •
Round 7: (60)	0 X 5 V 1 X 9 (X 5 V 1) * 3 X 9 (X 5 V 1) * 2
Round 8: (66)	0 X 3 V 1 X 12 (X 3 V 1 X 3) * 3 X 9 (X 3 V 1 X 3) * 2 •
Round 9: (72)	0 X 7 V 1 X 9 (X 7 V 1) * 3 X 9 (X 7 V 1) * 2 •
Round 10: (78)	0 X 4 V 1 X 13 (X 4 V 1 X 4) * 3 X 9 (X 4 V 1 X 4) * 2 •
Rounds 11-28: (78)	0 X 78 •
Round 29: (72)	0 (X 11 Λ 1) * 6 •
Round 30: (66)	0 X 5 Λ 1 (X 10 Λ 1) * 5 X 5 •
Round 31: (60)	0 (X 9 Λ 1) * 6 •
Round 32: (54)	0 X 4 Λ 1 (X 8 Λ 1) * 5 X 4 •
Round 33: (48)	0 (X 7 Λ 1) * 6 •
Round 34: (42)	0 X 3 Λ 1 (X 6 Λ 1) * 5 X 3 •
Round 35: (36)	0 (X 5 Λ 1) * 6 •
	Stuff and shape the Head. Leaving a 16" (40 cm) long tail, cut the yarn and finish off.

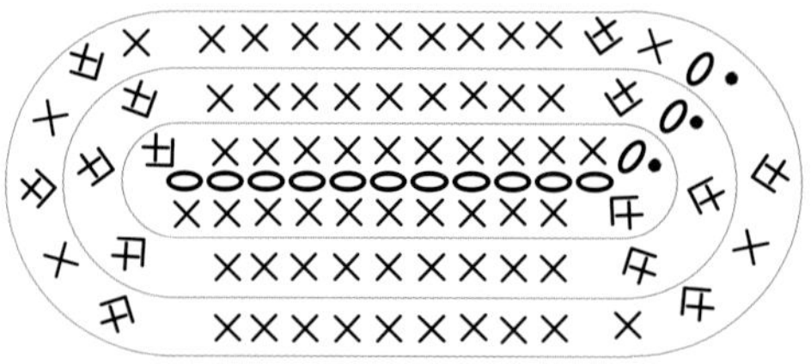

Hair * Please see Making Ovals on page 46.

[Brown]

	Chain stitch **11**
Round 1: (24)	0 (X 10 ⋎1) * 2 •
Round 2: (30)	0 ⋎1 X 9 ⋎3 X 9 ⋎2 •
Round 3: (36)	0 X 1 ⋎1 X 9 (X 1 ⋎1) * 3 X 9 (X 1 ⋎1) * 2 •
Round 4: (42)	0 X 1 ⋎1 X 10 (X 1 ⋎1 X 1) * 3 X 9 (X 1 ⋎1 X 1) * 2 •
Round 5: (48)	0 X 3 ⋎1 X 9 (X 3 ⋎1) * 3 X 9 (X 3 ⋎1) * 2 •
Round 6: (54)	0 X 2 ⋎1 X 11 (X 2 ⋎1 X 2) * 3 X 9 (X 2 ⋎1 X 2) * 2 •
Round 7: (60)	0 X 5 ⋎1 X 9 (X 5 ⋎1) * 3 X 9 (X 5 ⋎1) * 2 •
Round 8: (66)	0 X 3 ⋎1 X 12 (X 3 ⋎1 X 3) * 3 X 9 (X 3 ⋎1 X 3) * 2 •
Round 9: (72)	0 X 7 ⋎1 X 9 (X 7 ⋎1)* 3 X 9 (X 7 ⋎1) * 2 •
Round 10: (78)	0 X 4 ⋎1 X 13 (X 4 ⋎1 X 4) * 3 X 9 (X 4 ⋎1 X 4) * 2 •
Rounds 11-17: (78)	0 X 78 •
	Cut the yarn and finish off, hiding the tail on the inside. Refer to the Tip below for position of the first stitch, to work across back of the Head.
	* Please see Working in Rows on page 42.
Row 18: (54)	0 X 54
Rows 19-28: (54)	0 X 54
	Leaving a 16" (40 cm) long tail, cut the yarn and finish off.

TIP Back of Hair

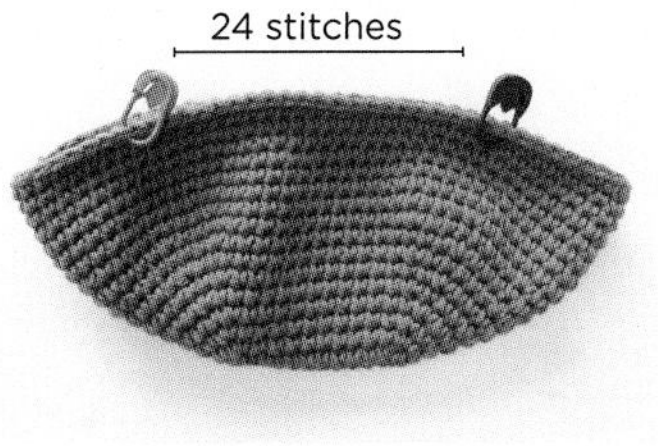

1 After finishing off at the end of Round 17, fold the finished piece in half and flatten it. On the front side, mark the center position using 2 markers, with 24 stitches between them.

2 Join the yarn to the marked stitch on the left and work in each stitch across the back to the other marker, leaving the front 24 stitches unworked.

3 Change direction and continue working in rows across these stitches for another 10 rows. When completed, leave a 16" (40 cm) long tail, cut the yarn and finish off.

Suspenders [Dark Gray]		
* Please see Working in Rows on page 42.	Row 1: (40)	Chain Stitch **40** Add 4 turning chains (buttonhole), start in 5th ch from hook **X 40** Finish off, leaving a 4" (10 cm) tail. Repeat for second suspender.

Face

- **Hair:** The front bangs should be 20 rounds up from neck join.
- **Eyes:** About 15 rounds up from neck join, with 12 stitches between them.
- **Eyebrows:** About 2 rounds above eyes.
- **Nose:** Between 13th & 14th round up from neck join.
- **Mouth:** Between 10th & 11th round from neck join.
- **Cheeks:** Between 9th & 14th round from neck join.

Suspender Buttons + Knees

- **Buttons:** On waistline with 15 stitches between them.
- **Knees:** Between Rounds 14 & 18 from toe tip.

Suspenders

- **Straps:** On waistline with 17 stitches between them.

» Head+Body

1 Sew the Head to the Body, and after about ⅔ of the way around, add more stuffing to the neck before finishing.

» Arms

2 Position the arms on either side of body and using the yarn tail, sew in place. Repeat for other arm.

» Hair

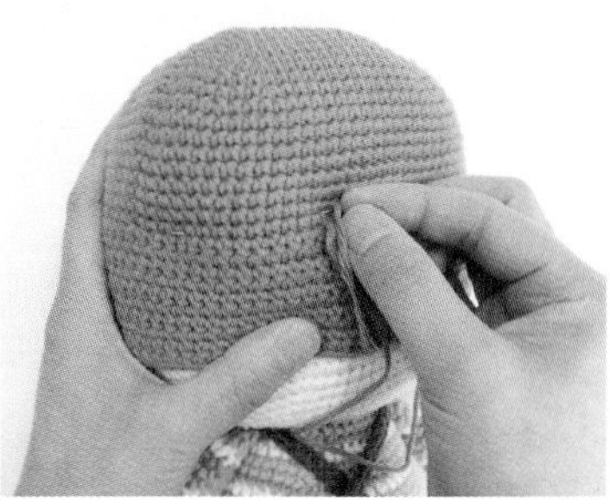

3 Thread the yarn tail onto a needle and first sew the bangs to the front of the head. Sew the remainder of the hair around the head, leaving the bottom rows loose, if you choose.

» Eyes

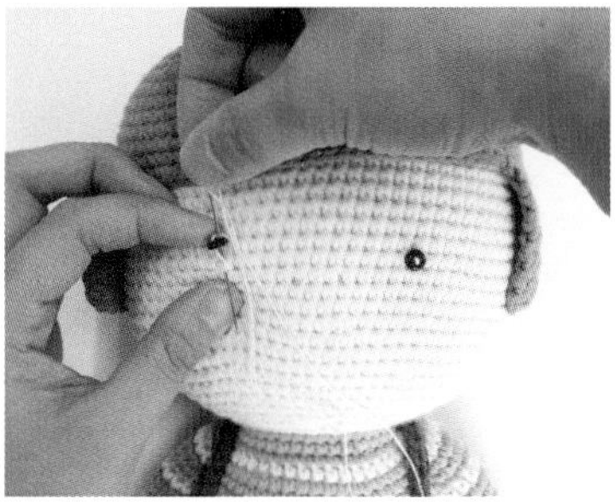

4 Mark the position of the Eyes with straight pins. Use white thread for sewing on the button eyes. Follow photo tutorial #2-5 of Bear Groom on page 79. Using white thread with a dark button, makes the eyes twinkle.

» Nose

5 Using the Flesh Color yarn, embroider the nose over 3 stitches. Make about 3 stitches to get a 3-D effect.

» Mouth

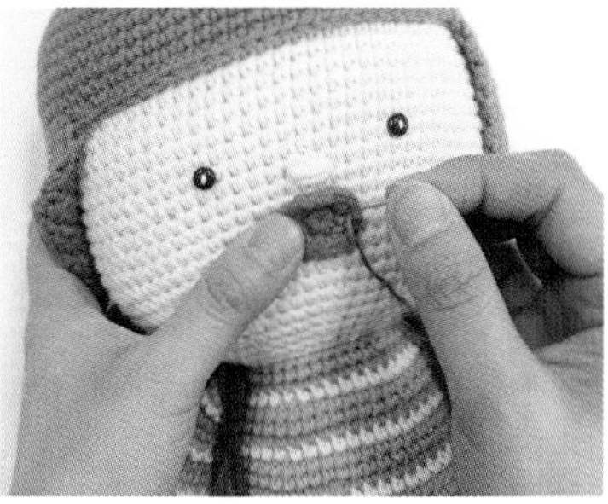

6 Split the yarn tail into 2 strands. Hide the one strand in the head. With the second strand, sew across the middle of the mouth to secure it to the head.

7 Pinch the upper and lower mouth together, making the lips 3-D.

» Cheeks

8 Split the yarn tail into 2 strands. Roll up the one strand and hide under the cheek. Using the second strand, sew the cheek in place. Repeat for other cheek.

» Eyebrows

9 Using brown thread, embroider the eyebrows as shown in the photo.

» Suspenders strap

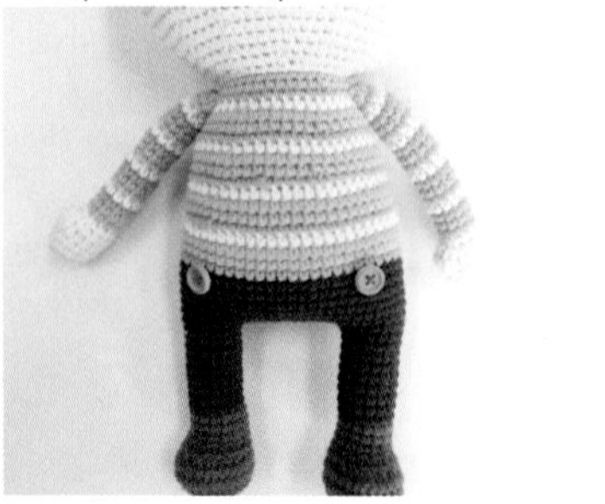

10 Mark the position of the buttons and follow photo tutorial #2-5 of Bear Groom on page 79.

11 Attach the suspenders on the back, following photo tutorial #6-13 of Bear Groom on page 80.

» Knees

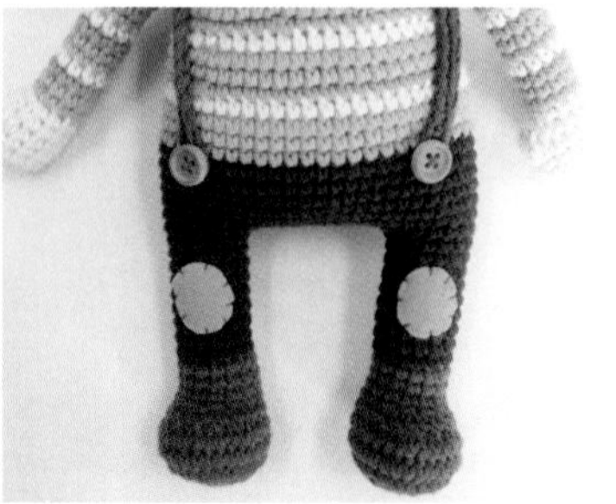

12 Cut the felt into 2 ovals about ¾" (2 cm) x 1" (2.5 cm) each. Using black thread, stitch a felt patch to each knee.

Head + Body

[Dark Brown]

Round 1: (6)	In starting ring X 6 •
Round 2: (8)	0 X 2 ⋎ 2 X 2 •
Round 3: (10)	0 X 3 ⋎ 2 X 3 •

[Brown]

Round 4: (12)	0 X 4 ⋎ 2 X 4 •
Round 5: (14)	0 X 5 ⋎ 2 X 5 •
Round 6: (16)	0 X 6 ⋎ 2 X 6 •
Round 7: (18)	0 X 7 ⋎ 2 X 7 •
Round 8: (22)	0 X 3 ⋎ 1 X 4 ⋎ 2 X 4 ⋎ 1 X 3 •
Round 9: (26)	0 X 4 ⋎ 1 X 5 ⋎ 2 X 5 ⋎ 1 X 4 •
Round 10: (30)	0 X 5 ⋎ 1 X 6 ⋎ 2 X 6 ⋎ 1 X 5 •
Round 11: (34)	0 X 6 ⋎ 1 X 7 ⋎ 2 X 7 ⋎ 1 X 6 •
Round 12: (38)	0 X 7 ⋎ 1 X 8 ⋎ 2 X 8 ⋎ 1 X 7 •
Round 13: (42)	0 X 8 ⋎ 1 X 9 ⋎ 2 X 9 ⋎ 1 X 8 •
Rounds 14-56: (42)	0 X 42 •
Round 57: (36)	0 (X 5 ⋏ 1) * 6 •
Round 58: (30)	0 X 2 ⋏ 1 (X 4 ⋏ 1) * 5 X 2 •
Round 59: (24)	0 (X 3 ⋏ 1) * 6 •
	Start stuffing.
Round 60: (18)	0 X 1 ⋏ 1 (X 2 ⋏ 1) * 5 X 1 •
Round 61: (12)	0 (X 1 ⋏ 1) * 6 •
Round 62: (6)	0 ⋏ 6 •
	Continue stuffing to fill the toy.
	Finish off and using the yarn tail, close the last round.

Ears

[Dark Brown]

Round 1: (6)	In starting ring X 6 •
Round 2: (12)	0 ⋎ 6 •
Round 3: (18)	0 (X 1 ⋎ 1) * 6 •
Rounds 4-7: (18)	0 X 18
Round 8: (16)	0 (X 7 ⋏ 1) * 2 •
Round 9: (14)	0 (X 6 ⋏ 1) * 2 •
Round 10: (12)	0 (X 5 ⋏ 1) * 2 •
Round 11: (10)	0 (X 4 ⋏ 1) * 2 •
Round 12: (10)	0 X 10 •
	Leaving a 16" (40 cm) long tail, cut the yarn and finish off.
	Repeat Rounds 1-12 for other Ear.

Legs

[Dark Brown]	Round 1: (6)	In starting ring **X 6** •
	Round 2: (12)	0 **⋎ 6** •
	Round 3: (12)	0 **Ꭓ 12** • (Don't miss the back post single crochet stitches!)
[Brown]	Round 4: (9)	0 **X 3 ⋏ 3 X 3**
	Rounds 5-6: (9)	0 **X 9** •
		Stuff about ⅓ full. Leaving a 16" (40 cm) long tail, cut the yarn and finish off. Repeat the instructions for each of the four Legs.

Tail

[Dark Brown]	Round 1: (6)	In starting ring **X 6** •
	Round 2: (12)	0 **⋎ 6** •
	Rounds 3-5: (12)	0 **X 12** •
	Round 6: (9)	0 **(X 2 ⋏ 1) * 3** •
	Rounds 7-8: (9)	0 **X 9** •
	Round 9: (6)	0 **(X 1 ⋏ 1) * 3** •
	Rounds 10-11: (6)	0 **X 6** •
		Stuff about ½ full. Leaving a 16" (40 cm) long tail, cut the yarn and finish off.

Hat

[Dark Pink]	Round 1: (6)	In starting ring **X 6** •
	Round 2: (12)	0 **⋎ 6** •
	Round 3: (12)	0 **X 12** •
[Dark Brown]	Round 4: (12)	0 **X 12** •
[Dark Pink]	Round 5: (18)	0 **(X 1 ⋎ 1) * 6** •
	Round 6: (24)	0 **X 1 ⋎ 1 (X 2 ⋎ 1) * 5 X 1** •
		Finish off, leaving a 16" (40 cm) tail.

Collar

* Please see Working in Rows on page 42.

[Light Green]		Chain Stitch **50**
	Row 1: (50)	Add 3 turning chains (buttonhole), start in 4th ch from hook **X** 50
		Finish off, leaving a 4" (10 cm) tail.

Face + Collar

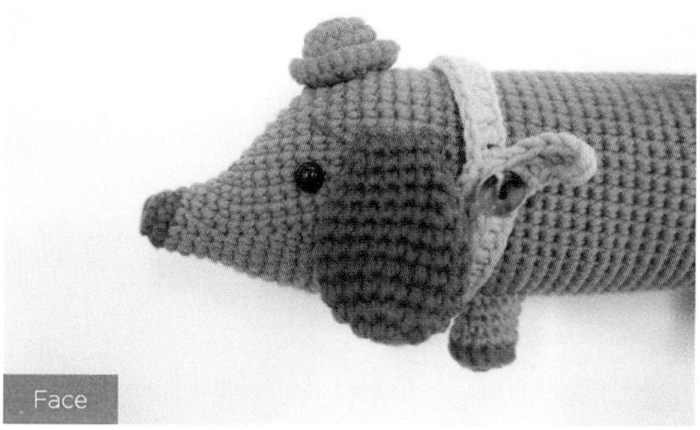

- **Ears:** Between 17th & 21st round from tip of nose, and 6 stitches down from top of head.
- **Eyes:** Between 13th & 14th round from tip of nose, with about 12 stitches between them.
- **Eyebrows:** About 14-15 rounds from tip of nose, 2 stitches up from eyes.
- **Collar:** About 23-24 rounds from tip of nose.

Tail

- **Tail:** About 6th round from closing round.

Legs

- **Front Legs:** Between Rounds 23 & 27 from tip of nose, 8 stitches between them.
- **Back Legs:** Between Rounds 48 & 51 from tip of nose, 10 stitches between them.

» Legs

1. Mark the position lengths of each leg with straight pins.

2. Fold the leg in half and flatten. Using the yarn tail, sew the leg to the body, first on the one side and then on the other side to secure it. Repeat for all four legs.

» Ears

3. Mark the position with straight pins. Using the yarn tail, sew the ear in place. Repeat for the other ear.

» Eyes + Eyebrows

4 Mark the position of the eyes with straight pins. Follow photo tutorial #14-17 of Wacky Bear on page 72.

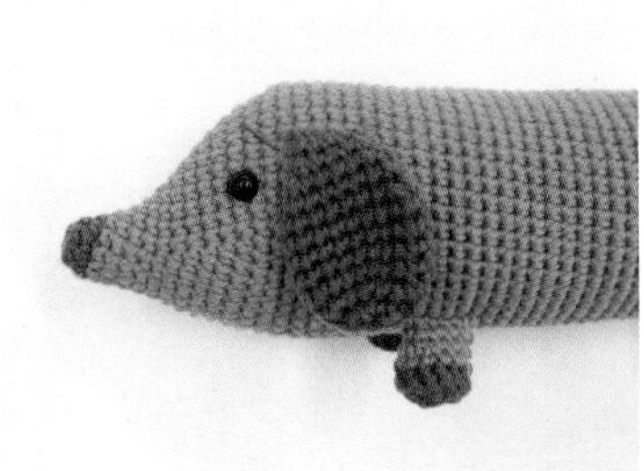

5 Identify the position of the eyebrows, and embroider them using dark brown thread, and angling them downwards.

» Tail

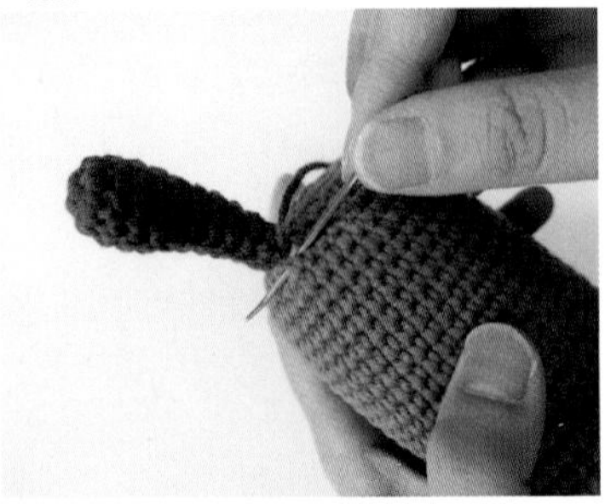

6 Stuff about ½ of the tail. Find the position, and using the yarn tail, sew it in place.

» Hat

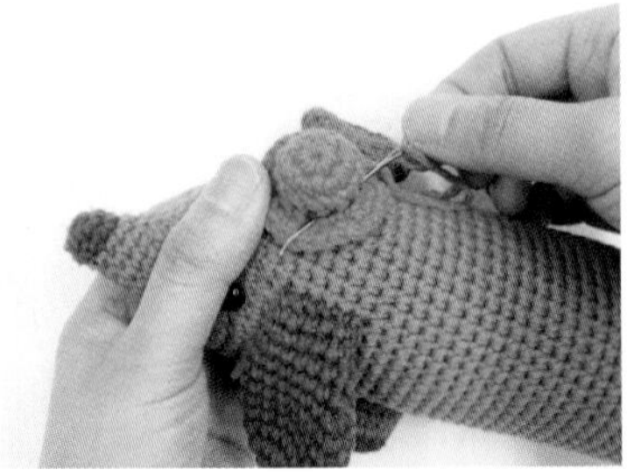

7 Thread the yarn tail onto a needle and bring it out between rounds 4 & 5. Position it on top of the head between the ears and sew it in place.

» Collar

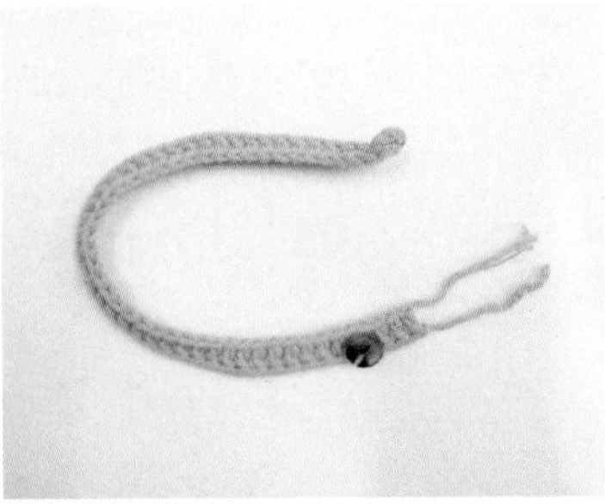

8 Sew a button on the 4th stitch from end of row.

9 Place the collar in position and sew the tail ends to the body, following photo tutorial #6-13 of the Groom Bear's Suspenders on page 80. Fasten the button to keep collar in place.

TRAVELLING
IN SPACE

The robot, RXKOY716 (affectionately known as Ricky), was developed in the year 2910 as a babysitter for human children on Mars. All went well for ten years, and then one day in 2920, while looking after a very active child, Ricky had a bad fall and landed on his head. When he woke up, he found he was on a rocket ship heading back to Earth. He looked out the window, and saw the beautiful view of the Universe and decided to become an astronaut.

11 | Ricky Robot (11" / 28 cm)

Yarn: Medium Weight (Worsted)
- Mustard
- Forest Green
- Moss Green

Hook: Size D-3 (3.25 mm)

Other: Yarn Needle
Stuffing
¾" (20 mm) Buttons - 2 (Eyes)
½" (13 mm) Buttons - 4 (for Arms & Legs)
½" (13 mm) Buttons - 2 (for decoration)
Sewing Thread & Needle

12 | Rocket Ship (6¾" / 17 cm)

Yarn: Medium Weight (Worsted)
- Mustard
- Forest Green
- Moss Green

Hook: Size D-3 (3.25 mm)

Other: Yarn Needle
Stuffing
5⁄16" (8 mm) Buttons – 3 (for decoration)
Sewing Thread & Needle

* Please see Working in Rows on page 42 for Ricky's Head.

Head - Front & Back
(Head 1, Head 2) [Mustard]

	Chain stitch **20**
Row 1: (20)	Add 1 turning chain, start in 2nd ch from hook **X 20**
Rows 2-17: (20)	**0 X 20**
	Cut the yarn and finish off Head 1. Repeat Rows 1-17 for Head 2.

Head Left & Right Sides
(Head 3, Head 4) [Forest Green]

	Chain stitch **10**
Row 1: (20)	Add 1 turning chain, start in 2nd ch from hook **X 10**
Rows 2-17: (20)	**0 X 10**
	Cut the yarn and finish off Head 3. Repeat Rows 1-17 for Head 4.

Head Top & Bottom
(Head 5, Head 6) [Moss Green]

	Chain stitch **20**
Row 1: (20)	Add 1 turning chain, start in 2nd ch from hook **X 20**
Rows 2-10: (20)	**0 X 20**
	Cut the yarn and finish off Head 5. Repeat Rows 1-10 for Head 6.

Head Antenna
[Forest Green]

Round 1: (6)	In starting ring **X 6**
Round 2: (12)	**0 ⩡ 6 •**
Round 3: (12)	**0 Ꭓ 12 •** (Don't miss the back post single crochet stitches!)
Round 4: (6)	**0 ⩢ 6 •** (Don't miss the back loop only!)
Round 5-9: (6)	**0 X 6 •**
	Leaving a 16" (40 cm) long tail, cut the yarn and finish off

Ears

[Moss Green]

Round 1: (6) In starting ring X 6 •
Round 2: (12) 0 ⋎ 6 •
Round 3: (12) 0 X̆ 12 • (Don't miss the front loop only.)

[Mustard]

Rounds 4-5: (12) 0 X 12 •

[Moss Green]

Round 6: (18) 0 (X̄ 1 ⋎̄ 1) * 6 •
Stuff about ⅔ full. Leaving a 16" (40 cm) long tail, cut the yarn and finish off.
Repeat Rounds 1-6 for other Ear.

Body

[Mustard]

Round 1: (6) In starting ring X 6 •
Round 2: (12) 0 ⋎ 6 •
Round 3: (18) 0 (X 1 ⋎ 1) * 6 •
Round 4: (24) 0 X 1 ⋎ 1 (X 2 ⋎ 1) * 5 X 1 •
Round 5: (30) 0 (X 3 ⋎ 1) * 6 •
Round 6: (36) 0 X 2 ⋎ 1 (X 4 ⋎ 1) * 5 X 2 •
Round 7: (36) 0 X̆ 36 •
Rounds 8-10: (36) 0 X 36 •

[Forest Green]

Rounds 11-17: (36) 0 X 36 •
Round 18: (33) 0 X 5 ⋏ 1 (X 10 ⋏ 1) * 2 X 5 •
Rounds 19-20: (33) 0 X 33 •
Round 21: (30) 0 (X 9 ⋏ 1) * 3 •
Rounds 22-23: (30) 0 X 30 •
Leaving a 16" (40 cm) long tail, cut the yarn and finish off.

Thumbs

[Mustard]

Rounds 1: (6) In starting ring X 6 •
Rounds 2-3: (6) 0 X 6 •
Cut the yarn and finish off, hiding the tail inside.
Repeat Rounds 1-3 for second thumb.

Arms

[Mustard]	Round 1: (6)	In starting ring X 6 •
	Round 2: (12)	0 ⩔6 •
	Rounds 3-4: (12)	0 X 12 •
	Round 5: (18)	0 X 6 (leave last 6 stitches).
		Starting in 2nd stitch on Thumb X 6
		On Arm, in remaining stitches X 6 •

[Joining Thumb to Hand]

	Round 6: (18)	0 X 18 •
	Round 7: (12)	0 (X 1 ⩓1) * 6 •
	Rounds 8-9: (12)	0 X 12 •
		Start stuffing the Arm, shaping the hand and thumb.
		For Rounds 10-21, alternate the 3 colors, working 2 rounds in each color.
[Moss Green, Forest Green, Mustard]	Rounds 10-21: (12)	0 X 12 •
[Moss Green]	Rounds 22-23: (12)	0 X 12 •
[Forest Green]	Rounds 24-26: (12)	0 X 12 •
		Start stuffing.
	Round 27: (6)	0 ⩓6 •
		Stuff the Arm. Finish off and using the yarn tail, close the last round.
		Repeat Rounds 1-27 for second Arm.

Legs

[Mustard]	Round 1: (6)	In starting ring X 6 •
	Round 2: (12)	0 ⋎X 6 •
	Round 3: (24)	0 ⋎X 12 •
	Round 4: (24)	0 X̧ 24 •
[Forest Green]	Rounds 5-6: (24)	0 X 24 •
	Round 7: (18)	0 X 6 ⋏X 6 X 6 •
	Round 8: (14)	0 X 5 ⋏X 4 X 5 •
	Rounds 9-11: (14)	X 14 •
[Moss Green]	Rounds 12-17: (14)	0 X 14 •
[Mustard]	Rounds 18-26: (14)	0 X 14 • Start stuffing.
	Round 27: (7)	0 ⋏X 7 • Stuff the Leg. Finish off and using the yarn tail, close the last round. Repeat Rounds 1-27 for second Leg.

Face + Antenna

- **Eyes:** About 10 rows from bottom, 8 stitches between them.
- **Mouth:** About 5-6 rows from bottom, across 13 stitches.
- **Scar:** Between 3rd and 5th row from top.
- **Antenna:** In the center at top of Head

Ears

- **Ears:** Between 7th & 11th row from bottom.

Arms + Legs

- **Arms:** Between 2nd & 3rd round from neckline.
- **Legs:** Between 9th & 10th round from bottom of body.

Decorations

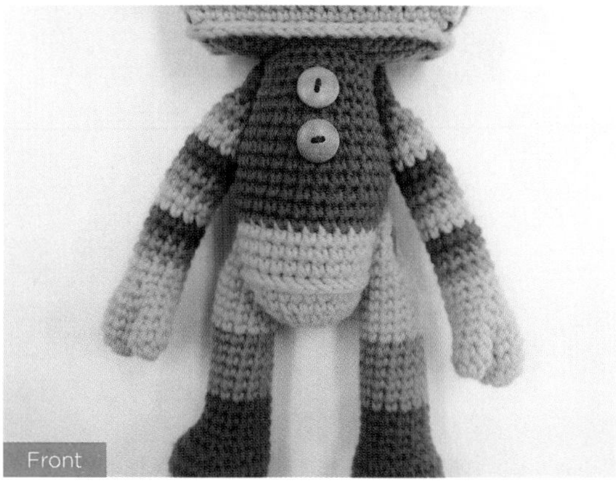

- **Buttons:** About the 4th and 7th round from neckline.

» Head Pieces

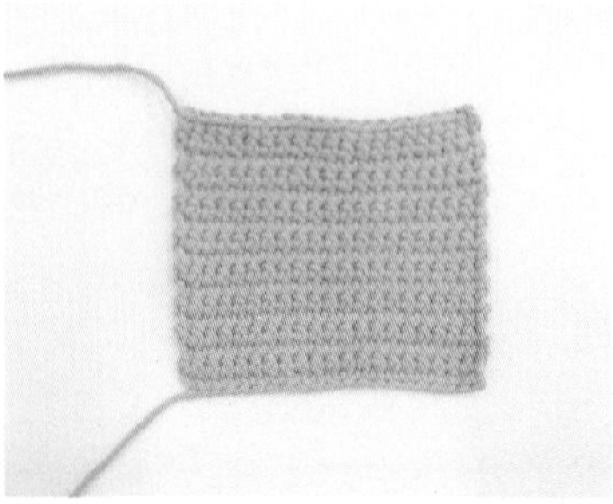

1. Before assembling the Head pieces, weave in all the tails on the wrong side of the pieces. Please see page 50 for Hiding the Yarn Tails.

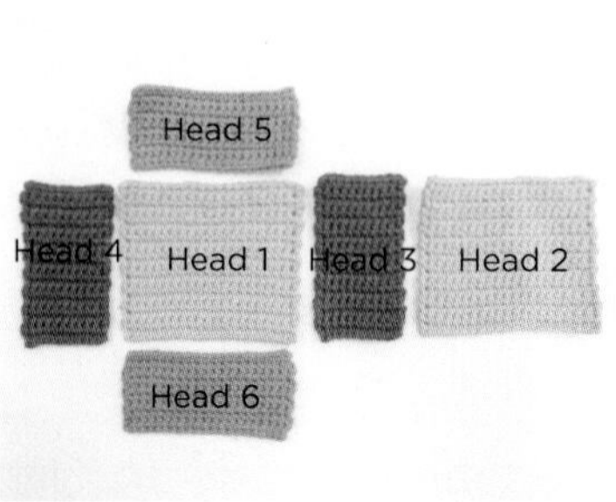

2. Repeat for all six Head pieces and lay them out as shown.

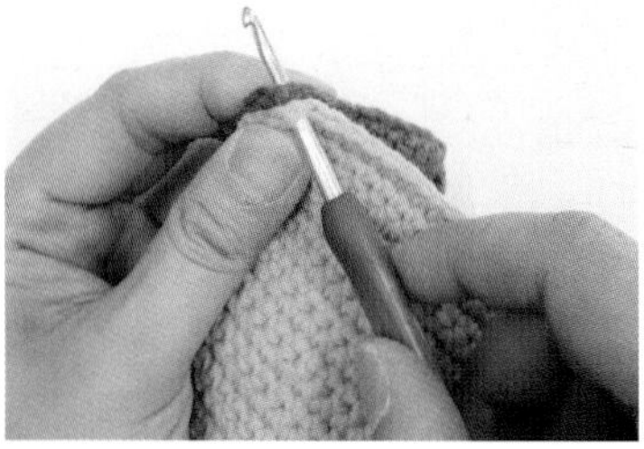

3. Holding Head 1 & Head 3 together, insert hook in first stitch through both pieces.

tip

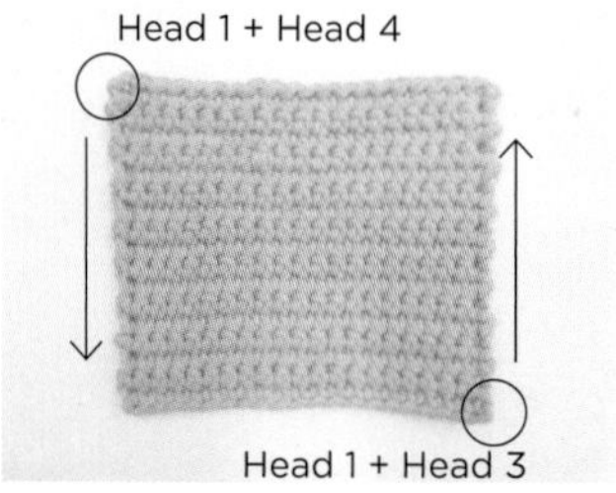

Note the location of the first stitch, and the direction of working, when connecting the head pieces together.

4. Pull a new strand of Mustard yarn through both pieces.

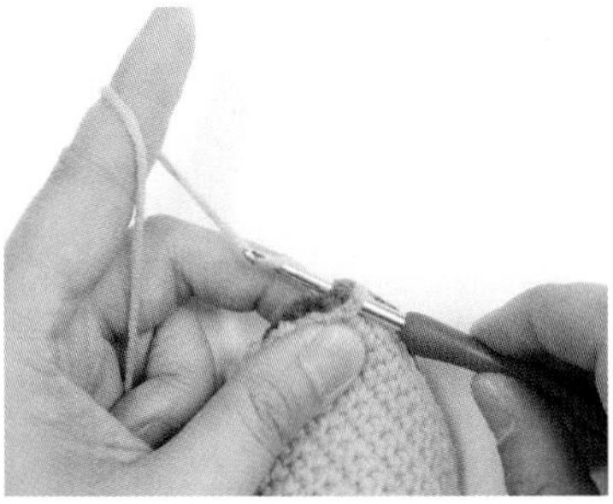

5 Make one raising chain stitch (**0**).

6 Place the tail on the inside between Head 1 and Head 3.

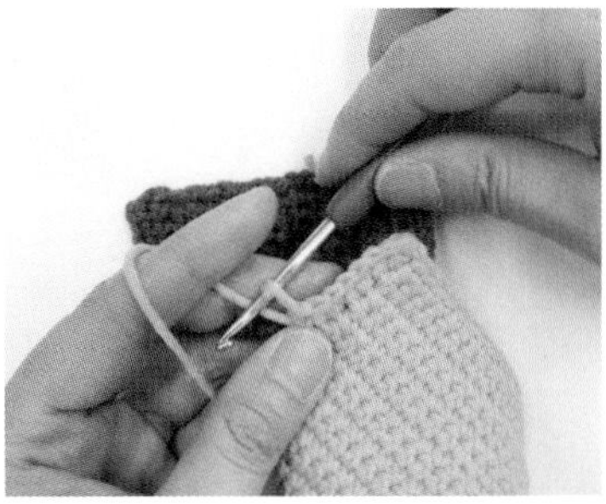

7 Work single crochet stitches (**X**) across to end.

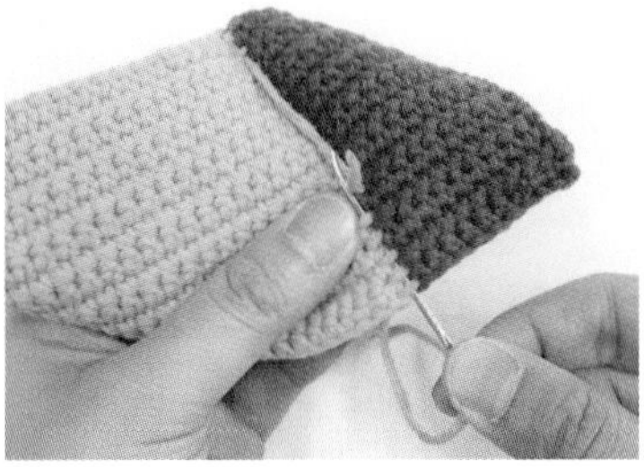

8 Leaving a short tail, cut the yarn and finish off. Using a needle, hide the the yarn tail on the inside.

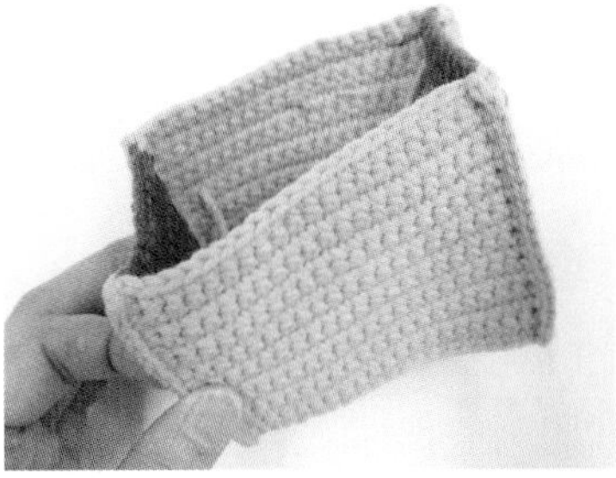

9 In the same way, join Head 1 to Head 4, and then join Head 2 to both Head 3 and Head 4.

» Top Head + Bottom Head

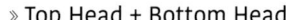

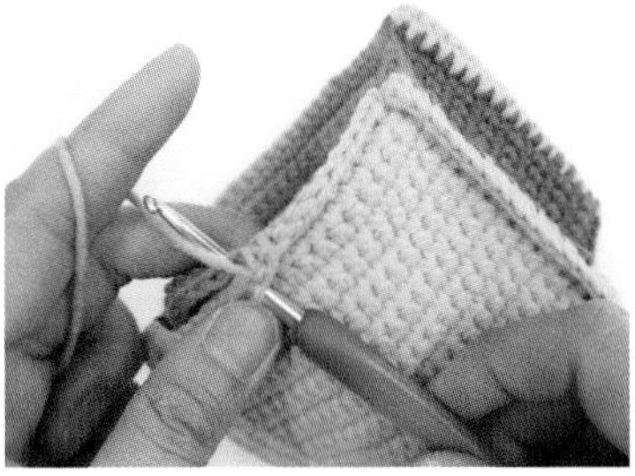

10 Join the Top Head (Head 5) by working single crochet stitches around all four sides.

tip

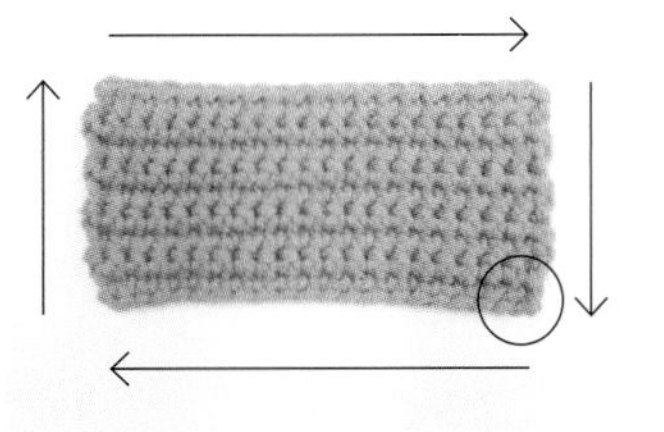

Note the location of the first stitch, and the direction of working around the pieces for Heads 5 & 6.

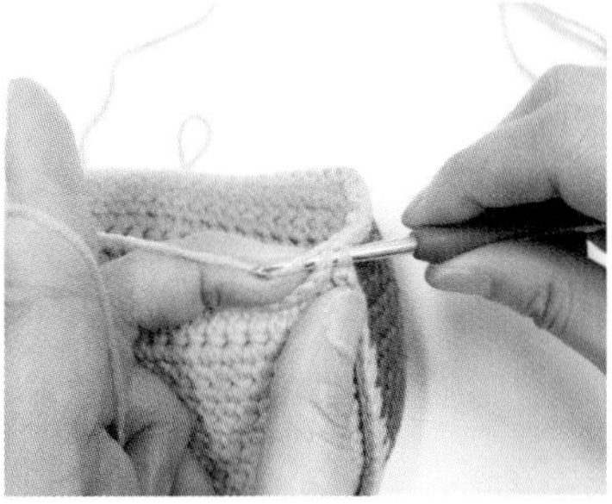

11 After working all around, join with a slip stitch (•) to the first stitch. Leaving a short tail, cut the yarn and finish off. Using a needle hide the yarn tail on the inside.

» Head + Body

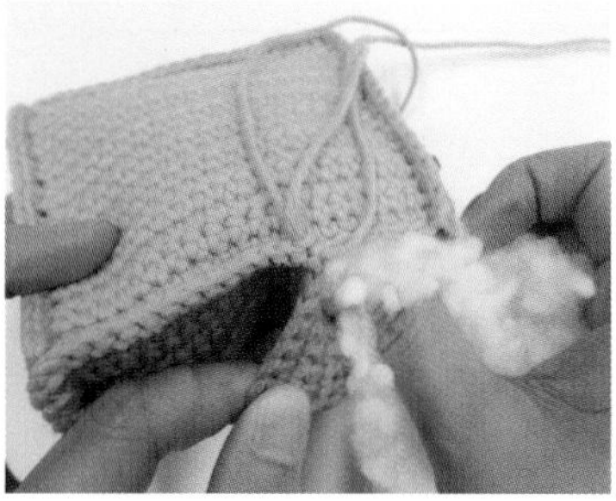

12 In the same way, join Head 6, but start stuffing after about ⅔ of the way around. Finish stuffing before completing the last 5 stitches. Join and finish off, hiding the yarn tail in the head.

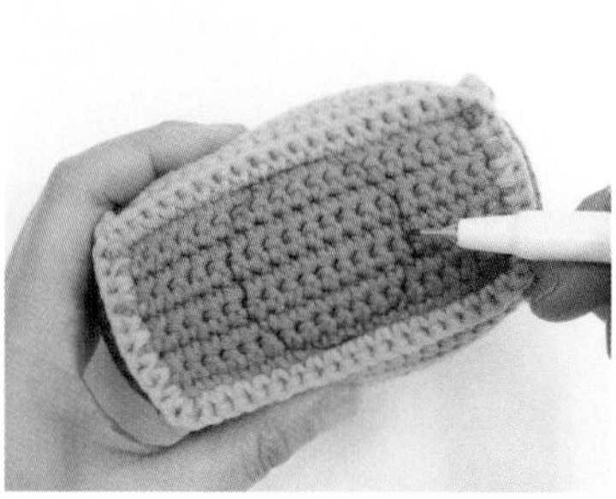

13 With a water-soluble pen, mark the position of the body on the underside of the head (Head 6).

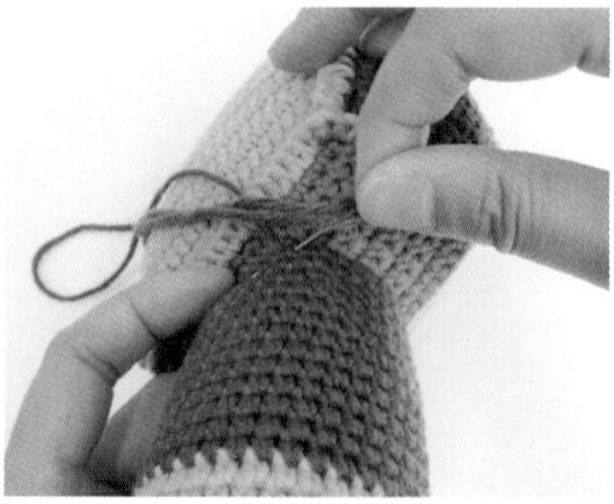

14 Using the yarn tail, sew the body to the head following the markings. After about ⅔ of the way around, add more stuffing to the neck before finishing.

» Antenna

15 Mark the position on the top of the head (Head 5) with a water-soluble pen. Using the yarn tail, sew the antenna in position.

» Ears

16 Using a water-soluble pen, mark the position of both ears on either side of head (Head 3 & Head 4). Using the yarn tail, bring the needle up between 5th & 6th Round on Ear, and sew ear in place. Repeat for other ear.

» Eyes

17 Using black thread, position and sew on the eyes.
Hint: Make the stitches in different directions on each button to change the facial expression.

» Mouth

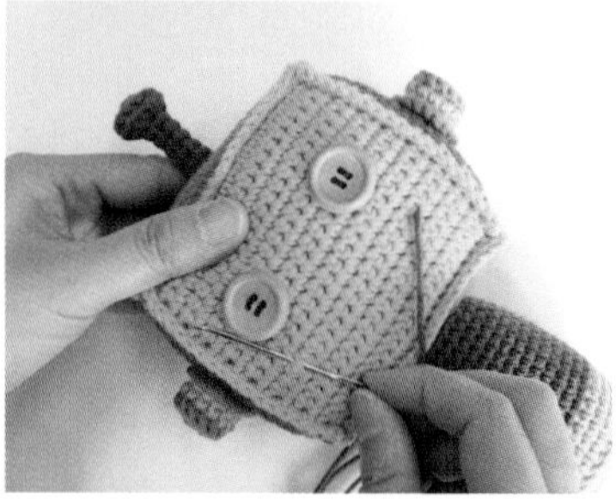

18 Using Forest Green yarn, embroider a mouth using straight stitches

» Scar

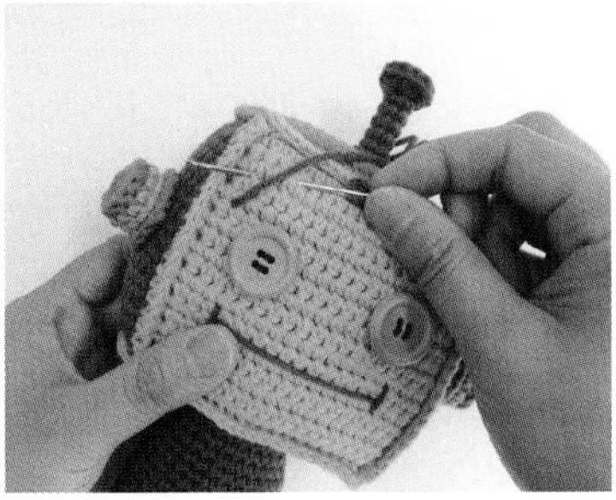

19 In the same way, embroider the scar on the forehead.

» Decorations

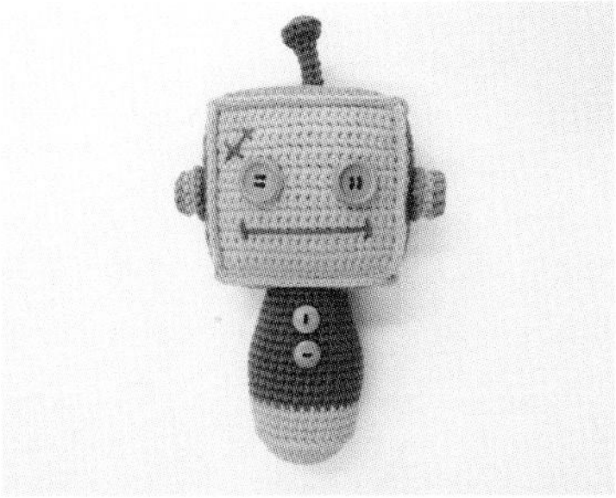

20 Position and sew on the buttons following photo tutorial #2-5 for Bear Groom on page 79.

» Arms + Legs

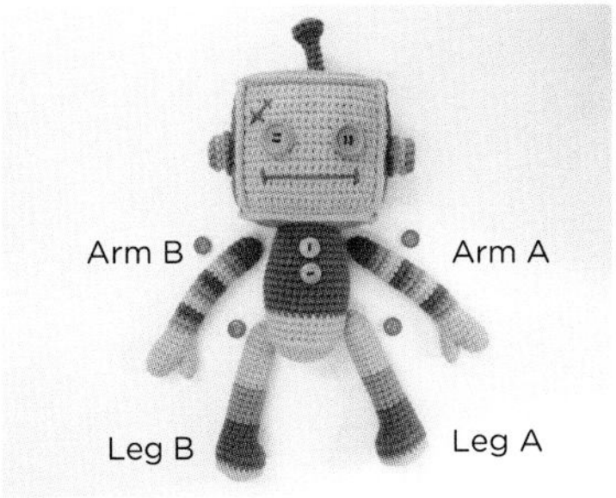

21 Each arm and leg is connected with a button, so that the limbs are movable. Position the limbs as shown.

22 Sew both arms on together by going through the one button, arm, body, other arm and other button. Repeat this 3-4 times to attach the arms firmly.

23 The legs are attached in the same way.

Body

[Forest Green]

Round 1: (6) In starting ring X 6 •
Round 2: (9) 0 (X 1 V 1) * 3 •
Round 3: (12) 0 X 1 V 1 (X 2 V 1) * 2 X 1 •
Round 4: (15) 0 (X 3 V 1) * 3 •
Round 5: (15) 0 X 15 •
Round 6: (18) 0 X 2 V 1 (X 4 V 1) * 2 X 2 •
Round 7: (18) 0 X 18 •
Round 8: (21) 0 (X 5 V 1) * 3 •

[Mustard]

Round 9: (21) 0 X 21 •
Round 10: (24) 0 X 3 V 1 (X 6 V 1) * 2 X 3 •
Round 11: (24) 0 X 24 •
Round 12: (27) 0 (X 7 V 1) * 3 •
Round 13: (27) 0 X 27 •
Round 14: (30) 0 X 4 V 1 (X 8 V 1) * 2 X 4 •
Rounds 15-16: (30) 0 X 30 •
Round 17: (33) 0 (X 9 V 1) * 3 •
Rounds 18-19: (33) 0 X 33 •
Round 20: (36) 0 X 5 V 1 (X 10 V 1) * 2 X 5 •
Round 21-22: (36) 0 X 36 •
Round 23: (39) 0 (X 11 V 1) * 3 •
Rounds 24-25: (39) 0 X 39 •
Round 26: (42) 0 X 6 V 1 (X 12 V 1) * 2 X 6 •
Round 27-29: (42) 0 X 42 •

[Forest Green]

Rounds 30-36: (42) 0 X 42 •
Round 37: (36) 0 (X 5 Λ 1) * 6 •
Round 38: (24) 0 (X̲ 1 Λ̲ 1) * 12 • (Don't miss the back loop only!)
Start stuffing.
Round 39: (18) 0 X 1 Λ 1 (X 2 Λ 1) * 5 X 1 •
Round 40: (12) 0 (X 1 Λ 1) * 6 •
Round 41: (6) 0 Λ 6 •
Continue stuffing to fill the doll.
Finish off and using the yarn tail, close the last round.

Fins

[Moss Green]

* Please see Making Ovals on page 46.

Chain stitch **12**

Round 1: (24) **0 ×24 •**

Rounds 2-5: (24) **0 ⩚1 ×9 ⩛2 ×9 ⩚1 •**

Stuff about ⅔ full. Leaving a 16" (40 cm) long tail, cut the yarn and finish off.

Repeat Rounds 1~5 for other Fin.

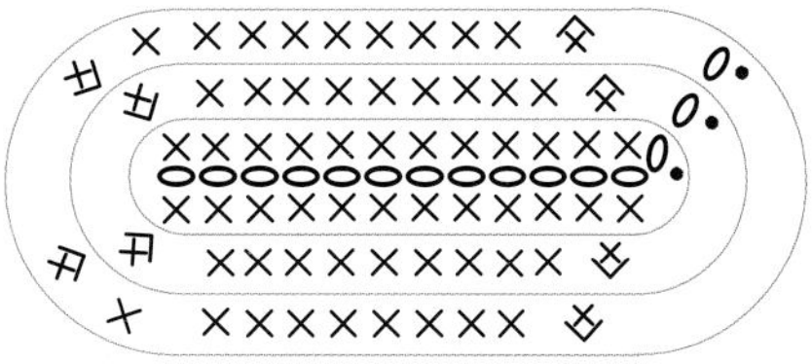

Window

[Mustard]

Round 1: (6) In starting ring **×6 •**

Round 2: (12) **0 ⩛6 •**

Round 3: (18) **0 (×1 ⩛1) * 6 •**

[Moss Green]

Round 4: (24) **0 ×1 ⩛1 (×2 ⩛1) * 5 ×1 •**

Round 5: (24) **0 ×̆ 24 •**

Leaving a 16" (40 cm) long tail, cut the yarn and finish off.

Window + Fins

- **Window:** Between 13th & 19th Round from top.
- **Fins:** Between 24th & 34th Round from top.
- **Buttons:** About 22nd, 25th, & 28th Round from top.

» Window

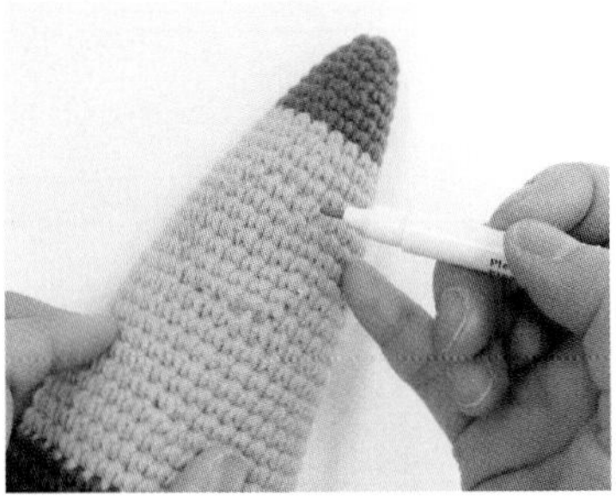

1 Mark the position of the window with a water-soluble pen.

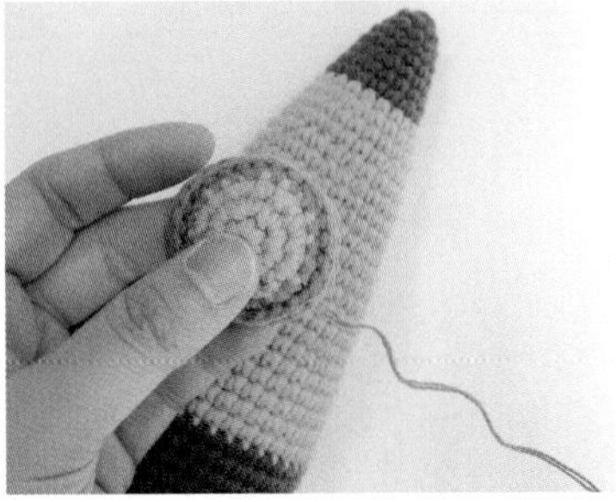

2 Split the yarn tail into 2 strands. Roll and hide the one strand under the window. Thread the second strand onto a needle.

3 Sew the window about ⅔ of the way around. Stuff the window before continuing to finish sewing.

» Decorations

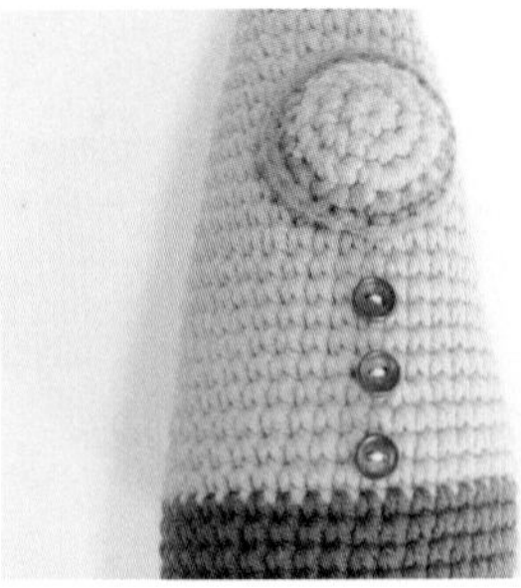

4 Mark the positions of the buttons with straight pins. Using white thread, sew on the three buttons.

» Fins

5 Using the water-soluble pen, mark the position of the fins on either side of the rocket. Stuff the fin, and thread the yarn tail onto a needle.

6 Position the fin and sew in place. Repeat for other fin.

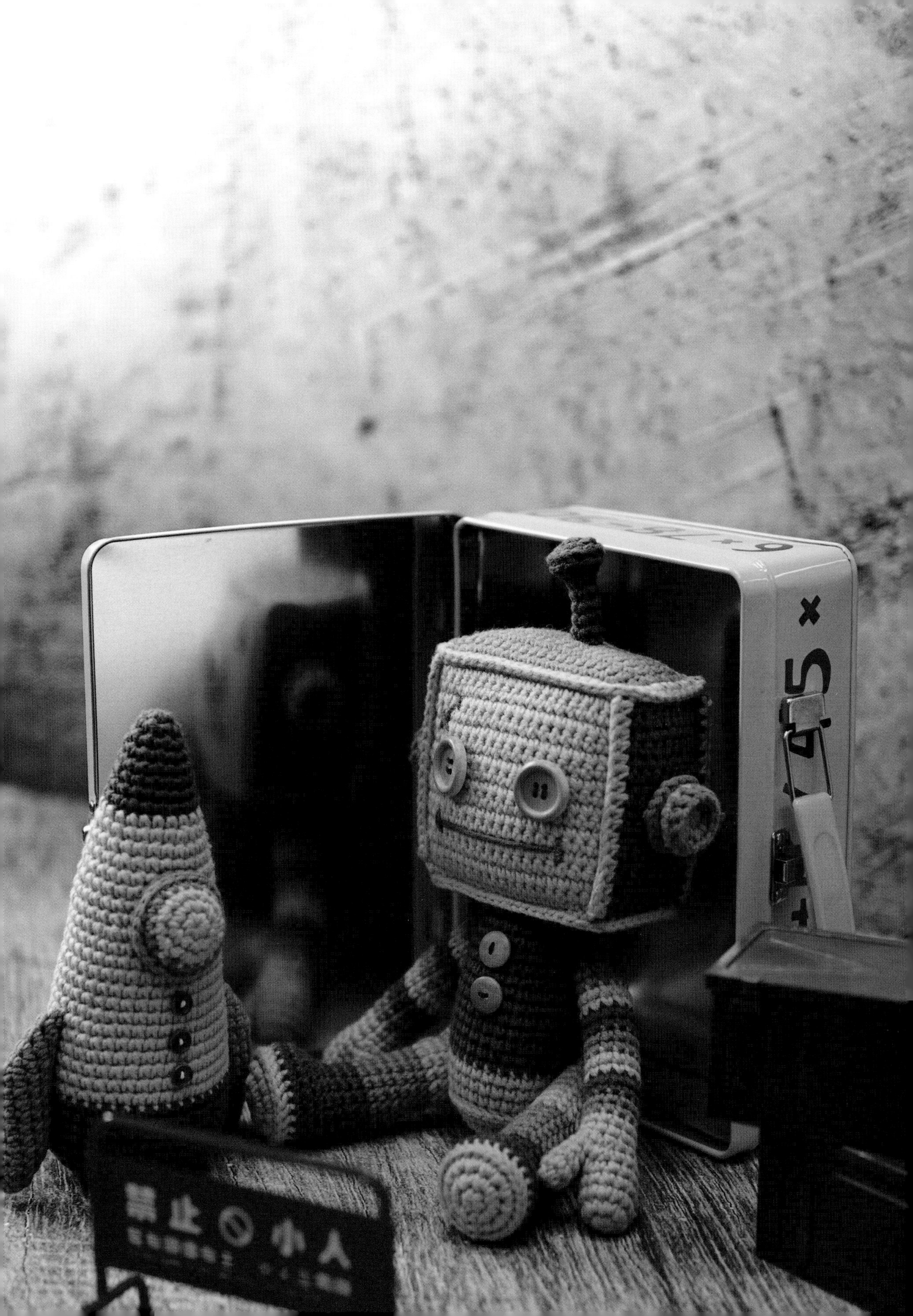
小人

The GREAT GATSBY

WARM AND COZY
TOGETHER

When the weather outside starts getting colder, the first thing I do is to snuggle up with Mister Hottie and his little dog, Dougie. They keep my feet warm in bed and I can cuddle up against them to keep my whole body warm. With these two friends keeping me comfy, I'm not afraid of the winter weather.

13 | Mister Hottie (Width - 7¾" / 20 cm; Height - 11¾" / 30 cm, excluding legs)

Yarn: Medium Weight (Worsted)
- Brown
- Beige
- Navy Blue
- Dark Brown
- Bright Blue
- Yellow
- Red
- Light Beige
- Pink

Hook: Size D-3 (3.25 mm)

Other: Yarn Needle
Stuffing
2 quarts (2 litre) Hot Water Bottle
½" (13 mm) Buttons – 2 (Suspenders)
Sewing Thread & Needle

14 | Dougie (Width - 6" / 15 cm; Height - 9" / 23 cm, excluding legs)

Yarn: Medium Weight (Worsted)
- Beige
- Dark Brown
- Navy Blue
- Bright Blue
- Yellow
- Red
- Light Beige

Hook: Size D-3 (3.25 mm)

Other: Yarn Needle
Stuffing
1½ pints (0.7 liter) Hot Water Bottle
5⁄16" (8 mm) Buttons – 2 (Eyes)
½" (13 mm) Button – 1 (Nose)
½" (13 mm) Buttons – 2 (Suspenders)
Sewing Thread & Needle

Legs + Body + Face

[Brown]

Round 1: (6)	In starting ring **X 6** •
Round 2: (12)	**0** **V 6** •
Round 3: (18)	**0** **(X 1 V 1) * 6** •
Round 4: (24)	**0** **X 6 V 6 X 6** •
Round 5: (24)	**0** **X 24** •
Round 6: (18)	**0** **X 6 Λ 6 X 6** •
Round 7: (14)	**0** **X 5 Λ 4 X 5** •
Round 8: (11)	**0** **X 4 Λ 3 X 4** •
Rounds 9-10: (11)	**0** **X 11** •

[Navy Blue]

Rounds 11-18: (11)	**0** **X 11** •
	At the end of Leg A, cut the yarn and finish off.
	Repeat Rounds 1~18 for Leg B, but do not finish off.
	Stuff each leg, shaping the feet.
Round 19: (82)	On Leg B **0** **X 9** (Leave the last 2 stitches unworked.)
	Chain Stitch **30**
	On Leg A, start in the 4th stitch **X 11**
	Working in the chains **X̲ 30** (Don't miss the back loop only!)
	In remaining stitches on Leg B **X 2** •
Round 20: (82)	On Leg B **0** **X 9**
	On chain **X̲ 30** (Don't miss the back loop only!)
	On Leg A and finish round **X 43** •
Rounds 21-29: (82)	**0** **X 82** •

[Yellow Bright Blue Dark Brown Light Beige]

	For rounds 30-41, alternate the 4 colors, working 1 round in each color.
Rounds 30-41: (82)	**0** **X 82** •

[Beige]

Rounds 42-58: (82)	**0** **X 82** •
	After Round 58, put this piece aside. After the arms and face are complete, continue with the Hair.

Arms

[Beige]		
	Round 1: (6)	In starting ring × **6** •
	Round 2: (12)	**0** ∨ **6** •
	Round 3-4: (12)	**0** × **12** •
	Round 5: (8)	**0** **(× 1 ∧ 1) * 4** •
[Light Beige Dark Brown Bright Blue Yellow]	Round 6-17: (8)	For Rounds 6-17, alternate the 4 colors, working 1 round in each color. **0** × **8** • Stuff the Arm about ⅔ full. Leaving a 16" (40 cm) long tail, cut the yarn and finish off. Repeat Rounds 1~17 for other Arm.

Mouth

[Red]		
	Round 1: (6)	In starting ring × **6** •
	Round 2: (12)	**0** ∨ **6** • Leaving a 16" (40 cm) long tail, cut the yarn and finish off.

Cheeks

[Pink]		
	Round 1: (6)	In starting ring × **6** •
	Round 2: (12)	**0** ∨ **6** •
	Round 3: (18)	**0** **(× 1 ∨ 1) * 6** • Leaving a 16" (40 cm) long tail, cut the yarn and finish off. Repeat Rounds 1-3 for other Cheek.

Suspenders

[Red]

* Please see Working in Rows on page 42.

	Chain stitch **24**
Row 1: (24)	Add 5 turning chains (buttonhole), start in 6th chain from hook × **24** Finish off, leaving a 4" (10 cm) tail. Repeat for second suspender.

Hair [Brown]

Complete the arm and face assembly (page 149-151) before continuing.

Round 59: (82) 0 X 82 •
Round 60: (82) 0 X̲ 82 (Don't miss the back loop only!)
Rounds 61-72: (82) 0 X 82 •
Round 73: (80) 0 X 8 ⋀1 X 39 ⋀1 X 31 •
Round 74: (78) 0 X 7 ⋀1 X 38 ⋀1 X 31 •
Round 75: (74) 0 X 6 ⋀2 X 35 ⋀2 X 29 •
Round 76: (70) 0 X 5 ⋀2 X 33 ⋀2 X 28 •
Round 77: (66) 0 X 4 ⋀2 X 31 ⋀2 X 27 •
Round 78: (62) 0 X 3 ⋀2 X 29 ⋀2 X 26 •
Round 79: (58) 0 X 2 ⋀2 X 27 ⋀2 X 25 •
Round 80: (52) 0 ⋀3 X 23 ⋀3 X 23 •
Rounds 81-90: (52) 0 X 52 •

Cut the yarn and finish off. Using yarn needle, weave in all the tails neatly on the inside.

Bangs [Brown]

With the Head pointing down, start at the back of head, and work in the front loops of Round 59.

Round 1: (84) 0 (X 40 V 1) * 2 •
Round 2: (84) 0 (X 1 [shell] 1) * 14 •

Cut the yarn and finish off. Using yarn needle, hide the tails.

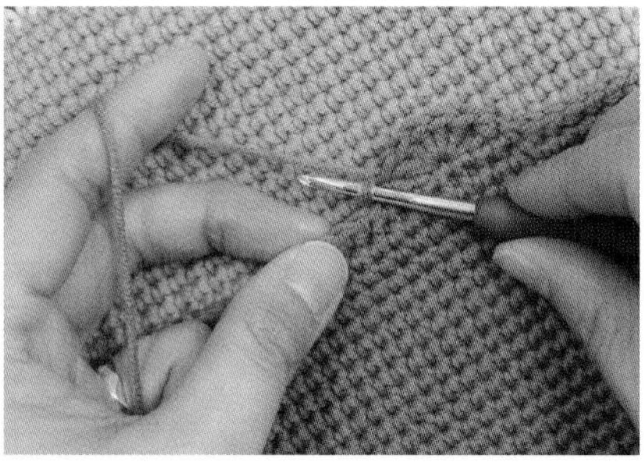
[Making Bangs]

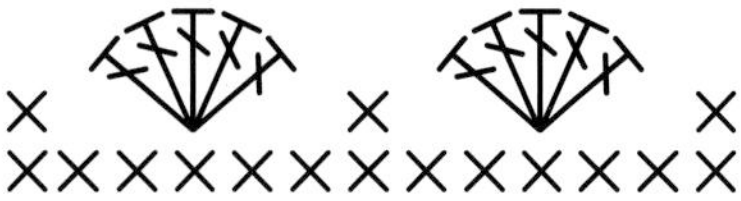

Face + Arms + Buttons

◦ **Eyes:** Over 10th & 11th round from neckline, 15 stitches between them.
◦ **Eyebrows:** About 2 rounds above eyes.
◦ **Nose:** Between 9th & 10th round from neckline.
◦ **Mouth:** Between 5th & 6th round from neckline.
◦ **Cheeks:** Between 5th & 10th round from neckline.
◦ **Arms:** On the round before neckline.
◦ **Buttons:** On the waistline with 28 stitches between them.

Suspenders

◦ **Straps:** On the waistline with 28 stitches between them.

» Arms

1 Using the tail, sew the arm in position. Repeat on other arm.

2 When the arms are attached, hide the tails on the inside.

tip

Mister Hottie and Dougie are open on the inside, so make sure all the stitching is neat and the tails sewn in. Refer to Hiding the Yarn Tails on page 50. This process is used for all the assembly.

» Suspenders

3 Attach the straps on the back, following photo tutorial #6-13 of Bear Groom on page 80.

4 Tie the tails in a neat knot on the inside.

5 Using a needle, hide the tails on the inside and trim the yarn.

6 Bring the suspenders up over the arms to the front. On the front, position and sew on the buttons following photo tutorial #2-5 of Bear Groom on page 79.

» Eyes

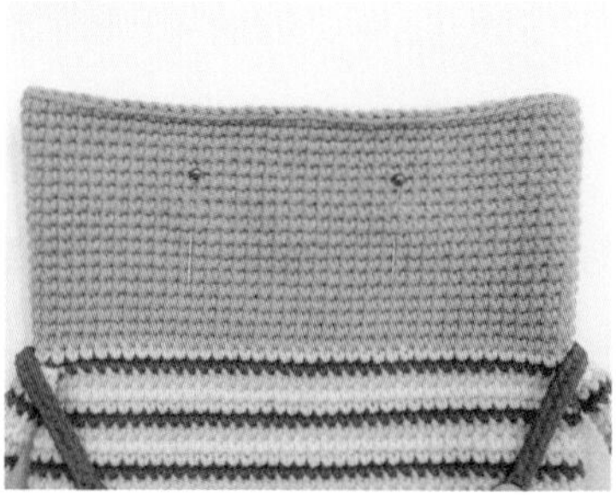

7 On the front, mark the position of the eyes with straight pins.

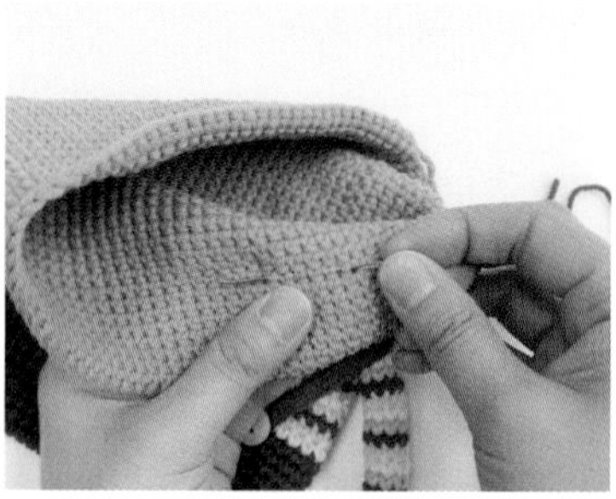

8 Using Navy Blue yarn, start sewing from the inside. Weave the yarn under about 5 stitches before bringing the needle out at the eye position.

9 You can see the stitches are hidden on the inside is neat and not visible on the outside. Tip:This method is recommended for a neater finish.

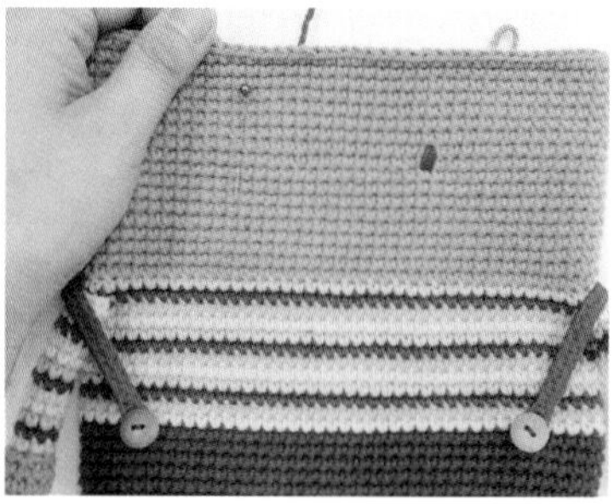

10 Embroider the eyes over 2 rounds using straight stitches. Make about 2-3 stitches in the same place to make the eyes look 3-D.

11 Weave the yarn through the stitches on the inside to the next eye position and repeat for second eye. Weave in the tail and trim the yarn.

» Nose

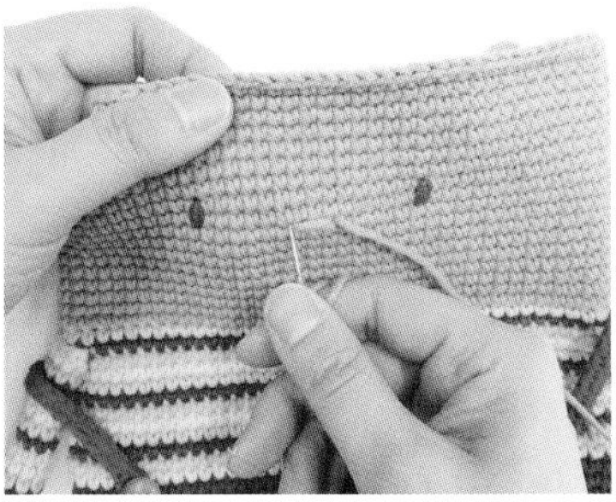

12 Mark the position of the nose with straight pins. Using Beige yarn, embroider the nose as you did the eyes.

» Mouth

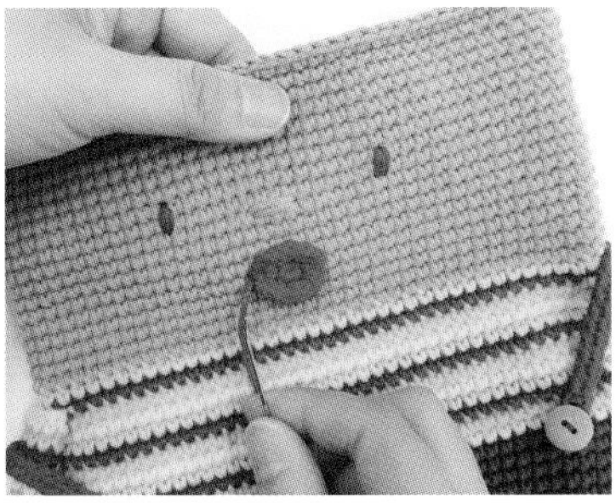

13 Place the mouth in position and sew across the center to secure. Refer to photo tutorial #6-7 of Benjy on page 123.

» Cheeks

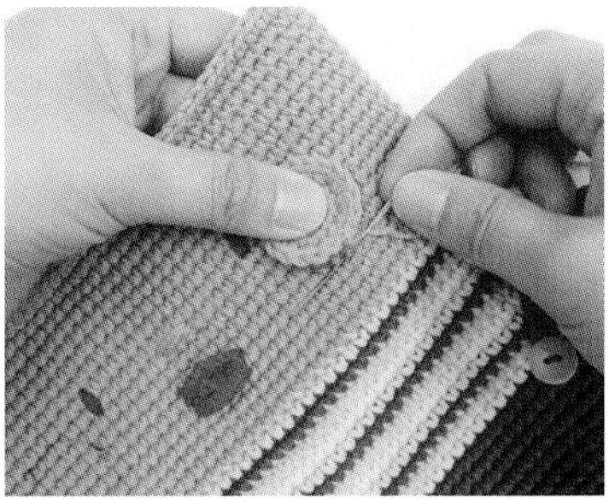

14 Split the yarn tail into 2 strands. Roll up the one strand and hide under the cheek. Using the second strand, sew the cheek in place. Repeat for other cheek.

» Eyebrows

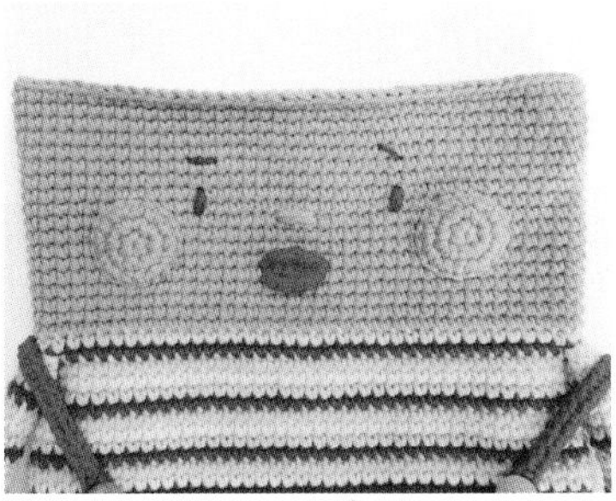

15 Using dark brown thread, embroider the eyebrows as shown in the photo. The face is now complete. Return to page 148 and continue with the Hair.

» Bangs

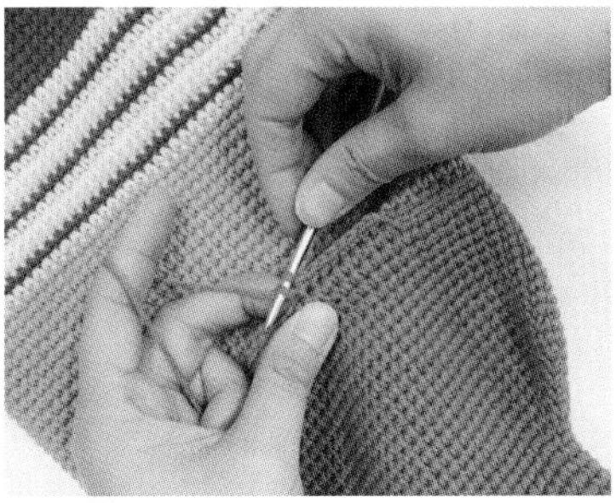

16 After the Hair is finished and all the tails neatly sewn in, turn the piece upside down with the head pointing downwards. Insert the hook in the front loop of the last stitch on Round 59. Working in the front loops only, single crochet (✕) around.

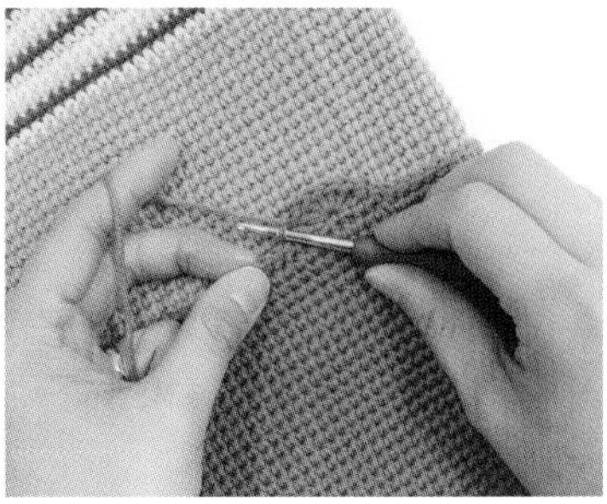

17 On the second round of the bangs, work 5-double crochet shells all around. (shell symbol) Hide all the tails on the inside. Mister Hottie is now finished.

Legs + Body + Face

[Dark Brown]

Round 1: (6) In starting ring × **6** •
Round 2: (12) 0 V **6** •
Round 3: (12) 0 × **12** •
Round 4: (8) 0 × **2** Λ **4** × **2** •
Round 5: (8) 0 × **8** •

[Navy Blue]

Rounds 6-7: (8) 0 × **8** •
At the end of Leg A, cut the yarn and finish off.
Repeat Rounds 1-7 for Leg B, but do not finish off.

Round 8: (66) On Leg B 0 × **6** • (Leave the last 2 stitches unworked.)
Chain Stitch **25**
On Leg A, start in the 3rd stitch × **8**
Working in the chains × **25** (Don't miss the back loop only)
In remaining stitches on Leg B × **2** •

Round 9: (66) On Leg B 0 × **6**
On chain × **25** (Don't miss the back loop only)
On Leg A and finish round × **35** •

Rounds 10-15: (66) 0 × **66** •

[Yellow, Bright Blue, Dark Brown, Light Beige]

For Rounds 16-27, alternate the 4 colors, working 1 round in each color.
Rounds 16-27: (66) 0 × **66** •

[Beige]

Rounds 28-47: (66) 0 × **66** •
Round 48: (64) 0 × **5** Λ **1** × **31** Λ **1** × **26** •
Round 49: (62) 0 × **5** Λ **1** × **30** Λ **1** × **25** •
Round 50: (60) 0 × **5** Λ **1** × **29** Λ **1** × **24** •
Round 51: (58) 0 × **4** Λ **1** × **28** Λ **1** × **24** •
Round 52: (54) 0 × **3** Λ **2** × **25** Λ **2** × **22** •
After Round 52, put this piece aside.
After the arms and face are complete, continue with the rest of the head.
Round 53: (48) 0 × **2** Λ **3** × **21** Λ **3** × **19** •
Round 54: (42) 0 Λ **3** × **18** Λ **3** × **18** •
Rounds 55-64: (42) 0 × **42** •
Cut the yarn and finish off. Using yarn needle, weave in all the tails neatly on the inside.

Arms

[Beige]	Round 1: (6)	In starting ring **X 6** •
	Round 2: (8)	**0 (X 2 V 1) * 2** •
	Round 3: (8)	**0 X 8** •
	Round 4: (6)	**0 (X 2 Λ 1) * 2** •
[Dark Brown, Bright Blue, Yellow, Light Beige]	Rounds 5-10: (6)	For Rounds 5-10, alternate the 4 colors, working 1 round in each color. **0 X 6** • Stuff the Arm about ⅔ full. Leaving a 16" (40 cm) long tail, cut the yarn and finish off. Repeat Rounds 1-10 for other Arm.

Ears

[Dark Brown]	Round 1: (6)	In starting ring **X 6** •
	Round 2: (12)	**0 V 6** •
	Round 3: (18)	**0 (X 1 V 1) * 6** •
	Round 4: (24)	**0 X 1 V 1 (X 2 V 1) * 5 X 1** •
	Rounds 5-7: (24)	**0 X 24** •
	Round 8: (22)	**0 (X 10 Λ 1) * 2** •
	Round 9: (20)	**0 (X 9 Λ 1) * 2** •
	Round 10: (18)	**0 (X 8 Λ 1) * 2** •
	Round 11: (16)	**0 (X 7 Λ 1) * 2** •
	Round 12: (14)	**0 (X 6 Λ 1) * 2** •
	Round 13: (12)	**0 (X 5 Λ 1) * 2** • Leaving a 16" (40 cm) long tail, cut the yarn and finish off. Repeat Rounds 1-13 for other Ear.

Suspenders

[Red]		Chain Stitch **24**
	Row 1: (24)	Add 4 turning chains (buttonhole), start in 5th chain from hook **X 24** Finish off, leaving a 4" (10 cm) tail. Repeat for second suspender.

* Please see Working in Rows on page 42.

Eye Patch

[Dark Brown]

Round 1: (6)	In starting ring ✕6 •	
Round 2: (12)	0 ✕̌6 •	
Round 3: (18)	0 (✕1 ✕̌1) * 6 •	
Round 4: (24)	0 ✕1 ✕̌1 (✕2 ✕̌1) * 5 ✕1 •	
	Leaving a 16" (40 cm) long tail, cut the yarn and finish off.	

Face + Buttons

◦ **Eyes:** About 12 rounds up from neckline, 13 stitches between them.
◦ **Nose:** About 11 rounds up from neckline.
◦ **Eye Patch:** Between 8th & 16th round from neckline.
◦ **Mouth:** Between 5th & 10th round from neckline.
◦ **Eyebrows:** About 18-19 rounds up from neckline.

Suspenders

◦ **Straps:** On the waistline with 28 stitches between them.

» Arms

1. Using the tail, sew the arm in position. Repeat on other arm. Please refer to photo tutorial #1-2 on page 149.

» Suspenders

2. Attach the suspenders on the back, and the buttons on the front, following photo tutorial #3-6 on page 150.

» Ears

3. Mark the position of the ears with straight pins. Flatten the ear and using the tail sew the ear in place. Repeat for other ear.

4. When the ears are attached, hide the tails on the inside.

» Eye Patch + Eyes

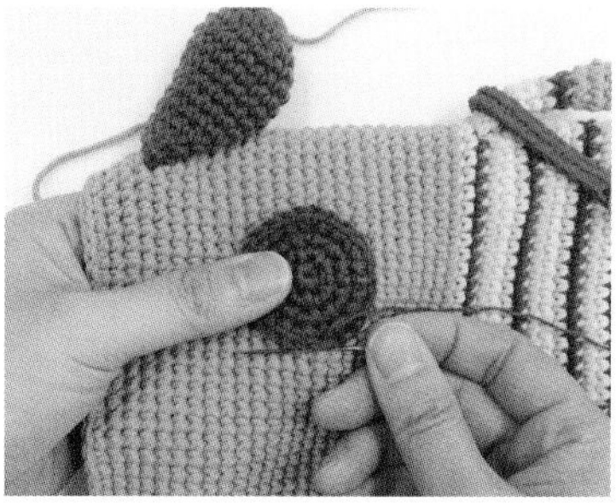

5. Split the yarn tail into 2 strands. Roll up the one strand and hide under the patch. Using the second strand, sew the patch in position.

6. Using white thread, sew on the eye buttons following photo tutorial #2-5 of Bear Groom on page 79. Using white thread with a dark button, makes the eyes twinkle.

» Eyebrows + Mouth

7. Using dark brown thread, embroider the eyebrows and mouth as shown in the photo.

» Nose

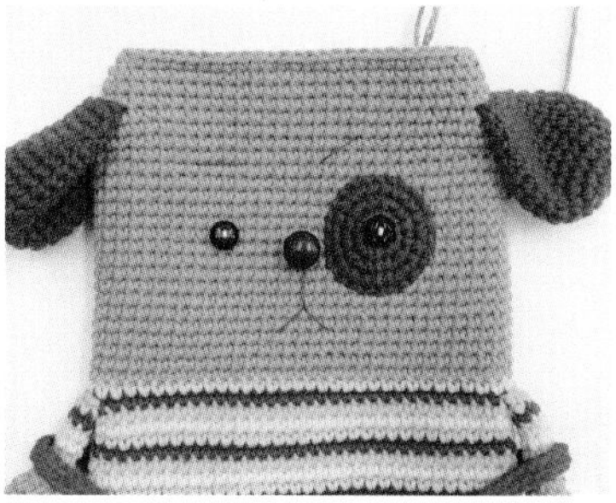

8. Pinch the top of the mouth and sew on the nose button. The face is now complete. Return to page 152 and continue with the head to finish Dougie the dog.

HEMINGWAY
THE OLD MAN AND THE SEA
Le Petit Prince
Le Petit Prince

CAFÉ **COUPLE**

Today Caleb and Clara are having their first date. They are meeting at their favorite book café. While reading together, Clara gently leans on Caleb's shoulder. Caleb's heart starts thumping so fast, he can hardly read another word!

15 | Caleb (18½ " / 47 cm)

Yarn: Medium Weight (Worsted)
- Flesh Color
- Dark Brown
- Cream
- Light Yellow
- Brown
- Dark Mint
- Light Mint
- Light Gray
- Light Pink

Hook: Size D-3 (3.25 mm)

Other: Yarn Needle
- Stuffing
- ½" (13 mm) Buttons - 2 (Suspenders)
- ½" (13 mm) Buttons - 1 (Nose)
- 5⁄16" (8 mm) Buttons - 2 (Shoes)
- Sewing Thread & Needle

16 | Clara (18½ " / 47 cm)

Yarn: Medium Weight (Worsted)
- Beige
- Dark Brown
- Cream
- Light Yellow
- Light Gray
- Mustard
- Light Pink
- Pink
- Dark Pink

Hook: Size D-3 (3.25 mm)

Other: Yarn Needle
- Stuffing
- ½" (13 mm) Buttons - 2 (Suspenders)
- ½" (13 mm) Buttons - 1 (Nose)
- 5⁄16" (8 mm) Buttons - 2 (Shoes)
- Sewing Thread & Needle

Caleb

Feet (Socks) + Legs

*Please see Making Ovals on page 46.

[Cream]

Chain stitch **8**

Round 1: (18) **0 (× 7 V 1) * 2 •**

Round 2: (24) **0 V 1 × 6 V 3 × 6 V 2 •**

Round 3: (30) **0 × 1 V 1 × 6 (× 1 V 1) * 3 × 6 (× 1 V 1) * 2 •**

Round 4: (30) **0 × 30 •**

Round 5: (24) **0 × 6 (× 1 Λ 1) * 6 × 6 •**

Round 6: (18) **0 × 6 Λ 6 × 6 •**

Rounds 7-8: (18) **0 × 18 •**

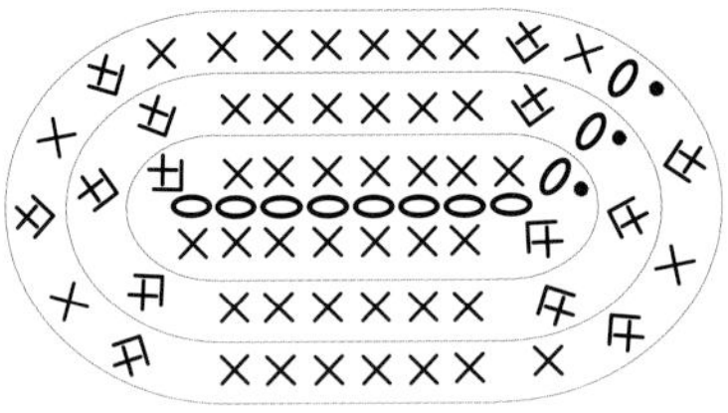

[Light Yellow
Light Mint
Light Gray]

For Rounds 9-17, alternate the 3 colors, working 1 round in each color.

Rounds 9-17: (18) **0 × 18 •**

[Cream]

Round 18: (18) **0 × 18 •**

Round 19-1: (18) **0 $\overline{\times}$ 18 •** (Don't miss the front loop only!)

Round 20-1: (18) **0 × 18 •**

Cut the yarn and finish off, hiding the tail on the inside.

[Flesh Color]

Insert the hook in the back loop of the first stitch on Round 18 and pull the yarn through.

Round 19-2: (18) **0 $\underline{\times}$ 18 •** (Don't miss the back loop only!)

Rounds 20-46: (18) **0 × 18 •**

Stuff and shape the foot.

Continue stuffing, referring to Making the Leg Joint on page 163.

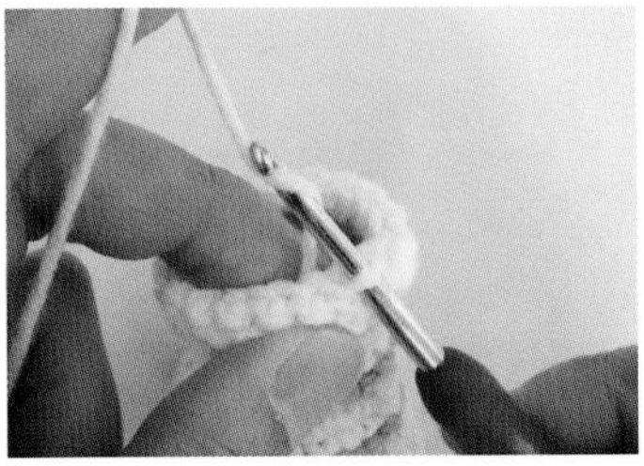

[Starting Caleb's Leg]

[Cream]

Round 47-52: (18) 0 ✕18 •

At the end of Leg A, stuff the leg ⅔ full. Cut the yarn and finish off, hiding the tail on the inside.

Repeat Rounds 1~52 for Leg B.

Finish stuffing, referring to Making the Leg Joints on page 163.

Joining the Legs

[Cream]

With the back of both flattened legs facing you, start in the 5th stitch from the inside on Leg B.

Round 53: (54) On Leg B **0** **✕14** (Leave the last 4 stitches unworked.)

Chain Stitch **9**

On flattened Leg A, start in the first stitch on inside edge **✕18**

Working in the chains **✕̲ 9** (Don't miss the back loop only!)

In remaining stitches on Leg B **✕4** •

Round 54: (54) On Leg B **0** **✕14**

On chain **✕̲ 9** (Don't miss the back loop only!)

On Leg A and finish round **✕31** •

Rounds 55-59: (54) **0** **✕54** •

TIP

Joining the Legs

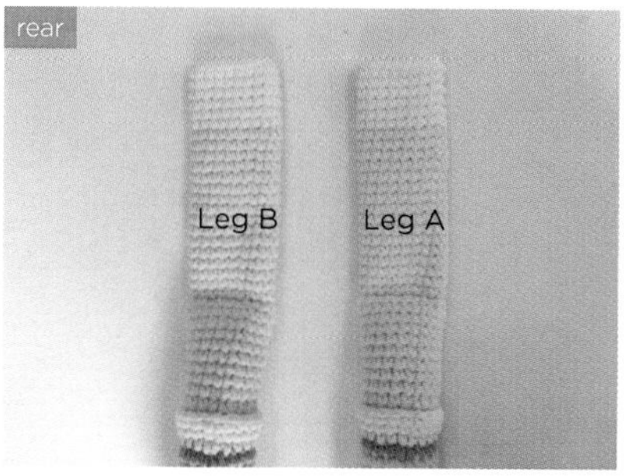

① Flatten the tops of the legs and place side by side with the back of the legs facing you. Pull the yarn through the 5th stitch from the inside edge on Leg B, work 14 single crochets (✕) around and then make 9 chain stitches (○).

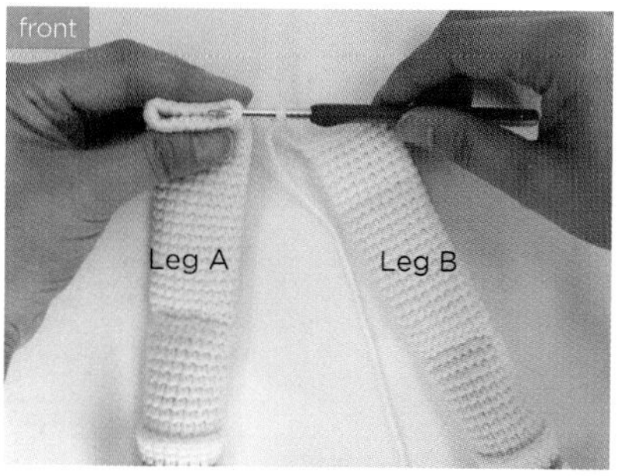

② On Leg A, work the first stitch at the inside edge and work 18 single crochets (✕) around to join the two legs.

Body + Head

[Light Yellow
Light Mint
Light Gray
Dark Mint]

For Rounds 60-83, alternate the 4 colors, working 3 rounds in each color.

Rounds 60-83: (54) 0 X 54 •

Start stuffing.

[Flesh Color]

Rounds 84-100: (54)	0 X 54 •
Round 101: (48)	0 (X 7 ⋀ 1) * 6 •
Round 102: (42)	0 X 3 ⋀ 1 (X 6 ⋀ 1) * 5 X 3 •
Round 103: (36)	0 (X 5 ⋀ 1) * 6 •
Round 104: (30)	0 X 2 ⋀ 1 (X 4 ⋀ 1) * 5 X 2 •
Round 105: (24)	0 (X 3 ⋀ 1) * 6 •

Continue stuffing to fill the doll.

Round 106: (18)	0 X 1 ⋀ 1 (X 2 ⋀ 1) * 5 X 1 •
Round 107: (12)	0 (X 1 ⋀ 1) * 6 •
Round 108: (6)	0 ⋀ 6 •

Finish off and using the yarn tail, close the last round.

Arms

[Flesh Color]

Round 1: (6)	In starting ring X 6 •
Round 2: (12)	0 V 6 •
Rounds 3-4: (12)	0 X 12 •
Round 5: (14)	0 X 5 V 2 X 5 •
Round 6: (12)	0 X 5 ⋀ 2 X 5 •
Round 7: (12)	0 X 12 •

[Dark Mint,
Light Gray,
Light Mint,
Light Yellow]

For Rounds 8-37, alternate the 4 colors, working 3 rounds in each color.

Rounds 8 - 37: (12) 0 X 12 •

Stuff about ⅔ full. Leaving a 16" (40 cm) long tail, cut the yarn and finish off.
Repeat Rounds 1-37 for other Arm.

Hair

[Brown]

Round 1: (6) In starting ring × 6 •
Round 2: (12) 0 ⋎ 6 •
Round 3: (18) 0 (× 1 ⋎ 1) * 6 •
Round 4: (24) 0 × 1 ⋎ 1 (× 2 ⋎ 1) * 5 × 1 •
Round 5: (30) 0 (× 3 ⋎ 1) * 6 •
Round 6: (36) 0 × 2 ⋎ 1 (× 4 ⋎ 1) * 5 × 2 •
Round 7: (42) 0 (× 5 ⋎ 1) * 6 •
Round 8: (48) 0 × 3 ⋎ 1 (× 6 ⋎ 1) * 5 × 3 •
Round 9: (54) 0 (× 7 ⋎ 1) * 6 •
Rounds 10-16: (54) 0 × 54 •
Round 17: (54) 0 × 1 T 3 Ŧ 8 T 4 × 38 •
Rows 18-21: (34) Working in rows 0 × 34
Leaving a 16" (40 cm) long tail, cut the yarn and finish off.

Shoes

* Please see Making Ovals on page 46.

[Light Gray]

Chain stitch 8
Round 1: (18) 0 (× 7 ⋎ 1) * 2 •
Round 2: (24) 0 ⋎ 1 × 6 ⋎ 3 × 6 ⋎ 2 •
Round 3: (30) 0 × 1 ⋎ 1 × 6 (× 1 ⋎ 1) * 3 × 6 (× 1 ⋎ 1) * 2 •
Round 4: (36) 0 × 2 ⋎ 1 × 6 (× 2 ⋎ 1) * 3 × 6 (× 2 ⋎ 1) * 2 •
Round 5: (36) 0 Č 36 •

[Dark Brown]

Round 6: (36) 0 × 36 •
Round 7: (24) 0 × 6 ⩓ 3 Ⱥ 6 ⩓ 3 × 6 •
Round 8: (24) 0 × 24 •
Cut the yarn and finish off, hiding the tail on the inside.

Repeat Rounds 1~8 for other Shoe.

Shoe Straps

[Dark Brown]

* Please see Working in Rows on page 42.

Row 1: (10)

Chain Stitch **10**

Add 4 turning chains (buttonhole), start in 5th chain from hook **X 10**

Finish off, leaving a 4" (10 cm) tail.

Repeat for second strap.

Pants

[Dark Brown]

* Please see Making Tubes on page 47.

Chain stitch **27**

Join with a slip stitch (•) to the first chain.

Rounds 1-11: (27)

0 X 27 •

At the end of Pants Leg A, cut the yarn and finish off.

Repeat Rounds 1~11 for Pants Leg B, but do not finish off.

Round 12: (54)

On Leg B **0 X 26** (Leave the last stitch unworked.)

On Leg A, start in the second stitch **X 27**

In remaining stitch on Leg B **X 1 •**

Rounds 13~12: (54)

0 X 54 •

Cut the yarn and finish off, hiding the tail on the inside.

Suspenders

[Dark Brown]

* Please see Working in Rows on page 42.

Row 1: (50)

Chain Stitch **50**

Add 5 turning chains (buttonhole), start in 6th chain from hook **X 50**

Finish off, leaving a 4" (10 cm) tail.

Repeat for second suspender.

Face

- **Hair:** The front bangs should be 12 rounds up from neckline.
- **Eyes:** About 8-9 rounds up from neckline, with 10 stitches between them.
- **Eyebrows:** About 1-2 rounds above eyes.
- **Nose:** About 8 rounds up from neckline.
- **Cheeks:** One round below eyes and one stitch out.

Arms

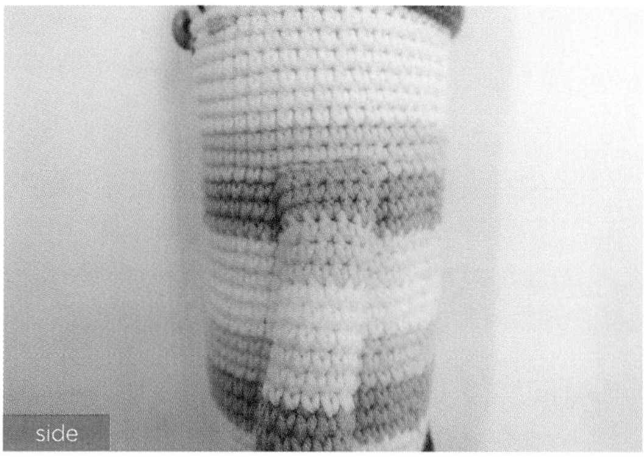

- **Arms:** About 2-3 rounds down from neckline.

Buttons + Suspenders

- **Buttons:** On the front, about 2 rounds down from waist with 14 stitches between them.
- **Straps:** On the back, about 2 rounds down from waist with 14 stitches between them.

» Making the Leg Joints

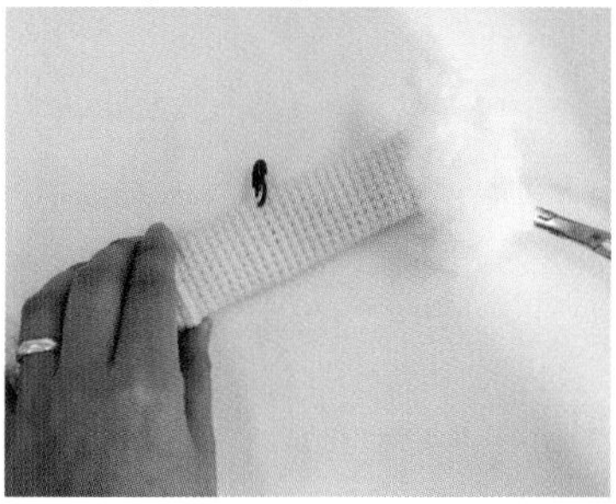

1. Mark the position of the joint with a stitch marker between Rounds 30 & 31 on the legs. Using a forceps, insert stuffing until the feet are firmly stuffed.

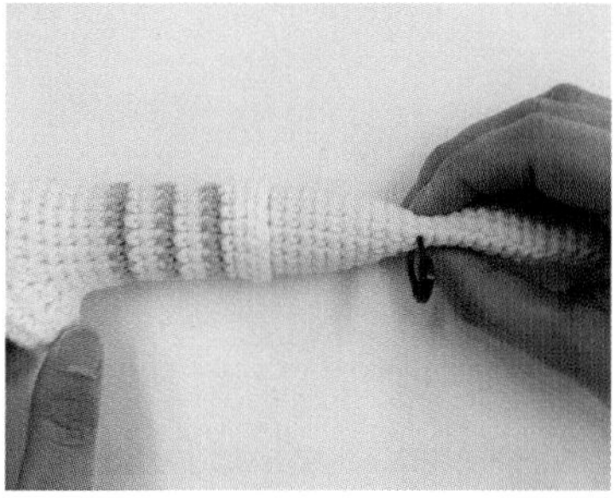

2. To make the leg bend easier, reduce the amount of stuffing near the joint, making sure the corners are stuffed and the leg bends freely.

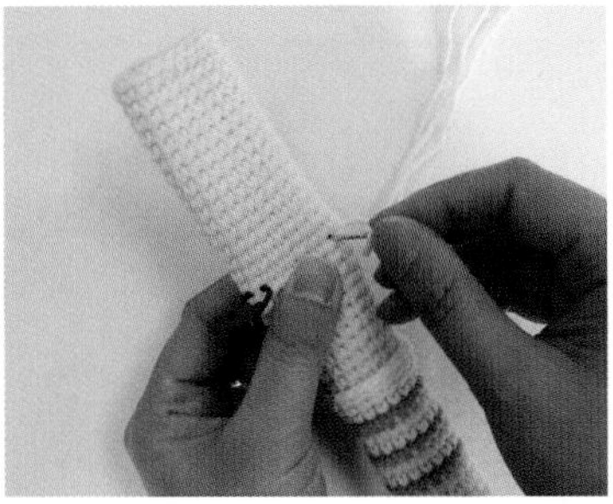

3 Flatten the leg and using Flesh Color yarn, sew across the marked round. Repeat for the other leg.

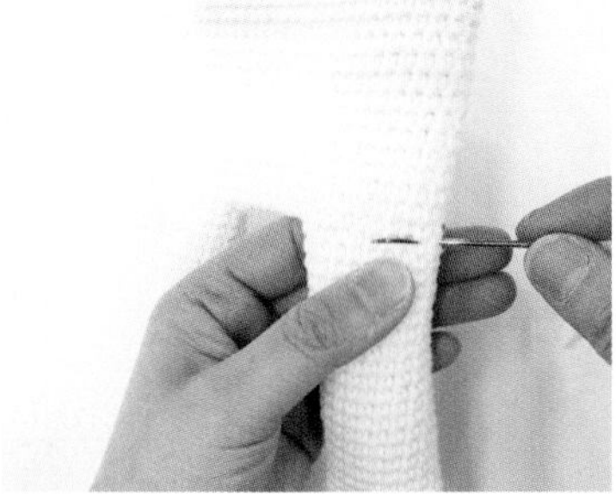

4 After Joining the Legs together, repeat #1-3 between Rounds 53 & 54 on the legs, using Cream yarn for stitching.

» **Arms**

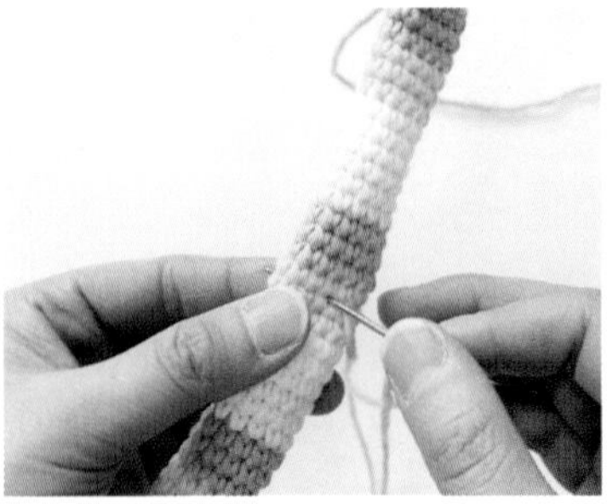

5 Stuff the arms about ⅔ full and sew across between Rounds 21-22 for arm joint.

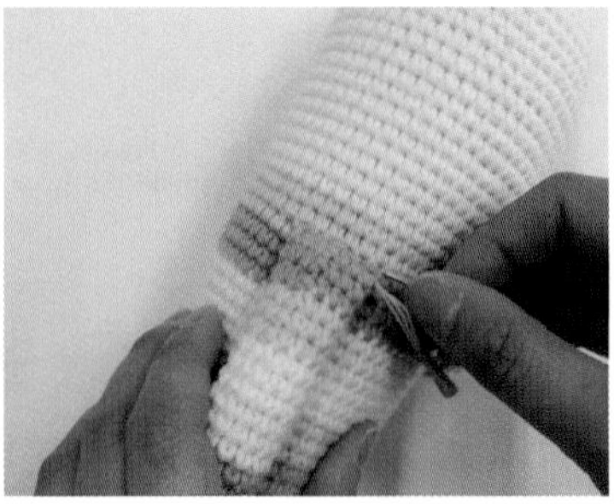

6 Using the yarn tail, sew the arms in position. Repeat for other arm.

» **Hair**

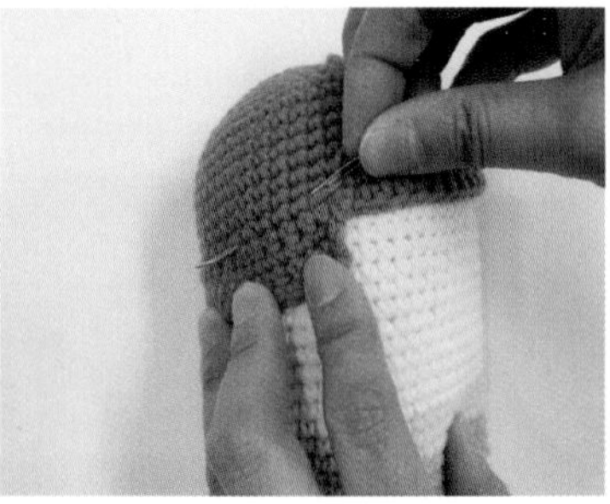

7 Thread the yarn tail onto a needle and first sew the bangs to the front of the head. Sew the remainder of the hair around the head.

» **Eyes**

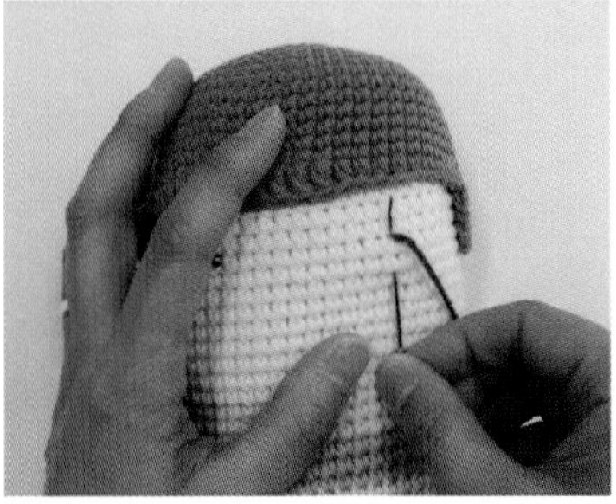

8 Mark the position of the Eyes with straight pins. Using Dark Brown yarn, embroider the eye over 2 rounds. Make about 3 stitches to get a 3-D effect.

» **Eyebrows**

9 Also mark the position with straight pins.Using Dark Brown yarn, embroider the eyebrows with one stitch.

» **Nose**

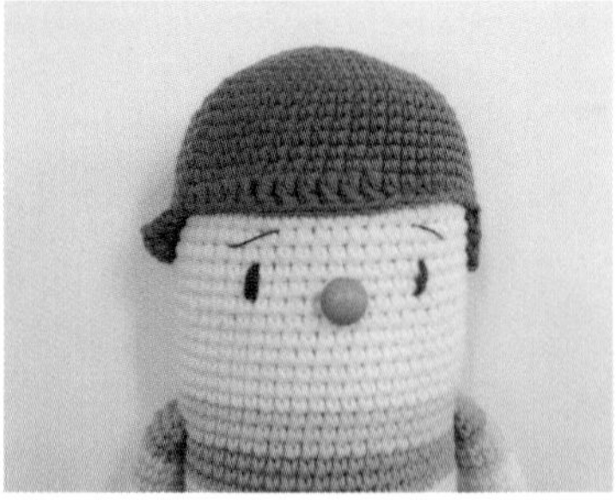

10 Mark the position of the Nose with a straight pin. Using knotted thread, insert needle in button and secure on thread, before sewing the nose in place.

» Cheeks

11 Using Light Pink yarn, embroider the Cheeks in position, following photo tutorials #21-26 of Wacky Bear on page 73.

» Mouth

12 Using Red yarn, embroider the mouth as shown in the photo.

» Shoes + Straps

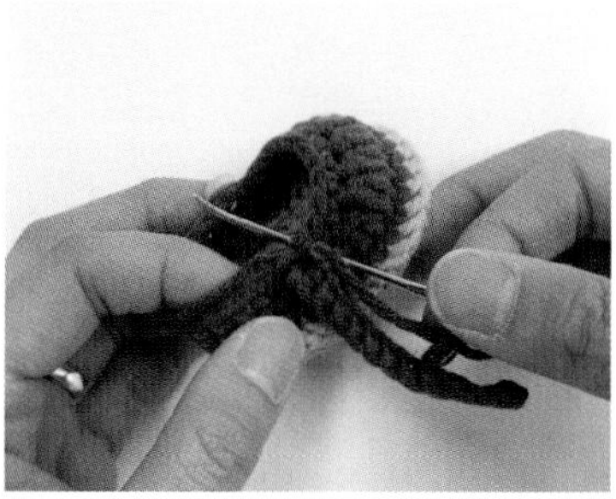

13 Using a needle, bring the two tails of the strap to the inside of the shoe.

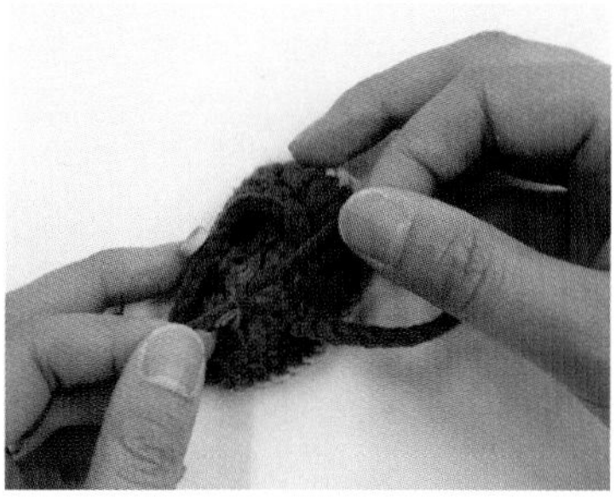

14 Tie the tails together in a knot on the inside.

15 Using a needle, hide the tails. Sew a button on the other side of the shoe and fasten the strap to complete the shoe. On the second shoe, reverse the strap and button positions.

» Pants + Suspenders

16 On the back of the pants, attach the suspenders, following #13-14 above.

17 On the front side, sew on the buttons. Cross the suspenders at the back and fasten to the buttons to complete the pants.

Feet (Socks) +Legs

* Please see Making Ovals on page 46.

[Cream]

Chain stitch **8**

Round 1: (18) — **0 (X 7 V 1) * 2 •**

Round 2: (24) — **0 V 1 X 6 V 3 X 6 V 2 •**

Round 3: (30) — **0 X 1 V 1 X 6 (X 1 V 1) * 3 X 6 (X 1 V 1) * 2 •**

Round 4: (30) — **0 X 30 •**

Round 5: (24) — **0 X 6 (X 1 Λ 1) * 6 X 6 •**

Round 6: (18) — **0 X 6 Λ 6 X 6 •**

Rounds 7-8: (18) — **0 X 18 •**

[Light Yellow
Light Pink
Light Gray]

From 9-17, alternate the 3 colors, working 1 round in each color.

Rounds 9-17: (18) — **0 X 18 •**

[Cream]

Round 18: (18) — **0 X 18 •**

Round 19-1: (18) — **0 $\overline{X}$ 18 •** (Don't miss the front loop only!)

Rounds 20-1: (18) — **0 X 18 •**

Cut the yarn and finish off, hiding the tail on the inside.

[Beige]

Insert the hook in the back loop of the first stitch on Round 18 and pull the yarn through.

Round 19-2: (18) — **0 $\underline{X}$ 18 •** (Don't miss the back loop only!)

Round 20-46: (18) — **0 X 18 •**

Stuff and shape the foot.

Continue stuffing, referring to Making the Leg Joint on page 163.

[Cream]

Rounds 47-52: (18) — **0 X 18 •**

At the end of Leg A, stuff the leg ⅔ full. Cut the yarn and finish off, hiding the tail on the inside.

Repeat Rounds 1-52 for Leg B.

Joining the Legs + Body + Head

[Cream]

With the back of both flattened legs facing you, start in the 5th stitch from the inside on Leg B.

Round 53: (54) On Leg B 0 × 14

Chain Stitch 9

On flattened Leg A, start in the first stitch on inside edge × 18

Working in the chains ⨯̲ 9

(Don't miss the back loop only!)

In remaining stitches on Leg B × 4 •

Round 54: (54) On Leg B 0 × 14

On chain ⨯̲ 9 (Don't miss the back loop only!)

On Leg A and finish round × 31 •

Rounds 55-59: (54) 0 × 54 •

Finish stuffing, referring to Making the Leg Joints on page 163.

[Light Yellow
Light Pink
Light Gray
Pink]

For Rounds 60-83, alternate the 4 colors, working 3 rounds in each color.

Rounds 60-83: (54) 0 × 54 •

Start stuffing.

[Dark Beige]

Round 84-100: (54) 0 × 54 •

Round 101: (48) 0 (× 7 ⩚1) * 6 •

Round 102: (42) 0 × 3 ⩚1 (× 6 ⩚1) * 5 × 3 •

Round 103: (36) 0 (× 5 ⩚1) * 6 •

Round 104: (30) 0 × 2 ⩚1 (× 4 ⩚1) * 5 × 2 •

Round 105: (24) 0 (× 3 ⩚1) * 6 •

Continue stuffing to fill the doll.

Round 106: (18) 0 × 1 ⩚1 (× 2 ⩚1) * 5 × 1 •

Round 107: (12) 0 (× 1 ⩚1) * 6 •

Round 108: (6) 0 ⩚6 •

Finish off and using the yarn tail, close the last round.

Arms

[Beige]

Round 1: (6) In starting ring X 6 •
Round 2: (12) 0 V * 6 •
Rounds 3-4: (12) 0 X 12 •
Round 5: (14) 0 X 5 V 2 X 5 •
Round 6: (12) 0 X 5 Λ 2 X 5 •
Round 7: (12) 0 X 12 •

[Medium Pink
Light Gray
Light Pink
Light Yellow]

For rounds 8-37, alternate the 4 colors, working 3 rounds in each color.

Rounds 8-37: (12) 0 X 12 •

Stuff about ⅔ full. Leaving a 16" (40 cm) long tail, cut the yarn and finish off.

Repeat Rounds 1-37 for other Arm.

Hair

[Mustard]

Round 1: (6) In starting ring X 6 •
Round 2: (12) 0 V * 6 •
Round 3: (18) 0 (X 1 V 1) * 6 •
Round 4: (24) 0 X 1 V 1 (X 2 V 1) * 5 X 1 •
Round 5: (30) 0 (X 3 V 1) * 6 •
Round 6: (36) 0 X 2 V 1 (X 4 V 1) * 5 X 2 •
Round 7: (42) 0 (X 5 V 1) * 6 •
Round 8: (48) 0 X 3 V 1 (X 6 V 1) * 5 X 3 •
Round 9: (54) 0 (X 7 V 1) * 6 •
Rounds 10-16: (54) 0 X 54 •
Round 17: (54) 0 (X 1 (shell) 1) * 9 •

Leaving a 16" (40 cm) long tail, cut the yarn and finish off.

Skirt Pants

[Dark Brown]

* Please see Making Tubes on page 47.

Please work (open) Pants first.

Chain stitch **27**

Join with a slip stitch (•) to the first chain.

Rounds 1-4: (27) — **0 X 27 •**

At the end of Pants Leg A, cut the yarn and finish off.

Repeat Rounds 1~4 for Pants Leg B, but do not finish off.

Round 5: (54) — On Leg B **0 X 26** (Leave the last stitch unworked.)

On Leg A, start in the second stitch **X 27**

In remaining stitch on Leg B **X 1 •**

Rounds 6-10: (54) — **0 X 54 •**

Round 11: (54) — **0 X̲ 54 •** (Don't miss the back loop only!)

Rounds 12-13: (54) — **0 X 54 •**

Cut the yarn and finish off, hiding the tail on the inside.

Holding the Pants upside down, start in the last stitch of Round 10 and work in the front loops only.

[Dark Brown]

[Starting Clara's Skirt]

Round 1: (54) — **0 X 54 •**

Round 2: (57) — **0 (X 17 V 1) * 3 •**

Round 3: (60) — **0 X 9 V 1 (X 18 V 1) * 2 X 9 •**

Round 4: (63) — **0 (X 19 V 1) * 3 •**

Round 5: (66) — **0 X 10 V 1 (X 20 V 1) * 2 X 10 •**

Round 6: (69) — **0 (X 21 V 1) * 3 •**

Round 7: (72) — **0 X 11 V 1 (X 22 V 1) * 2 X 11 •**

Round 8: (75) — **0 (X 23 V 1) * 3 •**

Round 9: (78) — **0 X 12 V 1 (X 24 V 1) * 2 X 12 •**

Round 10: (81) — **0 (X 25 V 1) * 3 •**

Round 11: (84) — **0 X 13 V 1 (X 26 V 1) * 2 X 13 •**

Suspenders

[Dark Brown]

* Please see Working in Rows on page 42.

Row 1: (50)

Chain Stitch **50**

Add 5 turning chains (buttonhole), start in 6th chain from hook **✕50**

Finish off, leaving a 4" (10 cm) tail.

Repeat for the second suspender.

Shoes *Please see Making Ovals on page 46.

[Light Gray]

Chain stitch **8**

Round 1: (18)	**0**	**(✕7 V1) * 2 •**
Round 2: (24)	**0**	**V1 ✕6 V3 ✕6 V2 •**
Round 3: (30)	**0**	**✕1 V1 ✕6 (✕1 V1) * 3 ✕6 (✕1 V1) * 2 •**
Round 4: (36)	**0**	**✕2 V1 ✕6 (✕2 V1) * 3 ✕6 (✕2 V1) * 2 •**
Round 5: (36)	**0**	**✕Ͻ36 •**

[Dark Pink]

Round 6: (36)	**0**	**✕36 •**
Round 7: (24)	**0**	**✕6 Λ3 Ⱥ6 Λ3 ✕6 •**
Round 8: (24)	**0**	**✕24 •**

Cut the yarn and finish off, hiding the tail on the inside.

Repeat Rounds 1~8 for other Shoe.

Shoe Straps * Please see Working in Rows on page 42.

[Dark Pink]

Row 1: (10)

Chain Stitch **10**

Add 4 turning chains (buttonhole), start in 5th chain from hook **✕10**

Finish off, leaving a 4" (10 cm) tail.

Repeat for second strap.

» Hair + Face + Arms

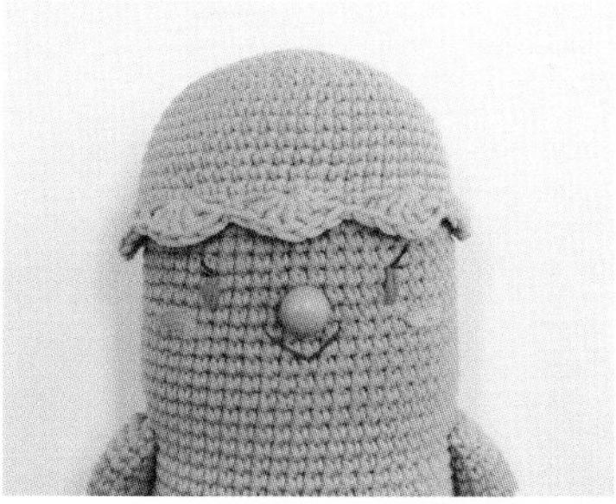

1 Finish the doll using the same positioning for the Hair, Face and Arms, following the photo tutorials #1-17 of Caleb on pages 163-165.

» Hair Braids

2 Mark the center of the bangs with a stitch marker.

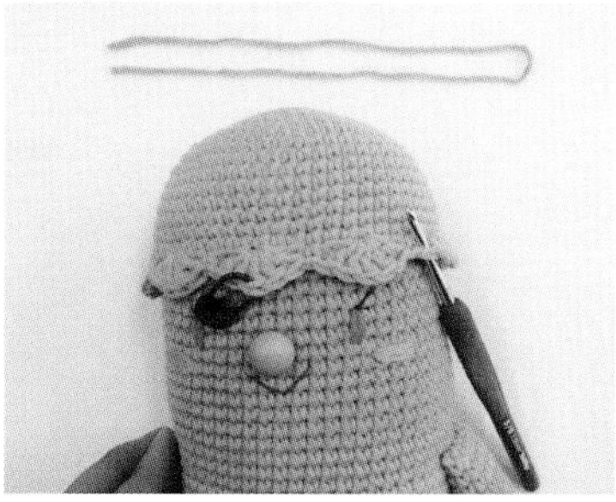

3 Cut the Mustard yarn into 12" (30.5 cm) long strands. Insert the hook in the 10th stitch from the marker.

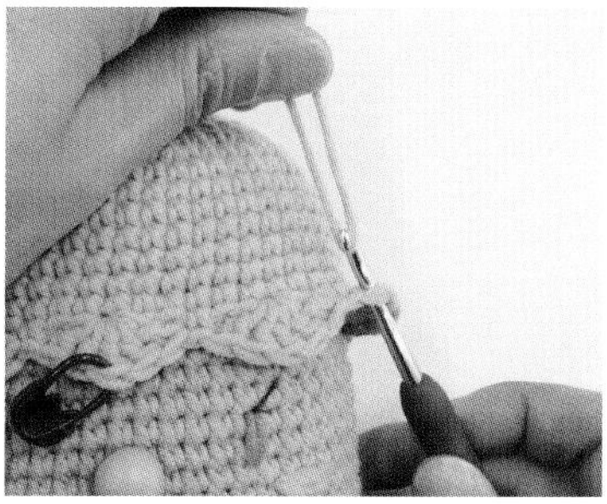

4 Fold one strand in half and place the fold on the hook.

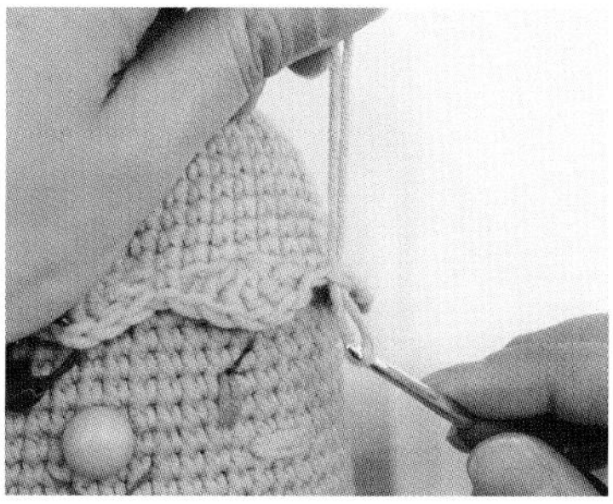

5 Pull the yarn through the stitch, forming a loop.

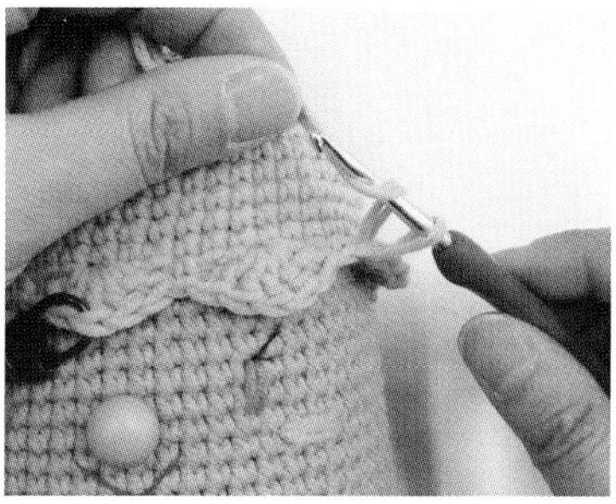

6 Wrap the yarn tails around the hook.

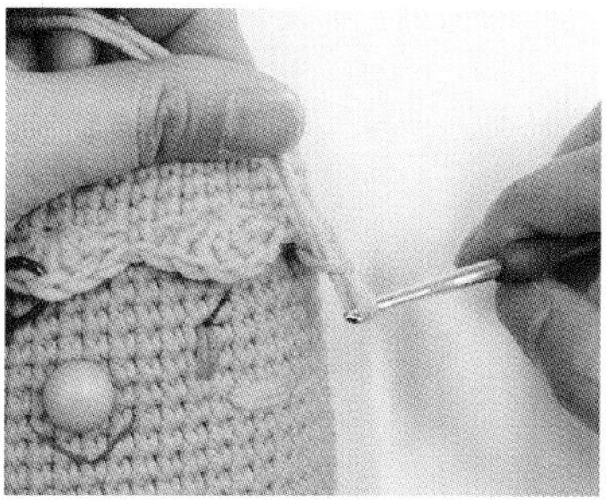

7 Pull the yarn tails through the loop.

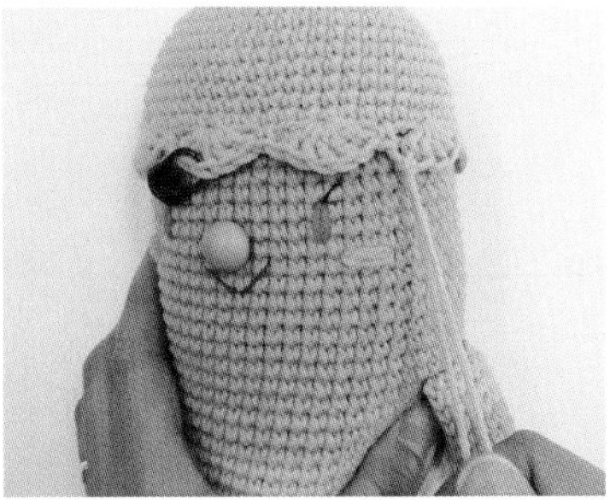

8 Gently tug to secure the yarn.

9 Do the same in the next 11 stitches so there are 12 strands of hair.

10 Braid the hair strands together, and fasten using Dark Pink yarn, tied in a bow. Repeat on the other side of the head.